M000219163

Sydney & New South Wales

Darroch Donald

Credits

Footprint credits
Editor: Jo Williams
Production and Layout: Jo Williams
Maps: Kevin Feeney

Managing Director: Andy Riddle
Commercial Director: Patrick Dawson
Publisher: Alan Murphy
Publishing Managers: Felicity Laughton, Nicola Gibbs, Jo Williams
Marketing and Partnerships Director: Liz Harper
Trade Product Manager: Diane McEntee
Advertising: Renu Sibal, Elizabeth Taylor
Trade Product Co-ordinator: Kirsty Holmes

Photography credits
Front cover: Dreamstime
Back cover: Shutterstock

Printed in Great Britain by CPI Antony Rowe, Chippenham, Wiltshire

Every effort has been made to ensure that the facts in this guidebook are accurate. However, travellers should still obtain advice from consulates, airlines, etc about travel and visa requirements before travelling. The authors and publishers cannot accept responsibility for any loss, injury or inconvenience however caused.

Publishing information
Footprint *Focus Sydney & New South Wales*
1st edition
© Footprint Handbooks Ltd
August 2012

ISBN: 978 1 908206 75 6
CIP DATA: A catalogue record for this book is available from the British Library

® Footprint Handbooks and the Footprint mark are a registered trademark of Footprint Handbooks Ltd

Published by Footprint
6 Riverside Court
Lower Bristol Road
Bath BA2 3DZ, UK
T +44 (0)1225 469141
F +44 (0)1225 469461
footprinttravelguides.com

Distributed in the USA by Globe Pequot Press, Guilford, Connecticut

The content of Footprint *Focus Sydney & New South Wales* has been taken directly from Footprint's *East Coast Australia Handbook* which was researched and written by Darroch Donald.

Contents

Sydney has come a long way since January 1788, when Captain Arthur Phillip, commander of the 'First Fleet', weighed anchor in Port Jackson and declared the entire continent a British penal colony. Where once was a collection of sorry-looking shacks and lock-ups full of desperate, hopeless convicts, stands a forest of glistening modern high-rises. In their shadow, hordes of free-spirited, cosmopolitan city workers have every reason to be proud of their beautiful city, one that, in their eyes, is the 'real' capital of Australia.

One of the best things about Australia's largest city is that you are never too far away from water. To the south are the little-known coastal towns of Jervis Bay, Batemans Bay and Narooma, gateways to the greatest concentration of parks in the state.

Less than two hours from Sydney is the Greater Blue Mountains region. Named after the visual effects of sunlight on eucalyptus oil released by the cloak of gum trees that liberally swathes the valleys and plateau, the 'Blueys' now attract over one million visitors a year, who delight in the stunning vistas, walk the many tracks or simply relax in the many characterful hotels and B&Bs.

The north coast of New South Wales stretches almost 900 km from Sydney to Tweed Heads, a seemingly endless string of beautiful beaches, bays and headlands, blue sea and national parks. There are so many stunning natural features that, after a while, they all seem to merge into one golden memory of sun-drenched sands and crystal clear waters, with the constant soundtrack of rolling surf.

As a general guide, from south to north, extended stops in Nelson Bay (Port Stephens), Myall Lakes National park, Port Macquarie, South West Rocks, Coffs Harbour, Bundjalung National Park, and, of course, Byron Bay, are all recommended.

Also, try to break up the journey with the odd trip inland, especially to Bellingen, the Dorrigo and New England National Parks and the numerous other superb national parks in the Rainbow Region, inland from Byron Bay.

Planning your trip

Best time to visit Sydney and New South Wales

One of the joys of the East Coast is that at any time of year there is always some section where the weather is just right. The converse, of course, is that those particular about their destination need good timing. Generally, accommodation and tourist sites stay open year round. Watch out for school holidays and peak seasons, when some areas get completely booked out months in advance. School holidays tend to take place from mid-December to late January, a week or two around Easter, a couple of weeks in June and July and another couple during September and October. If planning a long trip, say three months or more, try to make spring or autumn the core of your time. Also note that during big sporting events such as cricket (summer) and rugby tests (winter) as well as the Aussie Rules football finals (again in spring), you are strongly advised to book transport tickets and accommodation as far ahead as possible. ▸▸ *See Public holidays, page 17.*

Climate
As a general rule of thumb, the further north you travel, and the further in time from July, the hotter it gets. And hot means very hot: days over 40°C regularly occur in summer in the arid regions. Australia is the driest inhabited continent and most areas are currently suffering the longest and most protracted drought on record. Drought or no drought, virtually nowhere further than 250 km inland gets more than an average of 600 mm of rain a year. About half the continent, in a band across the south and west, gets less than 300 mm and much of it is desert. Naturally, the East Coast see much higher rainfall. For comprehensive weather forecasts, see www.bom.gov.au.

Getting to Sydney and New South Wales

Air
There are international flights direct to Sydney. It is usually possible to book internal Australian flights when booking your international ticket, at lower prices than on arrival. Some do not even require a stated departure and arrival point. If you have plans to fly within New South Wales check this out prior to booking.

Fares depend on the season, with prices higher during December and January unless booked well in advance. Mid-year sees the cheapest fares. Qantas, www.qantas.com.au, is Australia's main international and domestic airline and flies from most international capitals and major cities. That said, with the advent of the global financial crisis, competition is fiercer than ever, and Qantas is struggling in international and domestic markets against other airlines like Emirates, V Australia and Tiger Airways. Most other international major airlines have flights to Australia from their home countries.

Departure tax There are currently a number of departure taxes levied by individual airports (such as noise tax) and the government. All taxes are included in the cost of a ticket.

Transport in Sydney and New South Wales

Public transport is generally good and efficient and often easier than driving. Most cities have good metropolitan bus services, though some are curiously unaware of tourist traffic and there is many an important outlying attraction poorly served by public transport, or even missed off the bus routes completely. Some cities are compact enough for this to be a minor irritation, others are so spread out that the visitor must invest in an expensive tourist bus service or taxis. In such places staying at a hostel or B&B with free or low-cost bike hire can save a lot of money. Bear in mind that when it comes to public transport in the major centres, Australia is hardly comparable to Japan or to a lesser extent Europe or North America.

By far the best way of seeing the East Coast is under your own steam, or with a tour operator with an in-depth itinerary. See Tour operators sections and individual town and city sections for details. The further from the cities you go, the more patchy and irregular public transport becomes. All the states have networks based on a combination of air, bus and train. Some of these services connect up at border towns but check first. If you are short on time and long on funds, flying can save a lot of time, money and effort within New South Wales. In some cases it is the only real option. Most other interstate options involve long-distance buses, and on a few routes, trains. Train fares and domestic air travel can be considerably cheaper if booked in advance and on the net. For flights within Australia, try www.webjet.com.au.

Air
Qantas, T131313, www.qantas.com.au, **Tiger Airways**, T03-9335 3033, www.tigerairways.com, Jetstar, T131538, www.jetstar.com.au, and **Virgin Blue**, T136789, www.virginblue.com.au, link most state capitals to each other and to many of the larger towns and main tourist destinations. There are also several regional airways operating smaller planes on specialist routes including **Regional Express (REX)**, T131713, www.regionalexpress.com.au. Domestic fares have dropped dramatically in recent years. But bear in mind with budget airlines advertised fares do not take into account cargo baggage, for which you will pay significantly more. For up-to-date information on whether a destination is served by scheduled or charter flights, contact your destination's tourist office or each airline direct.

Bear in mind that many provincial airports may not be staffed when you arrive. Check with the local tourist office regarding transport from the airport to the town.

Rail
Train travel up and down the East Coast is a viable mode of transport and can be a delightful way to get from A to B, especially if you are short of time. Given the distances between the main centres, Australia lends itself to rail travel and you may find routes with such evocative names as **Sunlander** and **Spirit of the Outback** irresistible. That said, a car or coach is a better option if you wish to explore or get off the beaten track. The East Coast offers endless beaches and numerous national parks that are well away from any railway stations. Also, note that overnight travel by rail is possible, though often expensive, if you wish to have the comfort of your own compartment and to do it in style.

In New South Wales, **Countrylink**, T132232 (within Australia), www.countrylink .nsw.gov.au, offers rail and rail/coach services state-wide and to Brisbane. There are several Countrylink travel centres at principal stations in Sydney including the Sydney Central Railway Station, T02-99379 3800. A useful website for travel throughout New South Wales is www.webwombat.com.au/transport/nsw.htm.

Road

Bus State and interstate bus services offer the most cost-effective way of constructing an itinerary for a single traveller. A large selection of bus services can be found at www.buslines.com.au. Always check the journey duration and time of arrival, as some routes can take days, with just a couple of short meal stops. Many coaches are equipped with videos but you may also want something to read. It's also a good idea to take warm clothing, socks, a pillow, toothbrush and earplugs. There's a good chance you'll arrive in the late evening or the early hours of the morning. If so, book accommodation ahead and, if possible, transfer transportation.

The main operator throughout New South Wales is **Greyhound Pioneer**, T1300 473946, www.greyhound.com.au (referred to simply as Greyhound throughout this guide). Their networks follow all the main interstate highways up and down the coast with offshoots including the Blue Mountains, New England (Hunter Valley) and so on. As well as scheduled routes, they offer a range of passes. There are also many other smaller regional companies. Most are listed under the relevant destinations. **Countrylink**, T132232, www.countrylink.info, also offers coach services to some centres in conjunction with rail schedules.

Greyhound offer a wide variety of passes with several jump-on, jump-off options. The **Day Passes** system has three options: the **Standard Day Pass** allows you to travel anywhere on the Greyhound network for the number of consecutive days you choose with a pre-set kilometre limit. You can buy a pass for three days (1000 km limit, $154), five days (1500 km limit, $223), seven days (2000 km limit, $286), 10 days (3000 km limit, $398), 20 days (6000 km limit, $755), 30 days (10,000 km, $1030). The **Flexi Day Pass** gives you total flexibility without a kilometre restriction. Customers purchase the number of days' travel required (10, 15 or 21) and have up to 60 days to use the travelling days purchased, while The **Fixed Day Pass** gives you freedom to travel for a consecutive number of days (10, 15 and 21) without a kilometre restriction.

The **Explorer Pass** commits you to a set one-way or circular route and is valid for between 30 and 365 days.

Other passes include the **Mini Traveller**, which provides travel between two popular destinations; in between you can hop on and hop off as much as you like in the one direction, over 45 days. From Cairns to Sydney will cost around $408.

Backpacker buses There are now several operators who make the assumption that the most important part of your trip is the journey. These companies combine the roles of travel operator and tour guide, taking from two to five times longer than scheduled services (a good indicator of just how much they get off the highway). They are worth considering, especially if you are travelling alone. In terms of style, price and what is included, they vary greatly and it is important to clarify this prior to booking. Some offer transport and commentary only, others include accommodation and some meals, a few specialize in 4WD and bush camping. A few, including **Oz Experience** (see below) offer jump-on, jump-off packages and are priced more on distance. The main backpacker bus company in NSW is **Oz Experience**, T1300 300028, www.ozexperience.com.

Car If you live in a small and populous country, travelling by car in Australia will be an enlightening experience, as well as an enervating one. Distances are huge and travelling times between the major cities, towns and sights can seem endless, so put on some tunes and make driving part of the whole holiday experience.

You should consider buying a car if you are travelling for more than three months. Consider a campervan if hiring or buying. Traffic congestion is rarely an issue on the East Coast route – only Sydney has anything like the traffic of many other countries, so driving itineraries can be based on covering a planned distance each day, up to, say, 100 km for each solid hour's driving. The key factor in planning is distance. It is pretty stress-free and as the distances can be huge, drivers can get bored and sleepy. There are a lot of single-vehicle accidents in Australia, many the result of driver fatigue.

The other major factor when planning is the type of roads you may need to use. Many country roads are unsealed, usually meaning a stony or sand surface. When recently graded (levelled and compacted) they can be almost as pleasant to drive on as sealed roads, but even then there are reduced levels of handling. After grading, unsealed roads deteriorate over time. Potholes form, they can become impassable when wet and corrugations usually develop, especially on national park roads, with heavy usage. These are regular ripples in the road surface, at right angles to the road direction, that can go on for tens of kilometres. Small ones simply cause an irritating judder, large ones can reduce tolerable driving speeds to 10-20 kph. Generally, the bigger the wheel size and the longer the wheel base, the more comfortable the journey over corrugations will be. Many unsealed roads can be negotiated with a two wheel-drive (2WD) low-clearance vehicle but the ride will be a lot more comfortable, and safer, in a 4WD high-clearance one. Most 2WD hire cars are uninsured if driven on unsealed roads. Some unsealed roads (especially in the outback) are designated as 4WD-only or tracks, though individual definitions can differ according to the map or authority you consult. If in doubt, stick to the roads you are certain are safe for your vehicle and you are sufficiently prepared for. With careful preparation, however, and the right vehicles (convoys are recommended), traversing the major outback tracks is an awesome experience.

If you stray far from the coast, and certainly anywhere outback, prepare carefully. Carry essential spares and tools such as fan belts, hoses, gaffer tape, a tyre repair kit, extra car jack, extra spare wheel and tyre, spade, decent tool kit, oil and coolant and a fuel can. Membership of the NRMA (NSW) or the RACQ (QLD) is recommended (see below), as is informing someone of your intended itinerary. Above all carry plenty of spare water, at least 10 litres per person, 20 if possible. As far as the best make of vehicle for the outback, in Australia it is the iconic Toyota Landcruiser every time. Break down in a cruiser and the chances are spare parts can be sourced quite easily, without waiting days for foreign hard-to-come-by items. Break down in a Mitsubishi Delica and you may as well look for a job and get married to a local.

To drive in Australia you must have a current driving licence. Foreign nationals also need an international driving licence, available from your national motoring organization. In Australia you drive on the left. Speed limits vary between states, with maximum urban limits of 50-60 kph and maximum country limits of 100-120 kph. Speeding penalties include a fine and police allow little leeway. Seatbelts are compulsory for drivers and passengers. Driving under the influence of alcohol is illegal over certain (very small) limits and penalties are severe.

Driving safely

→ If you stray from the coast and 'go outback', watch out for large animals such as kangaroos and emus. Hitting a kangaroo, emu or sheep can write off the vehicle and cause injury. Dawn and dusk are the worst times so try to avoid travelling then. Do not expect any animal to get out of your way. Many, through sheer angst, will head towards the vehicle or run into its path at the last second.

→ On country and outback roads you will also meet road trains (trucks up to four times the size you are most probably used to). Overtake them with great care.

→ If you're on a single-track bitumen road or an unsealed road pull right over when a road train comes the other way. Not only can dust cause zero visibility but you will also minimize the possibility of stones pinging up and damaging your windows.

→ If travelling in the outback always carry extra water and food. If you do break down and are out of mobile coverage DO NOT leave your vehicle. Stay with it and on the road until help arrives.

→ Drive only in full daylight if possible.

→ Always check with the hire company where you can and cannot take your 4WD vehicle (some will not allow them off graded roads or on sand, like Fraser Island) and also what your liability will be in the case of an accident.

→ To minimize costs on long journeys: ensure correct tyre pressures, avoid using air conditioning if possible, pack luggage in the car rather than on the roof, check the oil regularly and stick to 90-100 kph.

→ Some hire companies offer one-way hire on certain models and under certain conditions.

→ The general breakdown number for all associations is T131111.

→ For excellent travel route planning along the East Coast consult the Travel Planner section on the RACQ website, www.racq.com.au.

Fuel costs were approximately half that in Britain and twice that in the US, but due to the increase in the price of crude are following the global trend and rising rapidly. Diesel was traditionally more expensive than unleaded, but it's less prone to price fluctuations and in recent times can actually beat unleaded. When budgeting, allow at least $15 for every estimated 100 km. A trip around the eastern circuit can easily involve driving 20,000 km. Picking an economical vehicle and conserving fuel can save hundreds of dollars.

Every state has a breakdown service that is affiliated to the **Australian Automobile Association (AAA)**, www.aaa.asn.au, with which your home country organization may have a reciprocal link. You need to join one of the state associations: in New South Wales **NRMA**, T132132, www.nrma.com.au. Note also that you may be covered for only about 100 km (depending on the scheme) of towing distance and that without cover towing services are very expensive. Given the sheer distances you are likely to cover by car, joining an automobile organization is highly recommended but read the fine print with regard to levels of membership in relation to coverage outside metropolitan areas and in the outback.

Car rental costs vary considerably according to where you hire from (it's cheaper in the big cities, though small local companies can have good deals), what you hire and the mileage/insurance terms. You may be better off making arrangements in your own country for a fly/drive deal. Watch out for kilometre caps: some can be as low as 100 km per day. The minimum you can expect to pay in Australia is around $250 a week for a small car. Drivers need to be over 21. At peak times it can be impossible to get a car at short notice and some companies may dispose of a booked car within as little as half an hour of you not showing up for an agreed pick-up time. If you've booked a car but are going to be late, ensure that you let them know before the pick-up time.

Cycling Long-term bicycle hire is rarely available and touring cyclists should plan to bring their own bike or buy in Australia. Bicycle hire is available in most towns and cities and companies are listed in the relevant sections of this book. If you do plan on touring the coast by bicycle, the website www.cycling.org.au is recommended.

Hitchhiking While not strictly illegal in New South Wales, hitchhiking is not advised. This is not to say that hitching is more dangerous in Australia than elsewhere else.

Where to stay in Sydney and New South Wales

East Coast Australia presents a diverse and attractive range of accommodation options, from cheap national park campsites to luxurious Great Barrier Reef island retreats. The real beauty here, given the weather and the environment, is that travelling on a budget does not detract from the enjoyment of the trip. On the contrary, this is a place where a night under canvas in any of the national parks is an absolute delight.

Booking accommodation in advance is highly recommended, especially in peak seasons. Booking online will usually secure the best rates. Check if your accommodation has air conditioning (a/c) when booking as rooms without air conditioning are almost impossible to sleep in during hot weather. Note that single rooms are relatively scarce. Twin or double rooms let to a single occupant are rarely half the price and you may even be charged the full cost for two people.

Hotels, lodges, motels and resorts

At the top end of the scale, especially in Sydney, there are some impressive international-standard hotels, with luxurious facilities, attentive service and often outstanding locations. For example, the Park Hyatt in Sydney, www.hyatt.com.au.

Rooms in hotels and lodges will typically start in our **$$$$** range. In the main cities are a few less expensive hotels in the **$$$** range. Most 'hotels' outside of the major towns are pubs with upstairs or external accommodation. If upstairs, a room is likely to have access to shared bathroom facilities, while external rooms are usually standard en suite motel units. The quality of pub-hotel accommodation varies considerably but is usually a budget option (**$$**). Linen is almost always supplied.

Motels in Australia are usually depressingly anonymous but dependably clean and safe and offer the cheapest en suite rooms. Most have dining facilities and free, secure parking. Some fall into our **$$** range, most will be a **$$$**. Linen is always supplied.

B&Bs and self-catering

Bed and breakfast (B&B) is in some ways quite different from the British model. Not expensive, but rarely a budget option, most fall into our **$$** range. They offer very comfortable accommodation in usually upmarket, sometimes historic houses. Rooms are usually en suite

Price codes

Where to stay

$$$$	over US$200
$$$	US$111-200
$$	US$50-110
$	Under US$50

Prices are in Australian dollars and include taxes and service charge, but not meals. They are based on a double room, except in the **$** range, where prices are almost always per person.

Restaurants

$$$	Expensive	over US$35
$$	Mid-range	US$25-35
$	Cheap	under US$25

Prices refer to the cost of a two-course meal, not including drinks.

or have access to a private bathroom. Most hosts are friendly and informative. Some B&Bs are actually semi or fully self-contained cottages or cabins with breakfast provisions supplied. Larger ones may have full kitchens. As well as private houses, caravan parks and hostels and some resorts and motels provide self-contained, self-catering options with apartment-style units. Linen may not be supplied in self-catering accommodation.

A couple of good websites are www.bedandbreakfast.com.au, www.bbbook.com.au and www.bedandbreakfastnsw.com.

National parks, farms and stations

Some national parks and rural cattle and sheep stations have old settlers' or workers' homes that have been converted into tourist accommodation, which is usually self-contained. They are often magical places to stay and include many old lighthouse keepers' cottages and shearers' quarters. Stations may also invite guests to watch, or even get involved in, the day's activities. Transport to them can be difficult if you don't have your own vehicle. Linen is often not supplied in this sort of accommodation.

Hostels

For those travelling on a tight budget there is a large network of hostels offering cheap accommodation (**$**). These are also popular centres for backpackers and provide great opportunities for meeting fellow travellers. All hostels have kitchen and common room facilities, almost all now have internet and some have considerably more. A few, particularly in cities, will offer freebies including breakfast and pick-ups. Many are now open 24 hours, even if the front desk is closed at night. Standards vary considerably and it's well worth asking the opinions of other travellers. Most are effectively independent – even most YHAs are simply affiliates – but the best tend to be those that are owner-managed. Of several hostel associations, **YHA**, www.yha.org.au, and **NOMADS**, T02-9299 7710, www.nomadsworld.com, no membership fee, seem to keep the closest eye on their hostels, ensuring a consistency of quality. The **YMCA**, T03-9699 7655, www.ymca.org.au, and **YWCA**, T02-6230 5150, www.ywca.org.au, are usually a clean and quiet choice in the major cities. International visitors can obtain a **Hostelling International Card** (HIC) from any **YHA** hostel or travel centre: it's valid for one year and costs $32. For this you get a handbook of **YHA** hostels nationwide and around $3 off every night's accommodation. Some transport and tourist establishments also offer discounts to HIC holders. For more information, see www.hihostels.com.

Caravan and tourist parks

Almost every town will have at least one caravan park, with unpowered and powered sites varying from $25-40 (for two) for campers, caravans and campervans, an ablutions block and usually a camp kitchen or barbecues. Some will have permanently sited caravans (onsite vans) and cabins. Onsite vans are usually the cheapest option (**$**) for families or small groups wanting to self-cater. Cabins are usually more expensive (**$$-$**). Some will have televisions, en suite bathrooms, separate bedrooms with linen and well-equipped kitchens. Power is rated at the domestic level (240/250v AC), which is very convenient for those on a tight budget. Some useful organizations are: **Big 4**, T0300-738044/ T03-9811 9300, www.big4.com.au; **Family Parks of Australia**, T02-6021 0977, www.familyparks.com.au; and **Top Tourist Parks**, T08-8363 1901, www.toptourist.contact.com.au. Joining a park association will get you a discount in all parks that are association members.

If you intend to use motor parks, get hold of the latest editions of the tourist park guides published by the NMRA, RACV and RACQ. They are an essential resource.

Camping

Bush camping is the best way to experience the natural environment. Some national parks allow camping, mostly in designated areas only, with a few allowing limited bush camping. Facilities are usually minimal, with basic toilets, fireplaces and perhaps tank water; a few have barbecues and shower blocks. Payment is often by self-registration (around $6-15 per person) and barbecues often require $0.20, $0.50 or $1 coins, so have small notes and change ready. In many parks you will need a gas stove. If there are fireplaces you must bring your own wood as collecting wood within parks is prohibited. No fires may be lit, even stoves, during a total fire ban. Even if water is supposedly available it is not guaranteed so take a supply, as well as your own toilet paper. Camping in the national parks is strictly regulated. For details of the various rules, contact the National Parks Wildlife Service (NPWS).

Campervans

A popular choice for many visitors is to hire or buy a vehicle that can be slept in, combining the costs of accommodation and transport (although you will still need to book into caravan parks for power and ablutions). Ranging from the popular VW Kombi to enormous vans with integral bathrooms, they can be hired from as little as $60 per day to a de luxe 4WD model for as much as $800. A van for two people at around $130 per day compares well with hiring a car and staying in hostels and allows greater freedom. High-clearance, 4WD campervans are also available and increase travel possibilities yet further. Kombis can usually be bought from about $2500. An even cheaper, though less comfortable, alternative is to buy a van or station wagon (estate car) from around $2000 that is big enough to lay out a sleeping mat and bag in.

Sales outlets Apollo, T+800 3260 5466, www.apollocarrentals.com.au; **Backpacker**, T03-8379 8893, www.backpackercampervans.com; **Britz**, T03-8379 8890, www.britz.com.au; **Getabout**, T02-9380 5536, www.getaboutoz.com; **Maui**, T03-8379 8891 (T800 2008 0801), www.maui.com.au; **Wicked**, T07-3634 9000, www.wickedcampers.com.au. The latter are proving immensely popular with the backpacker set and you will see their vivid, arty vans everywhere.

Food and drink in Sydney and New South Wales

The quintessential image of Australian cooking may be of throwing some meat on the barbie but Australia actually has a dynamic and vibrant cuisine all its own. Freed from the bland English 'meat and two veg' straitjacket in the 1980s by the skills and cuisines of Chinese, Thai, Vietnamese, Italian, Greek, Lebanese and other immigrants, Australia has developed a fusion cuisine that takes elements from their cultures and mixes them into something new and original.

Asian ingredients are easily found in major cities because of the country's large Asian population. Australia makes its own dairy products so cheese or cream may come from Tasmania's King Island, Western Australia's Margaret River or the Atherton Tablelands in Far North Queensland. There is plenty of seafood, including some unfamiliar creatures such as the delicious Moreton bugs (crabs), yabbies and crayfish. Mussels, oysters and abalone are all also harvested locally. Fish is a treat too: snapper, dhufish, coral trout and red emperor or the dense, flavoursome flesh of freshwater fish such as barramundi and Murray cod. Freshness is a major feature of modern Australian cuisine, using local produce and cooking it simply to preserve the intrinsic flavour. Native animals are used, such as kangaroo, emu and crocodile, and native plants that Aboriginal people have been eating for thousands of years such as quandong, wattle seed or lemon myrtle leaf. A word of warning, however: this gourmet experience is mostly restricted to cities and large towns. There are pockets of foodie heaven in the country but these are usually associated with wine regions and are the exception rather than the rule.

Eating out

Eating habits in Australia are essentially the same as in most Western countries and are of course affected by the climate. The barbecue on the beach or in the back garden is an Aussie classic but you will find that most eating out during daylight hours takes place outdoors. Weekend brunch is hugely popular, especially in the cities, and often takes up the whole morning. Sydney and Melbourne are the undisputed gourmet capitals, where you will find the very best of modern Australian cuisine as well as everything from Mexican to Mongolian, Jamaican to Japanese. Restaurants are common even in the smallest towns, but the smaller the town the lower the quality, though not usually the price. Chinese and Thai restaurants are very common, with most other cuisines appearing only in the larger towns and cities. Corporate hotels and motels almost all have attached restaurants, as do traditional pubs, which also serve counter meals. Some may have a more imaginative menu or better quality fare than the local restaurants. Most restaurants are licensed, others BYO only, in which case you provide wine or beer and the restaurant provides glasses. Despite the corkage fee this still makes for a better deal than paying the huge mark-up on alcohol. Sadly, Australians have taken to fast food as enthusiastically as anywhere else in the world.

Alongside these are food courts, found in the shopping malls of cities and larger towns. Also in the budget bracket are the delis and milk bars, serving hot takeaways together with sandwiches, cakes and snacks.

Drinks

Australian **wine** will need no introduction to most readers. Many of the best-known labels, including **Penfolds** and **Jacob's Creek**, are produced in South Australia but there are dozens of recognized wine regions right across the southern third of Australia, where the climate is favourable for grape growing and the soil sufficient to produce high-standard grapes. The industry has a creditable history in such a young country, with several wineries boasting a tradition of a century or more, but it is only in the last 25 years that Australia has become one of the major players on the international scene, due in part to its variety and quality. There are no restrictions, as there are in parts of Europe, on what grape varieties are grown where, when they are harvested and how they are blended.

Visiting a winery is an essential part of any visit to the country, and a day or two's tasting expedition is a scenic and cultural as well as an epicurean delight. Cellar doors range from modern marble and glass temples to venerable, century-old former barns of stone and wood, often boasting some of the best restaurants in the country. In New South Wales the Hunter Valley provides one of the best vineyard experiences in the world with more than a 100 wineries, world-class B&Bs and tours ranging from cycling to horse-drawn carriage.

Australians themselves drink more and more wine and less beer. The average rate of consumption is now 20 litres per person per year, compared to eight litres in 1970. Beer has dropped from an annual 135 litres per person in 1980 to 95 litres now. The price of wine, however, is unexpectedly high given the relatively low cost of food and beer. Visitors from Britain will find Australian wines hardly any cheaper at the cellar door than back home in the supermarket.

The vast majority of **beer** drunk by Australians is lager, despite often being called 'ale' or 'bitter'. The big brands such as **VB** (Victoria), **Tooheys** (NSW) and **Castlemaine XXXX** (QLD) are fairly homogenous but refreshing on a hot day. If your palate is just a touch more refined, hunt out some of the imported beers on tap that are predominantly found in the pseudo-Irish pubs in almost all the main coastal towns. Beer tends to be around 4-5% alcohol, with the popular and surprisingly pleasant-tasting 'mid' varieties about 3.5%, and 'light' beers about 2-2.5%. Drink driving laws are strict and the best bet is to not drink alcohol at all if you are driving. As well as being available on draught in pubs, beer can also be bought from bottleshops (bottle-o's) in cases (slabs) of 24-36 cans (tinnies or tubes) or bottles (stubbies) of 375 ml each. This is by far the cheapest way of buying beer (often under $4 per can or bottle).

Essentials A-Z

Accident & emergency

Dial 000 for the emergency services. The 3 main professional emergency services are supported by several others, including the **State Emergency Service (SES)**, **Country Fire Service (CFS)**, **Surf Life Saving Australia (SLSA)**, **Sea-search and Rescue** and **St John's Ambulance**. The SES is prominent in coordinating search and rescue operations. The CFS provides invaluable support in fighting and controlling bush fires. These services, though professionally trained, are mostly provided by volunteers.

Electricity

The current in Australia is 240/250v AC. Plugs have 2- or 3-blade pins and adaptors are widely available.

Embassies and high commissions

For a list of Australian embassies and high commissions worldwide, see http://embassy.goabroad.com.

Health
Before you go

Ideally, you should see your GP or travel clinic at least 6 weeks before your departure for general advice on travel risks, malaria and vaccinations. No vaccinations are required or recommended for travel to Australia unless travelling from a yellow fever-infected country in Africa or South America. Check with your local Australian Embassy for further advice. A tetanus booster is advisable, however, if you have one due. Make sure you have travel insurance, get a dental check (especially if you are going to be away for more than a month), know your own blood group and, if you suffer a long-term condition such as diabetes or epilepsy, make sure someone knows or that you have a Medic Alert

bracelet/necklace with this information on it.

A-Z of health risks

There are three main threats to health in Australia: the powerful sun, dengue fever and poisonous snakes and spiders.

For **sun protection**, a decent wide-brimmed hat and factor 30 suncream (cheap in Australian supermarkets) are essential. Follow the Australians with their Slip, Slap, Slop campaign: slip on a shirt, slap on a hat and slop on the sunscreen.

Dengue can be contracted throughout Australia. In travellers this can cause a severe flu-like illness, which includes symptoms of fever, lethargy, enlarged lymph glands and muscle pains. It starts suddenly, lasts for 2-3 days, seems to get better for 2-3 days and then kicks in again for another 2-3 days. It is usually all over in an unpleasant week. The mosquitoes that carry the dengue virus bite during the day, unlike the malaria mosquitoes, which sadly means that repellent application and covered limbs are a 24-hr issue. Check your accommodation for flower pots and shallow pools of water since these are where the dengue-carrying mosquitoes breed.

In the case of **snakes and spiders**, check loo seats, boots and the area around you if you're visiting the bush. A bite itself does not mean that anything has been injected into you. However, a commonsense approach is to clean the area of the bite (never have it sutured early on) and get someone to take you to a medical facility fast. The most common poisonous spider is the tiny, shy redback, which has a shiny black body with distinct red markings. It regularly hides under rocks or in garden sheds and garages. Outside toilets are also a favourite. Far more dangerous, though restricted to the Sydney area only, is the Sydney funnel-web, a larger and more aggressive customer, often found in outdoor loos. There are dozens of venomous snake species in Australia. Few are actively aggressive and even those only during certain key times of year, such as mating seasons, but all are easily provoked and for many an untreated bite can be fatal.

Australia has reciprocal arrangements with a few countries allowing citizens of those countries to receive free emergency treatment under the **Medicare** scheme. Citizens of New Zealand and the Republic of Ireland are entitled to free care as public patients in public hospitals and to subsidized medicines under the Pharmaceutical Benefits Scheme. Visitors from Finland, Italy, Malta, the Netherlands, Sweden and the UK also enjoy subsidized out-of-hospital treatment (ie visiting a doctor). If you qualify, contact your own national health scheme to check what documents you will require in Australia to claim **Medicare**. All visitors are, however, strongly advised to take out medical insurance for the duration of their visit.

Money
All dollars quoted in this guide are Australian unless specified otherwise. The Australian dollar ($) is divided into 100 cents (c). Coins come in denominations of 5c, 10c, 20c, 50c, $1 and $2. Banknotes come in denominations of $5, $10, $20, $50 and $100. The Australian dollar is currently at a record high – almost a dollar for a dollar US and, sadly for Britons, at a high against the pound. **Exchange rates** as of Jul 2012 were as follows: US$1 = A$0.98; £1 = A$1.53; €1 = A$1.24.

Banks, ATMs, credit and cash cards
The four major banks, the **ANZ**, **Challenge/Westpac**, **Commonwealth** and **NAB (National Australia Bank)** are usually the best places to change money and traveller's cheques, though bureaux de change tend to have slightly longer opening hours and often open at weekends. You can withdraw cash from ATMs with a cash card or credit card issued by most international banks and they can also be used at banks, post offices and bureaux de change. Most hotels, shops, tourist operators and restaurants in Australia accept the major credit cards, though some places may charge for using them. When booking always check if an operator accepts them. EFTPOS (the equivalent of Switch in the UK) is a way of paying for goods and services with a cash card. Unfortunately EFTPOS only works with cards linked directly to an Australian bank account. Bank opening hours are Mon-Fri, from around 0930 to 1630.

Traveller's cheques
The safest way to carry money is in traveller's cheques, though they are fast becoming superseded by the prevalence of credit cards and ATMs. **American Express**, **Thomas Cook** and **Visa** are the cheques most commonly accepted. Remember to keep a record of the cheque numbers and the cheques you've cashed separate from the cheques themselves. Traveller's cheques are accepted for exchange in banks, large hotels, post offices and large gift shops. Some insist that at least a portion of the amount be in exchange for goods or services. Commission when cashing traveller's cheques is usually 1% or a flat rate. Avoid changing money or cheques in hotels as rates are often poor.

Money transfers
If you need money urgently, the quickest way to have it sent is to have it wired to the nearest bank via **Western Union**, T1800 337377, www.travelex.com.au. Charges apply but on a sliding scale. Money can also be wired by **Amex** or **Thomas Cook**, though this may take a day or two, or transferred direct from bank to bank, but this again can take several days.

Within Australia use money orders to send money. See www.auspost.com.au.

Cost of travelling

Accommodation, particularly outside the main centres, is good value, though prices can rise uncomfortably in peak seasons. Transport varies considerably in price and can be a major factor in your travelling budget. Eating out can be indecently cheap. There are some restaurants in Sydney comparable with the world's best where $175 is enough to cover dinner for 2 people. The bill at many excellent establishments can be half that. Australian beer is about $4-8 and imported about $6-8 in most pubs and bars, as is a neat spirit or glass of wine. Wine will generally be around 1½ times to double the price in restaurants than it would be from a bottleshop. The minimum budget required, if staying in hostels or campsites, cooking for yourself, not drinking much and travelling relatively slowly, is about $80 per person per day, but this isn't going to be a lot of fun. Going on the odd tour, travelling faster and eating out occasionally will raise this to a more realistic $100-130. Those staying in modest B&Bs, hotels and motels as couples, eating out most nights and taking a few tours will need to reckon on about $220 per person per day. Costs in the major cities will be 20-50% higher. Non-hostelling single travellers should budget on spending around 60-70% of what a couple would spend.

Opening hours

Generally Mon-Fri 0830-1700. Many convenience stores and supermarkets are open daily. Late night shopping is generally either Thu or Fri. For banks, see above.

Public holidays

New Years Day; Australia Day (26 Jan); Good Friday; Easter Monday; Anzac Day (25 Apr); Queen's Birthday (Jun); Labour Day (Oct); Christmas Day; Boxing (Proclamation) Day.

Safety

Australia certainly has its dangers, but with a little common sense and basic precautions they are relatively easy to minimize. The most basic but important are the effects of the sun, see Health, page 15. In urban areas, as in almost any city in the world, there is always the possibility of muggings, alcohol-induced harassment or worse. The usual simple precautions apply, like keeping a careful eye and hand on belongings, not venturing out alone at night and avoiding dark, lonely areas. For information on road safety see page 8, or contact one of the AAA associations, see page 9.

Smoking

This is not permitted in restaurants, cafés or pubs where eating is a primary activity, or on any public transport.

Taxes

Most goods are subject to a Goods and Services Tax (GST) of 10%. Some shops can deduct the GST if you have a valid departure ticket. GST on goods over $300 purchased (per store) within 30 days before you leave are refundable on presentation of receipts and purchases at the GST refund booth at Sydney International Airport (boarding pass and passport are also required). For more information, T1300 363263.

Telephone

Most public payphones are operated by nationally owned Telstra, www.telstra.com. au. Some take phonecards, available from newsagents and post offices, and credit cards. A payphone call within Australia requires $0.40 or $0.50. If you are calling locally (within approximately 50 km) this lasts indefinitely but for only a few seconds outside the local area. Well worth considering if you are in Australia for any length of time is a pre-paid mobile phone.

Telstra and **Vodafone** give the best coverage and their phones are widely available from as little as $150, including some call time. There are also some smaller companies like '3' and **Optus** offering attractive deals. By far the cheapest way of calling overseas is to use an international pre-paid phone card (though they cannot be used from a mobile phone, or some of the blue and orange public phones). Available from city post offices and newsagents, every call made with them may initially cost about $1 (a local call plus connection) but subsequent per-minute costs are a fraction of Telstra or mobile phone charges.

There are no area phone codes. Use a state code if calling outside the state you are in. This is 02 for ACT/NSW (08 for Broken Hill). To call Eastern Australia from overseas, dial the international prefix followed by 61, then the state phone code minus the first 0, then the 8-digit number. To call overseas from Australia dial 0011 followed by the country code. Country codes include: Republic of Ireland 353; New Zealand 64; South Africa 27; the USA and Canada 1; the UK 44. Directory enquiries: 1223. International directory enquiries: 1225.

Telephones numbers starting with 1300 or 1800 are toll free within Australia. Where 2 telephone numbers are listed in this guide, this toll-free number appears in brackets.

Time
Australia covers 3 time zones: Queensland and New South Wales are in Eastern Standard GMT+10 hrs. NSW and Victoria operate daylight saving, which means that clocks go forward 1 hr from Oct and Mar.

Tipping
Tipping is not the norm in Australia, but a discretionary 5-10% tip for particularly good service will be appreciated.

Visas and immigration
Visas are subject to change, so check with your local Australian Embassy or High Commission. For a list of these, see http://embassy.goabroad.com. All travellers to Australia, except New Zealand citizens, must have a valid visa to enter Australia. These must be arranged prior to travel (allow 2 months) and cannot be organized at Australian airports. Tourist visas are free and are available from your local Australian Embassy or High Commission, or in some countries, in electronic format (an Electronic Travel Authority or ETA) from their websites and from selected travel agents and airlines. Passport holders eligible to apply for an ETA include those from Austria, Belgium, Canada, Denmark, France, Germany, the Irish Republic, Italy, Japan, Netherlands, Norway, Spain, Sweden, Switzerland, the UK and the USA. Tourist visas allow visits of up to 3 months within the year after the visa is issued. Multiple-entry 6-month tourist visas are also available to visitors from certain countries. Application forms can be downloaded from the embassy website or from www.immi.gov.au. Tourist visas do not allow the holder to work in Australia. See also www.immi.gov.au/visitors.

Weights and measures
The metric system is universally used.

Contents

Footprint features

Sydney & South NSW

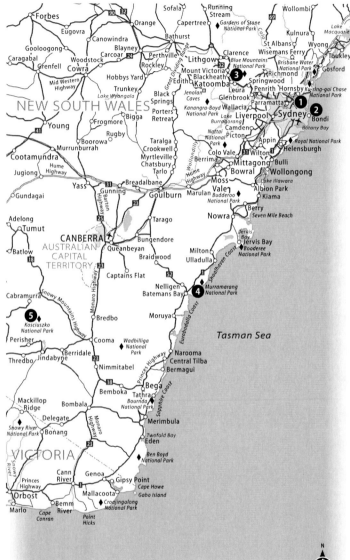

Sydney

Many adjectives and superlatives have been used to describe Sydney but the feelings stirred on seeing the city for the first time go beyond mere words. Seasoned travellers often complain that the world's great cities can seem a trifle disappointing; their icons somehow seeming smaller in reality than in the imagination. But not so Sydney. That first sighting of its majestic harbour from Circular Quay, with the grand Opera House and the mighty Harbour Bridge, is one that always exceeds expectations. Aussie writer and TV personality Clive James has described it as looking 'like crushed diamonds', but even without such analogies the marriage of natural and man-made aesthetics cannot fail to impress.

Over the last decade vast sums have also been spent on inner-city rejuvenation, transportation and state-of-the-art venues to host high profile international sporting events like the 2000 Olympics and 2003 Rugby World Cup, both of which were resounding successes and only added to the city's global reputation. Yet even without such events, this is a city whose inhabitants know that their lifestyle is one of the best in the world and their metropolis one of the most impacting anywhere. It's hardly surprising then that Sydney also has a whole lot to offer tourists, from its fascinating museums and galleries and world-class restaurants and beaches to its renowned 24-hour entertainment.

Arriving in Sydney → For listings, see pages 43-65.

Getting there
Kingsford Smith Airport ⓘ *9 km south of the city centre, www.sydneyairport.com*, has excellent facilities and its negotiation is straightforward. There is a **Tourism New South Wales** ⓘ *T9667 9386*, information desk in the main arrivals concourse where help is at hand to organize transport and accommodation bookings, flight arrival information and airport facilities. There are ATMs, foreign exchange outlets, car hire, a post office and medical centre (open 0400-2300). The domestic terminal is a short distance west of the international terminal.

Public transport to the city centre is available within a short walk of the terminal building. The fastest and most convenient method is via the **Airport Link** rail service every 10-15 minutes ($15). Taxis are available outside the terminal (south). A trip to the centre takes 30 minutes, $50. Various independent shuttle operators and courtesy accommodation shuttles also operate door-to-door from outside the terminal building, including **Kingsford Smith Transport** ① *T9666 9988*, which runs every 20-30 minutes anywhere in the city ($14 one way and $23 return).

All interstate and NSW state destination trains arrive and depart from Sydney's **Central Railway Station** on Eddy Avenue, T131500. **Countrylink** ① *T132232, www.country link.info*, is the main interstate operator with a combination of coach and rail to all the main interstate and NSW destinations. They have a travel centre at Central Station (open 0630-2200), while Town Hall Station, Wynyard Station, Circular Quay and Bondi Junction all have on-the-spot **CityRail** information booths. The main **coach terminal** is in the Central Railway Station; **Greyhound** ① *T1300 473946, www.greyhound.com.au, daily 0730-1830*. Left luggage and showers are also available.

Getting around

Public transport in Sydney is generally efficient and convenient. The great hub of public transportation in the city centre revolves around Circular Quay at the base of the CBD. It is from there that most ferry (**Sydney Ferries**) and many suburban rail (**CityRail**) and bus

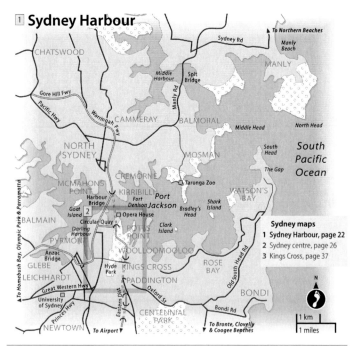

① Sydney Harbour

Sydney maps
1 Sydney Harbour, page 22
2 Sydney centre, page 26
3 Kings Cross, page 37

1 km
1 miles

Don't miss ...

(Sydney Buses) services operate. The State Transit Authority (STA) owns and operates the principal suburban ferry and bus services. Other principal terminals are Wynyard on York Street for northbound bus and rail services, Town Hall on George Street and the Central Railway Station. For information about all public transport, T131500 (0600-2200), www.131500.com.au. For discount passes, see box on page 63. Once in the city, ferry and rail route maps are available from information centres. The free leaflet *CBD Access Map Sydney*, available from the VICs or information booths, is a very useful map and guide for the disabled. ➤➤ *See Transport, page 62.*

Tourist information
Beyond the visitor information booth at the airport international arrivals terminal, the first stop for any visitor should be the **Sydney Visitors Centre** ① *Level 1, corner Argyle St and Playfair St, the Rocks, T9240 8788, www.therocks.com.au, daily 0930-1730.* The centre provides information, brochures, maps and reservations for hotels, tours, cruises, restaurants and other city-based activities. There is another **VIC** ① *Darling Harbour, 33 Wheat Rd, T9240 8788, www.sydneyvisitorcentre.com.au.* It offers similar services to the Rocks centre but has an emphasis on sights and activities within Darling Harbour itself. Neither centre issues public transport tickets. Manly, Parramatta, Homebush Bay and Bondi also have local information centres while small manned information booths are located on the corner of Pitt Street and Alfred Street, Circular Quay; opposite St Andrew's Cathedral near the Town Hall on George Street; and on Martin Place, near Elizabeth Street.

The main daily newspaper in Sydney is the excellent *Sydney Morning Herald*, which has comprehensive entertainment listings daily (see the pull-out *Metro* section on Friday) and regular city features. There are some excellent, free tourist brochures including the *Sydney Official Guide*, *This Week in Sydney*, *Where Magazine*, the very interesting suburb-oriented *Sydney Monthly* and, for the backpacker, *TNT* (NSW Edition), www.tntdownunder.com. For entertainment look out for *Drum Media*, www.drummedia.com.au, and *3-D World*, www.threedworld.com.au. All these and others are available from the main VICs, city centre information booths or from cafés, newsagents and bookshops.

Circular Quay and the Rocks ➔ *For listings, see pages 43-65.*

Sydney is without doubt one of the most beautiful cities in the world and the main reasons for this are its harbour, Opera House and Harbour Bridge. The first thing you must do on arrival, even before you throw your bags on a bed and sleep off the jet lag, is get yourself down to Circular Quay, day or night. Circular Quay also provides the main walkway from the historic and commercial Rocks area to the Opera House and the Botanical Gardens beyond. It's a great place to linger, take photographs or pause to enjoy the many bizarre street performers that come and go with the tides.

Sydney Opera House

① Information T9250 7777, bookings T9250 7111, www.sydneyoperahouse.com, lines open Mon-Sat 0900-2030 for the latest schedules, and for tours, see below. See also page 56.

Even the fiercest critics of modern architecture cannot fail to be impressed by the magnificent Sydney Opera House. Built in 1973, it is the result of a revolutionary design by Danish architect, Jorn Utzon, and every day, since this bizarre edifice was created, people have flocked to admire it. At times the steps and concourse seem more like the nave of some futuristic cathedral than the outside of an arts venue, with hordes of worshippers gazing in reverential awe. With such adoration it was perhaps inevitable that the great Aussie icon would join the international A-list of man-made creations, being awarded World Heritage Site status in 2007. The Opera House is best viewed not only intimately from close up, but also from afar. Some of the best spots are from Macquarie Point (end of the Domain on the western edge of Farm Cove) especially at dawn, and from the Park Hyatt Hotel on the eastern edge of Circular Quay. Also any ferry trip eastbound from Circular Quay will reveal the structure in many of its multi-faceted forms.

The Opera House has five performance venues ranging from the main, 2690-capacity Concert Hall to the small Playhouse Theatre. Combined, they host about 2500 performances annually – everything from Bach to Billy Connolly. The Opera House is the principal performance venue for Opera Australia, the Australian Ballet Company, the Sydney Dance Company, the Sydney Symphony Orchestra and the Sydney Theatre Company. There are two tours and three performance packages available. The **Essential Tour** *① every 30 mins, 1 hr, daily 0900-1700, $35, children and concessions $25*, provides an insider's view of selected theatres and foyers. The **Backstage Tour** *① T9250 7777, 2 hrs, daily 0700, $150*, as the name suggests, takes you behind the scenes and includes breakfast in the staff restaurant. Other performance packages combine a range of performance, dining and tour options.

From the Opera House to the Rocks

At the eastern edge of the quay, the **Opera Quays** façade provides many tempting, if expensive, cafés and restaurants as well as an art gallery and a cinema. After dark and on a warm summer's evening this surely has to be one of the best places on the planet for a convivial beer or G&T. Look out for the **Writers Walk**, a series of plaques on the main concourse with quotes from famous Australian writers.

The **Justice and Police Museum** *① corner of Albert St and Phillip St, T9252 1144, www.hht.nsw.gov.au, Sat-Sun 1000-1700, Sat-Thu in Jan, $8, children $4*, housed in the former 1856 Water Police Court, features a magistrates' court and former police cells, as well as a gallery and historical displays showcasing the antics and fate of some of Sydney's most notorious criminals. Nearby, facing the quay, is the former 1840 **Customs House** which now houses a major public library, several exhibition spaces, café-bars and on the top floor the long established and popular **Café Sydney**, see page 48. The ground floor –

Sydney Harbour's wildlife

Amidst all the human activity on Sydney Harbour you may be surprised to learn that it is not unusual to see a penguin dodging the wakes of boats in the inner harbour. Incredible as it may seem, little blue penguins live and breed in Sydney Harbour, and at the harbour mouth, in late winter and spring, migrating humpback whales are also regularly seen. Also, around the Rocks at dusk and after dark, keep your eye open for huge flying foxes (fruit bats). These sometimes stray from the large colony resident in the Botanical Gardens.

or city lounge as it is dubbed – comes complete with a newspaper and magazine salon, TV wall, internet access, information desk and a giant model of the Sydney CBD embedded beneath a glass floor.

At the southwestern corner of Circular Quay it is hard to miss the rather grand art deco **Museum of Contemporary Art** ⓘ *T9245 2400, www.mca.com.au, 1000-1700, free with a small charge for some visiting exhibitions, tours Mon-Fri 1100 and 1300, Sat-Sun 1100, 1300 and 1500.* Opened in 1991, it maintains a collection of some of Australia's best contemporary works, together with works by renowned international artists like Warhol and Hockney. The museum also hosts national and international exhibitions on a regular basis.

A little further towards the Harbour Bridge is the rather incongruous **Cadman's Cottage**, overlooking the futuristic Overseas Passenger Terminal. Built in 1816, it is the oldest surviving residence in Sydney and was originally the former base for Governor Macquarie's boat crew. The cottage is named after the coxswain of the boat crew, John Cadman, who was transported to Australia for stealing a horse. The cottage is now the base for the **Sydney Harbour National Park Information Centre** ⓘ *110 George St, T9247 5033, www.nationalparks.nsw.gov.au, Mon-Fri 0930-1630, Sat-Sun 1000-1630, free,* which is the main booking office and departure point for a number of harbour and island tours, see page 62.

The Rocks

Below the Bradfield Highway, which now carries a constant flow of traffic across the Harbour Bridge, is the historic Rocks village. It was the first site settled by European convicts and troops as early as 1788 and, despite being given a major facelift in recent decades (and losing its erstwhile reputation as the haunt of prostitutes, drunks and criminals), still retains much of its original architectural charm. Old and new is married in an eclectic array of shops, galleries, arcades, cafés and some mighty fine pubs and restaurants.

By far the best way to see the Rocks properly is to join one of the official **Rocks Walking Tours**, which give an entertaining and informative insight into the past and present, see page 120. **Rocks Market**, held every weekend, is perhaps the most popular in Sydney. It features a fine array of authentic arts, crafts, bric-a-brac and souvenirs. For live entertainment head for the **Rocks Square** where you'll find jazz, classical or contemporary music every day from midday for two hours. The **Rocks Discovery Museum** ⓘ *Kendal Lane, T9240 8680 www.rocksdiscoverymuseum.com.au, daily 1000-1700, free (Discovery Dig $5),* houses various highly interactive historical exhibits specific to the Rocks. During school holiday periods the 45-minute Discovery Dig offers kids the

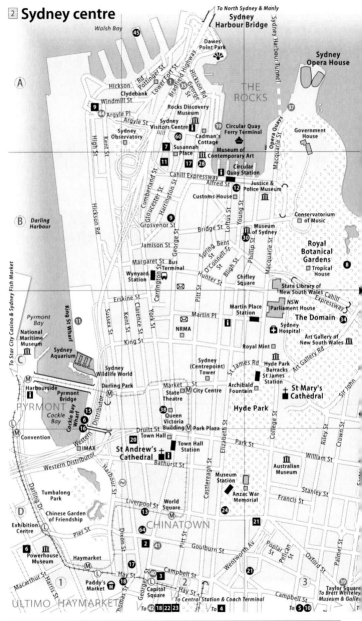

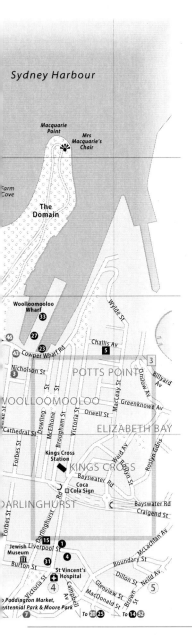

N

200 metres
200 yards

Where to stay 🛏

Alfred Park Budget
   Accommodation 4 D2
Australian Heritage
   Hotel 7 A2
B&B Sydney Harbour
   11 B2
Base Backpackers 20 D2
Capitol Square 3 D2
Challis Lodge 5 C4
Glasgow Arms 6 D1
Kangaroo Bakpak 1 D4
Lord Nelson 9 A1
Pensione 2 D2
Railway Square YHA
   23 D2
Royal Sovereign 15 D4
Russell 17 B2
Sydney Central YHA
   18 D2
Wake Up 22 D2
YHA The Rocks 7 B2
Y on the Park
   (YWCA) 21 D3

Restaurants 🍴

BBQ King 64 D2
Bill's Café 4 D4
Bill's Surry Hills 5 D3
Blackbird Café 6 C1
Botanical Gardens
   Café 8 B3
Brooklyn Hotel 9 B2
Café Sydney 12 B2
Casa Asturiana 13 D2
Chinta Ria – The
   Temple of Love 15 C1
Coast 16 C1
Dickson House
   Food Court 17 D2

Emperor's Garden
   Seafood 18 D2
Harry's Café de
   Wheels 23 C4
Hyde Park Café 24 D2
Indian Home Diner
   25 D4
La Renaissance 60 A2
Longrain 21 D3
Manta Ray 27 C4
MCA Café 28 B2
MG Garage 10 D3
MOS Café 30 B3
Oh! Calcutta! 31 D4
Otto Italiano 33 C4
Pavilion on the Park
   34 C3
Rocks Café 28 B2
Royal Hotel 14 D5
The Tearoom 38 C2
Una's 1 D4
Wharf 45 A2

Bars & clubs 🍸

Albury Hotel 7 D4
Cargo 11 C1
Cruise 19 A2
Durty Nelly's 20 D4
Harbour View
   Hotel 1 A2
Hero of Waterloo 26 A2
Lord Dudley 32 D5
Lord Nelson 44 A1
Mercantile 35 A2
Opera Bar 37 A3
Oxford Hotel 39 D3
Paddy McGuires 40 D2
Scruffy Murphys 41 D2
Scubar 42 D2
Tilbury 3 C4
Water Bar 46 C4
Woolloomooloo
   Bay Hotel 43 C4

Ⓛ LightRail Station
Ⓜ MonoRail Station

chance to dress up as junior archaeologists and dig up objects in fake (rubber) soil with an expert on hand to unravel the stories behind their finds. To escape the crowds, head up Argyle Street, and the steps to Cumberland Street, taking a quick peek at the historic row of cottages at **Susannah Place**, 58-64 Gloucester Street, west side, below the popular Australian hotel and pub, before walking through the pedestrian walkway to **Observatory Park**. This offers some fine views of the bridge and is home to the **Sydney Observatory** ① *T9921 3485, www.sydneyobservatory.com.au, exhibition daily 1000-1700, free, space theatre daily Mon-Fri 1430 and 1330, Sat-Sun 1100, 1200, 1430 and 1530, $7, children $5, evening tour $15, children $10, concessions $12*, which is Australia's oldest (book ahead). There is an interesting exhibition here covering early aboriginal and European astronomy, as well as a 3D space theatre and telescope tours during the day and evening tours offering a chance to view the heavens. From Observatory Park it is a short walk further along Argyle Street to enjoy a small libation and a bite to eat at the **Lord Nelson**, Sydney's oldest pub, see page 53, before walking north down Lower Fort Street to **Dawes Point Park** with its dramatic bridge perspectives.

The Harbour Bridge

From near or far, above or below, day or night, the Harbour Bridge is impressive and imposing. The 'Coat Hanger', as it is often called, was opened in 1932, having taken nine years to build, and it remains one of the longest single-span bridges in the world. The deck supports eight lanes of traffic – accommodating around 150,000 vehicles a day – a railway line and a pedestrian walkway, and forms a crucial artery to the North Shore and beyond. For over six decades the best views from the bridge were accessed by foot from its 59-m-high deck, but now the **Bridge Climb** experience, which ascends the 134-m-high and 502-m-long span, has become one of the city's must-do activities, see page 61. Not as thrilling, but far cheaper, are the views on offer from the top of the **Southeastern Pylon Lookout**, which can be accessed from the eastern walkway and Cumberland Street, the Rocks. The pylon also houses the **Harbour Bridge Exhibition** ① *T9240 1100, www.pylonlookout.com.au, 1000-1700, $9.50, children $6.50*. From below, the best views of the bridge can be enjoyed from Hickson Road and Dawes Point (south side) and Milson's Point (north side).

Harbour Islands

Sydney Harbour is scattered with a number of interesting islands, most of which hold some historical significance. **Fort Denison**, just east of the Opera House, is the smallest, and by far the most notorious. Its proper name is Pinchgut Island – so called because it was originally used as an open-air jail and a place where inmates were abandoned for a week and supplied with nothing except bread and water. In 1796, the governor of NSW left a sobering warning to the new penal colony by displaying the body of executed murderer, Francis Morgan, from a gibbet on the island's highest point. The island was later converted to a fort in the 1850s (for fear of a Russian invasion during the Crimean War). There is a café and tours are available through the National Parks and Wildlife Services, from $27, T9247 5033. A little further east, off Darling Harbour, is **Clark Island**, a popular picnic retreat for those with their own transport (landing fee $6, must be pre-booked and pre-paid). East again, off Rose Bay, is **Shark Island**, so called because of its shape. It served as a former animal quarantine centre and public reserve, before becoming part of the Sydney Harbour National Park in 1975. Access is via Captain Cook Cruises leaving Circular Quay (Jetty 6) at the weekends (hourly from 0945-1645) $17 return, children $15, T9247 5033. West of the bridge is the largest of the harbour's islands, **Goat Island**, site of a former gunpowder station and barracks. For tours, contact the NPWS, T9247 5033, from $24.

City centre → *For listings, see pages 43-65.*

Many visitors find the city centre a chaotic place. It is cooler, owing to the high-rise blocks, but much noisier, disturbed by the collective din of corporate Sydney. Despite this, it is worth taking the plunge and joining the purposeful flood of humanity through its gargantuan corridors to discover some hidden gems.

Museum of Sydney
ⓘ *corner of Phillip St and Bridge St, T9251 5988, www.hht.nsw.gov.au, 0930-1700, $10, children $5, family $20.*
The Museum of Sydney (MOS) was opened in 1995 and is a clever and imaginative mix of old and new. Built on the original site of Governor Phillip's 1788 residence and incorporating some of the archaeological remains discovered there, it contains uncluttered and well-presented displays that explore the history and stories surrounding the creation and development of the city, from the first indigenous settlers, through the European invasion and up to the modern day. Art is an important aspect of this museum and as well as dynamic and temporary exhibitions incorporating a city theme there are some permanent pieces, the most prominent being the intriguing *Edge of the Trees*, a sculptural installation. There is also a shop and café.

Macquarie Street
Macquarie Street forms the eastern fringe of the CBD and is Sydney's most historic street and the site of many important and impressive buildings. Heading north to south, near the Opera House in its own expansive grounds is the **Government House** ⓘ *T9931 5222, Fri-Sun 1030-1500, guided tours only every ½ hr from 1030, grounds open daily 1000-1600, free*, a Gothic revival building completed in 1837. The interior contains many period furnishings and features, giving an insight into the lifestyle of the former NSW governors and their families. Further up Macquarie Street, facing the Botanical Gardens, is the **State Library of New South Wales** ⓘ *T9273 1414, www.sl.nsw.gov.au, Mon-Thu 0900-2200, Fri 0900-1700, Sat 1000-1700*. Its architecture speaks for itself, but housed within its walls are some very significant historical documents, including most of the diaries of the First Fleet. Also worth a look is the foyer floor of the **Mitchell Library** entrance, one of three Melocco Brothers' mosaic floor decorations in the city. The library hosts visiting exhibitions that are almost always worth visiting and offers an ongoing programme of films, workshops and seminars. There is a shop and café on site.

Next door, the original north wing of the 1816 Sydney Hospital, formerly known as the Rum Hospital, is now the **NSW Parliament House**. Free tours are offered when parliament is not in session, and when it is you can visit the public gallery. The south wing of the hospital gave way to the **Royal Mint** ⓘ *small museum display, Mon-Fri 0900-1700, free*, in 1854 during the gold rush. The **Hyde Park Barracks**, on the northern edge of Hyde Park, were commissioned in 1816 by Governor Macquarie to house male convicts, and later utilized as an orphanage and an asylum. The renovated buildings now house a modern museum displaying the history of the Barracks and the work of the architect Francis Greenway. Various themed tours are available, from $10, children $5.

Central Business District (CBD)

Sydneysiders are very fond of the **Sydney (Centrepoint) Tower** ① *100 Market St, T8223 3800, observation deck Sun-Fri 0900-2230, Sat 0900-2330, $25, children $15, family $65*. This slightly dated landmark, built in 1981, has a distinctive 2239-tonne golden turret. The view from one of Australia's highest buildings is mighty impressive. As well as enjoying the stunning vistas from the tower's observation deck, you can also experience a virtual 'Great Australian Expedition' tour or dine in one of two revolving restaurants. The more adventurous can even brave outdoors and experience **Skywalk** ① *day, dusk or night from $65, T9333 9200, www.skywalk.com.au*, a glass-floored platform. Given the high price of entry to the observation deck alone, make sure that you keep an eye on the weather forecast and pick a clear day.

While you are on Market Street it is worth taking a peek at the impressive interior of the 1929 **State Theatre** ① *49 Market St, T9373 6852, www.statetheatre.com.au*. Much of its charm is instantly on view in the entrance foyer, but the 20,000-piece glass chandelier and Wurlitzer organ housed in the auditorium steal the show. Just around the corner from the State Theatre, on George Street, taking up an entire city block, is the grand **Queen Victoria Building** ① *T9264 9209, www.qvb.com.au, Mon-Wed and Fri-Sat 0900-1800, Thu 0900-2100, Sun 1100-1700, tours available with pre-booking*. Built in 1898 to celebrate Queen Victoria's Golden Jubilee and to replace the original Sydney Markets, the QVB (as it is known) is a prime shopping venue, containing three floors of boutique outlets, but the spectacular interior is well worth a look in itself. At the northern end is the four-tonne **Great Australian Clock**, the world's largest hanging animated turret clock. It is a stunning creation that took four years to build at a cost of $1.5 million. When activated with a $4 donation (which goes to charity), the clock comes alive with moving scenes and figurines. At the southern end is the equally impressive **Royal Clock**, which includes the execution of King Charles I. There are also galleries, historical displays, restaurants and cafés.

Across the street from the QVB is the **Town Hall** ① *corner of George St and Druitt St, T9265 9819, 0900-1700, free, pre-booked tours T4285 5685*, built in 1888. It also has an impressive interior, the highlight of which is the 8000-pipe organ, reputed to be the largest in the world. Next door to the Town Hall is **St Andrew's Cathedral** ① *T9265 1661, free*, built between 1819 and 1868, with regular choir performances.

Hyde Park and around

Hyde Park is a great place to escape the mania of the city and includes the historic grandeur of the 1932 Archibald Fountain and 1934 **Anzac War Memorial**. It's also great for people watching. At the northeastern edge of the park, on College Street, is **Saint Mary's Cathedral** ① *crypt 1000-1600*, which is well worth a look inside. It has an impressive and wonderfully peaceful interior, with the highlight being the Melocco Brothers' mosaic floor in the crypt. Further south along College Street is the **Australian Museum** ① *T9320 6000, www.austmus.gov.au, 0930-1700, $12, children $6, family $30 (exhibitions extra), Explorer bus, stop 6*, established in 1827, but doing a fine job of keeping pace with the cutting edge of technology, especially the modern Biodiversity and Indigenous Australians displays. Try to coincide your visit to the Indigenous Australians section with the live didgeridoo playing and informative lectures. Kids will love the Search and Discover section and Kidspace, a state-of-the-art mini museum for the under 5s.

Royal Botanical Gardens and Macquarie Point

The 30-ha **Botanical Gardens** ① *0700-sunset, free*, offer a wonderful sanctuary of peace and greenery only a short stroll east of the city centre. They boast a fine array of mainly native plants and trees, an intriguing pyramid-shaped **Tropical House** ① *1000-1600, small fee*, roses and succulent gardens, rare and threatened species and decorative ponds, as well as a resident colony of wild flying foxes (fruit bats). There is a visitors' centre and shop located in the southeastern corner of the park. There you can pick up a self-guided tour leaflet or join a free organized tour at 1030 daily. A specialist Aboriginal tour, exploring the significance of the site to the Cadigal (the original Aboriginal inhabitants) and the first European settlers' desperate attempts to cultivate the site, is available on request. The **Botanical Gardens Restaurant** is one of the best places to observe the bats. You'll see lots of tropical ibis birds around the gardens – the descendants of a tiny group that escaped from Taronga Zoo.

From the Botanical Gardens it is a short stroll to Macquarie Point, which offers one of the best views of the Opera House and Harbour Bridge. Mrs Macquarie's Chair is the spot where the first governor's wife came to reflect upon the new settlement. One can only imagine what her reaction would be now.

The Domain and the Art Gallery of New South Wales

① *Art Gallery Rd, The Domain, T9225 1744, www.artgallery.nsw.gov.au, 1000-1700 and Wed 1700-2100, free (small charge for some visiting exhibitions), Explorer bus stop 12.*

Inside its grand façade, Australia's largest gallery houses the permanent works of many of the country's most revered contemporary artists as well as a collection of more familiar international names like Monet and Picasso. The Yiribana Gallery, in stark contrast, showcases a fine collection of Aboriginal and Torres Strait Islander works and is a major highlight. The Asian Gallery is also well worth a look. The main gallery features a dynamic programme of major visiting exhibitions, and there is a great bookshop and café. Be sure not to miss the quirky and monumental matchsticks installation by the late Brett Whiteley, one of the city's most celebrated artists, behind the main building. More of his work can be seen at the Brett Whiteley Museum in Surry Hills, see page 36. The Domain, the pleasant open park between the Art Gallery and Macquarie Place, was declared a public space in 1810. It is used as a free concert venue especially over Christmas and during the Sydney Festival.

Darling Harbour and Chinatown → *For listings, see pages 43-65.*

Created to celebrate Sydney's Bicentennial in 1988, revitalized Darling Harbour was delivered with much aplomb and has proved such a success that even the waves seem to show their appreciation. Day and night, ferries and catamarans bring hordes of visitors to marvel at its modern architecture and aquatic attractions or to revel in its casino and trendy waterside bars and restaurants. Framed against the backdrop of the CBD, it is intricately colourful, urban and angular. In contrast, the Chinese Garden of Friendship towards the southwestern fringe provides a little serenity before giving way to the old and chaotic enclave of Chinatown, the epicentre of Sydney's Asian community and the city's most notable living monument to its cosmopolitan populace.

Sydney Aquarium

ⓘ *Aquarium Pier, T8251 7800, www.sydneyaquarium.com.au, 0900-2200, $35, children $18, concessions $23, Explorer bus stop 24.*

This modern, well-presented aquarium has over 650 species, but it's not all about fish. On show is an imaginative array of habitats housing saltwater crocodiles, frogs, seals, penguins and platypuses. The highlight of the aquarium is the Great Barrier Reef Oceanarium: a huge tank that gives you an incredible insight into the world's largest living thing. Of course, many visit the aquarium to come face-to-face with some of Australia's deadliest sea creatures, without getting their feet, or indeed their underwear, wet. There is no doubt that such beauty and diversity has its dark side, as the notorious box jellyfish, cone shell or rockfish will reveal.

Sydney Wildlife World

ⓘ *T9333 9288, www.sydneywildlifeworld.com.au, 0900-2200, $35, children $18, (VIP guided tours available from $185 for two), Explorer bus stop 24.*

Established in 2006, this highly commercial attraction has 65 exhibits hosting 100 native Australian species and offers a more convenient and less time-consuming alternative to Taronga Zoo. Far more compact, it showcases nine impressive habitat exhibits, from the 'Flight Canyon' to the 'Nocturnal', housing all the usual suspects from the ubiquitous koala to the lesser-known and eminently appealing bilby. Although commercial profit is of course the primary goal here, cynics can rest assured that Sydney Wildlife World, in partnership with the Australian Wildlife Conservancy, has established the Sydney Wildlife World Conservation Foundation, through which funds will be raised to help safeguard Australia's threatened wildlife and ecosystems.

National Maritime Museum

ⓘ *2 Murray St, T9298 3777, www.anmm.gov.au, 0930-1700, free except warship and submarine $20, children and concessions $10; heritage galleries and James Craig $12, children and concessions $7; heritage galleries and Endeavour $18, children $9; combination ticket (all attractions) $32, children and concessions $17. It is easily reached on foot across the Pyrmont Bridge, or by Monorail, LightRail or Explorer bus, stop No 21.*

The museum, designed to look like the sails of a ship, offers a fine mix of old and new. For many, its biggest attractions are without doubt the warship *HMAS Vampire* and the submarine *HMAS Onslow*, the centrepieces of a fleet of old vessels sitting outside on the harbour. Both can be thoroughly explored with the help of volunteer guides. The museum interior contains a range of displays exploring Australia's close links with all things nautical, from the early navigators and the First Fleet, to the ocean liners that brought many waves of immigrants. Don't miss the beautifully restored replica of the *Endeavour*, Captain Cook's famous ship of discovery, and the 1874 square-rigger, the *James Craig*, both of which are moored to the north of the museum at Wharf 7. Other museum attractions include a café, sailing lessons and a range of short cruises on historical vessels. Occasionally you can even take a multi-day voyage on board the *Endeavour* – but at a price!

Sydney Fish Market

ⓘ *T9004 1100, www.sydneyfishmarket.com.au, tours operate Mon, Thu and Fri from 0645, from $20, children $10 (book ahead on T9004 1143). Sydney Light Rail runs by, or catch bus 443 from Circular Quay or 501 from Town Hall, Explorer bus stop 19.*

For anyone interested in sea creatures, the spectacle of the Sydney Fish Market is recommended. Every morning from 0530, nearly 3000 crates of seafood are auctioned to a lively bunch of 200 buyers using a computerized clock system. The best way to see the action, and more importantly the incredible diversity of species, is to join a tour group, which will give you access to the auction floor. Normally the general public are confined to the viewing deck high above the floor. Also within the market complex are cafés, some excellent seafood eateries and a superb array of open markets where seafood can be bought at competitive prices.

Powerhouse Museum

ⓘ *500 Harris St, Ultimo, T9217 0111, www.powerhousemuseum.com, 1000-1700, $10, children $5, concessions $6. Monorail, LightRail or Explorer bus stop No 18.*

With nearly 400,000 items collected over 120 years, the Powerhouse is the state's largest museum and half a day is barely enough to cover its floors. Housed in the former Ultimo Power Station, there is an impressive range of memorabilia, from aircraft to musical instruments, mainly with an emphasis on Australian innovation and achievement, and covering a wide range of general topics from science and technology to transportation, social history, fashion and design. There's a shop and café on site.

Chinatown

The Chinese have been an integral part of Sydney culture since the gold rush of the mid-1800s, though today Chinatown is also the focus of many other Asian cultures, including Vietnamese, Thai, Korean and Japanese. The district offers a lively diversion, with its heart being the Dixon Street pedestrian precinct, between the two pagoda gates facing Goulburn Street and Hay Street. Here, and in the surrounding streets, you will find a wealth of Asian shops and restaurants. At the northwestern corner of Chinatown is the **Chinese Garden of Friendship** ⓘ *T9240 8888, www.chinesegarden.com.au, 0930-1700. $6, children $3, families $15,* which was gifted to NSW by its sister Chinese province, Guangdong, to celebrate the Australian Bicentenary in 1988. It contains all the usual beautiful craftsmanship, landscaping and aesthetics.

In stark contrast is **Paddy's Market** ⓘ *corner of Hay St and Thomas St, 0900-1700,* one of Sydney's largest, oldest and liveliest markets, though somewhat tacky.

City West → *For listings, see pages 43-65.*

Glebe

ⓘ *Bus from George St in the city (Nos 431 or 434).*

To the southwest of Darling Harbour, beyond Ultimo, and separated by the campus of **Sydney University** (Australia's oldest), are Glebe and Newtown. Glebe prides itself on having a New Age-village atmosphere, where a cosmopolitan, mainly student crowd sits in the laid-back cafés, browses old-style bookshops or bohemian fashion outlets or seeks the latest therapies in alternative health shops. The **Saturday market** ① *Glebe Public School, Glebe Point Rd, T0419-291449, Sat 0930-1630*, provides an outlet for local crafts people to sell their work as well as bric-a-brac, clothes, etc.

Newtown
① *Bus from Loftus St on Circular Quay, or George St (Nos 422, 423, 426, 428). The Newtown Railway Station is on the Inner West/Bankstown (to Liverpool) lines.*
South beyond the university is **King Street**, the hub of Newtown's idiosyncratic range of shops, cafés and restaurants. Here you can purchase anything from a black leather codpiece to an industrial-size brass Buddha, drool over the menus of a vast range of interesting eateries, or simply idle over a latte and watch a more alternative world go by. A few hours' exploration, Sunday brunch or an evening meal in Newtown's King Street is recommended. Don't miss **Gould's Book Arcade** at 32 King Street, www.goulds books.com.au, which is an experience in itself.

Leichhardt
① *Bus Nos 436-438 or 440 from Circular Quay.*
Although receiving less attention than the eccentricities of Glebe and Newtown, Leichhardt is a pleasant suburb, famous for its Italian connections and subsequently its eateries and cafés. There are numerous places on Norton Street to enjoy a fine espresso, gelato or the full lasagne. Try Leichhardt institution **Bar Italia** at No 169.

Balmain
① *Bus from the QVB, Nos 441-444, or ferry from Circular Quay, Wharf 5.*
Straddling Johnstons Bay and connecting Darling Harbour and Pyrmont with the peninsula suburb of Balmain is Sydney's second landmark bridge, the **Anzac Bridge**, opened in 1995. It is a modern and strangely attractive edifice, which makes an admirable attempt to compete with the mighty Harbour Bridge. The former working-class suburb of Balmain has undergone a quiet metamorphosis to become an area with some of the most sought after real estate in Sydney. The main drag of **Darling Street** now boasts an eclectic range of gift shops, modern cafés, restaurants and pubs, which provide a pleasant half-day escape from the city centre. Try the cosy **Sir William Wallace Hotel**, 31 Cameron Street, or the more traditional and historic 1857 **Dry Dock Hotel**, corner of Cameron and College streets. There's a popular Saturday market in the grounds of St Andrew's Church.

Sydney Olympic Park
① *Centre, corner of Showground Rd and Murray Rose Av, near Olympic Park Railway Station, T9714 7888, www.sydneyolympicpark.com.au, 0900-1700, by train or RiverCat from Circular Quay (Wharf 5) to Homebush Bay Wharf.*
Although the vast swathes of Sydney's Western Suburbs remain off the radar for the vast majority of tourists, there are a few major and minor sights worth a mention. Topping the list is the multi-million-dollar Sydney Olympic Park, about 14 km west of the centre, with its mighty stadium, the centrepiece of a vast array of architecturally stunning sports

venues and public amenities. Tours of the venues by bus or bike are available; see the visitors' centre at 1 Showground Road for details.

ANZ Stadium (formerly Stadium Australia) was the main focus of the games, being the venue for the opening and closing ceremonies, as well as track and field and soccer events. Although the Olympic flame has long been extinguished, it remains an important national venue for international and national Rugby Union, Rugby League, Aussie Rules football and soccer matches. Olympic Park was also the main venue for Catholic World Youth Day, and associated visit of Pope Benedict XVI in 2008, attracting well over 100,000 worshippers.

Next door is the state-of-the-art **Acer Arena**, which hosted basketball and gymnastics during the games and now offers a huge indoor arena for a range of public events from music concerts to Australia's largest agricultural show, the Royal Easter Show. Perhaps the most celebrated venue during the games was the **Aquatic Centre**, where the triumphant Aussie swimming team took on the world and won with the help of such stars as Ian Thorpe and Michael Klim. The complex still holds international swimming and diving events and is open to the public. The Olympic Park has many other state-of-the-art sports facilities and is surrounded by superb parkland. **Bicentennial Park** ① *T9714 7524*, is a 100-ha mix of dry land and conservation wetland and a popular spot for walking, jogging, birdwatching or simply feeding the ducks.

Parramatta and around
About 6 km further west from Homebush is Parramatta, often dubbed the city within the city, a culturally diverse centre that boasts some of the nation's most historic sites. After the First Fleeters failed in their desperate attempts to grow crops in what is now the city centre, they penetrated the upper reaches of the Parramatta River and established a farming settlement, first known as Rose Hill before reverting to its original Aboriginal name. The oldest European site is **Elizabeth Farm** ① *70 Alice St, Rosehill, T9635 9488, 0930-1600, $8, children $4, family $17*, a 1793 colonial homestead built for John and Elizabeth Macarthur, pioneers in the Australian wool industry. The homestead contains a number of interesting displays and is surrounded by a recreated 1830s garden. Also of interest is the 1799 **Old Government House** ① *T9635 8149, Tue-Fri 1000-1630, Sat-Sun 1030-1630, $9*, in Parramatta Park. It is Australia's oldest public building and houses a fine collection of colonial furniture. **Experiment Farm Cottage** ① *9 Ruse St, T9635 5655, Tue-Fri 1030-1530, Sat-Sun 1130-1530, $7*, is the site of the colonial government's first land grant to former convict James Ruse in 1791. The cottage itself dates from 1834. The **Parramatta River**, which quietly glides past the city, is without doubt its most attractive natural feature and it offers a number of heritage walking trails. These and many other historical details are displayed at the **Parramatta Heritage and VIC** ① *346a Church St, T8839 3311, www.parracity.nsw.gov.au, daily 0900-1700*.

City East → *For listings, see pages 43-65.*

Kings Cross
① *By bus Sydney Explorer stop No 9 or regular bus services Nos 311, 323-325, 327, 333.*
Even before arriving in Sydney you will have probably heard of Kings Cross, the notorious hub of Sydney nightlife and the long-established focus of sex, drugs and rock and roll. Situated

near the navy's Woolloomooloo docks, 'the Cross' (as it's often called) has been a favourite haunt of visiting sailors for years. The main drag, **Darlinghurst Road**, is the focus of the action, while Victoria Street is home to a rash of backpacker hostels. At the intersection of both, and the top of William Street, which connects the Cross with the city, is the huge Coca Cola sign, a popular meeting point. The best time to visit the Cross is in the early hours when the bars, the clubs and the ladies of the night are all in full swing. It is hugely popular with backpackers and Sydneysiders alike and can provide a great night out. It is also a great place to meet people, make contacts, find work and even buy a car.

Amid all the mania there are a number of notable and more sedate sights in and around Kings Cross. **Elizabeth Bay House** ⓘ *7 Onslow Av, Elizabeth Bay, T9356 3022, www.hht.nsw.gov.au, Tue-Sun 1000-1630, $8, children $4, family $17*, is a revival-style estate built by popular architect John Verge for Colonial Secretary Alexander Macleay in 1845. The interior is restored and faithfully furnished in accordance with the times and the house has a great outlook across the harbour.

Woolloomooloo

To the northwest of Kings Cross, through the quieter and more upmarket sanctuary of Potts Point, is the delightfully named suburb of Woolloomooloo. 'Woo' is the main east coast base for the Australian Navy and visiting sailors also weigh anchor here, heading straight for the Kings Cross souvenir shops. Other than the warships and a scattering of lively pubs, it is the **Woolloomooloo Wharf** and a pie cart that are the major attractions. The wharf has a rash of fine restaurants that are a popular dining alternative to the busy city centre. If the wharf restaurants are beyond your budget, nearby is one of Sydney's best cheap eateries. Harry's **Café de Wheels**, near the wharf entrance (see page 51), is an institution, selling its own range of meat, mash, pea and gravy pies 24 hours a day (well, almost).

Darlinghurst and Surry Hills

The lively suburb of Darlinghurst fringes the city to the east, Kings Cross to the north and Surry Hills to the south. Both Darlinghurst and Surry Hills offer some great restaurants and cafés with Darlinghurst Road and Victoria Street, just south of Kings Cross, being the main focus. Here you will find some of Sydney's most popular eateries. The **Jewish Museum** ⓘ *148 Darlinghurst Rd, T9360 7999, www.sydneyjewishmuseum.com.au, Sun-Thu 1000-1600, Fri 1000-1400, $10, children $7*, has displays featuring the Holocaust and the history of Judaism in Australia. To get to Darlinghurst, take bus No 311.

Surry Hills is a mainly residential district and does not have quite the pizzazz of Darlinghurst, but it is well known for its traditional Aussie pubs, which seem to dominate every street corner. One thing not to miss is the **Brett Whiteley Museum and Gallery** ⓘ *2 Raper St, T9225 1881, Sat-Sun 1000-1600, free*. The museum is the former studio and home of the late Whiteley, one of Sydney's most popular contemporary artists. Both places can be reached on foot from the city via William Street, Liverpool Street or Oxford Street or by bus Nos 311-399.

Paddington

ⓘ *By foot from southeast corner of Hyde Park via Oxford St, bus Nos 378-382.*
The big attraction in Paddington is **Oxford Street**, which stretches east from the city and southwest corner of Hyde Park to the northwest corner of Centennial Park and Bondi

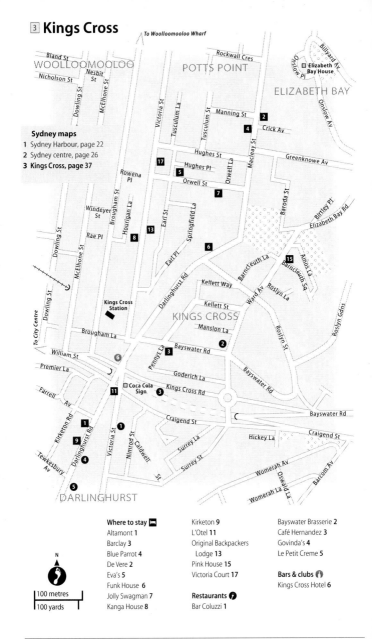

③ Kings Cross

To Woolloomooloo Wharf

WOOLLOOMOOLOO

Bland St
Nicholson St
Nesbit St
Dowling St
McElhone St

Rockwall Cres

POTTS POINT

Billyard Av
Onslow Av
Elizabeth Bay House

ELIZABETH BAY

Victoria St
Tusculum La
Tusculum St
Manning St
Crick Av
Macleay St
Greenknowe Av
Onslow Av

Sydney maps
1 Sydney Harbour, page 22
2 Sydney centre, page 26
3 Kings Cross, page 37

Rowena Pl
Hughes St
Hughes Pl
Orwell St
Orwell La
Baroda St
Birtley Pl
Elizabeth Bay Rd

Windeyer St
Brougham St
Hourigan La
Rae Pl
Earl St
Springfield La
Earl Pl

Dowling St
McElhone St
Darlinghurst Rd

Kings Cross Station

Barncleuth La
Barncleuth Sq
Amos La
Roslyn Gdns

Kellett Way
Kellett St
Ward Av
Roslyn La

To City Centre
Dowling St
Brougham La

KINGS CROSS
Mansion La
Bayswater Rd
Roslyn St

William St
Premier La
Farrell Av
Pennys La
Goderich La
Kings Cross Rd
Bayswater Rd

Coca Cola Sign

Bayswater Rd

Kirketon Rd
Darlinghurst Rd
Victoria St
Nimrod St
Caldwell St
Surrey La
Surrey St
Craigend St
Hickey La
Craigend St

Tewkesbury Av
Womerah Av
Oswald La
Barcom Av
Womerah La

DARLINGHURST

N

100 metres
100 yards

Junction. The city end of Oxford Street, surrounding Taylor Square, is one of the most happening areas of the city with a string of cheap eateries, cafés, restaurants, clubs and bars. It is also a major focus for the city's gay community. As Oxford Street heads west into Paddington proper it's lined with boutique clothes shops, art and bookshops, cafés and some good pubs. Many people coincide a visit to Oxford Street with the colourful **Paddington Market** ① *395 Oxford St, T9331 2923*, held every Saturday from 1000. Behind Oxford Street, heading north, are leafy suburbs lined with Victorian terrace houses, interspersed with commercial art galleries and old pubs, all of which are hallmarks of Paddington.

South of Oxford Street is the **Victoria Barracks**, a base for British and Australian Army battalions since 1848. It remains fully functional and visitors can see a flag-raising ceremony, and a marching band and join a guided tour on Thursdays at 1000.

Just to the south of the Barracks, in **Moore Park**, is the famous **Sydney Cricket Ground** (**SCG**) and, next door, the **Sydney Football Stadium** (**SFS**). The hallowed arena of the SCG is a veritable cathedral of cricket, considered by many as Australia's national sport. In winter the SCG is taken over by the Sydney Swans Australian Rules football team. The Sydney Football Stadium was, for many years, the focus of major national and international, Rugby Union, League and soccer matches but it now plays second fiddle to the mighty (and far less atmospheric) Telstra Stadium in Homebush. Tours of SCG and SFS are available to the public, Mon-Fri 1000, 1200 and 1400, Sat 1000, from $25, T1300 724737, www.sydneycricketground.com.au.

Fringing the two stadiums and Fox Studios Complex is **Centennial Park**, the city's largest green space. It provides a vast area for walking, cycling, horse riding, rollerblading and birdwatching. The Parklands Sports Centre also provides facilities for tennis, rollerhockey and basketball. In late summer there is a nightly outdoor **Moonlight Cinema** programme ① *www.moonlight.com.au*, which often showcases old classics.

Watson's Bay

① *Ferry from Circular Quay, Wharves 2 and 4, or bus No 342 or 325.*

Watson's Bay, on the leeward side of **South Head**, guarding the mouth of Sydney Harbour, provides an ideal city escape and is best reached by ferry from Circular Quay. As well as being home to one of Sydney's oldest and most famous seafood restaurants – **Doyle's** – it offers some quiet coves, attractive swimming beaches and peninsula walks. The best beaches are to be found at **Camp Cove** about 10 minutes' walk north of the ferry terminal. A little further north is **Lady Bay Beach**, which is very secluded and a popular naturist beach. The best walk in the area is the one- to two-hour jaunt to the 1858 **Hornby Lighthouse** and South Head itself, then south to the **HMAS Watson Naval Chapel** and the area known as **The Gap**. The area also boasts some interesting historical sites. Camp Cove was used by Governor Phillip as an overnight stop before reaching Port Jackson in the Inner Harbour. **Vaucluse House** ① *Wentworth Rd, T9388 7922, Tue-Sun 1000-1630, $8, children $4, family $17*, was built in 1827 and is a fine example of an early colonial estate. Many people spend a morning exploring Watson's Bay before enjoying a leisurely lunch at Doyle's, which sits just above the beach and ferry terminal on Marine Parade, or next door at the **Watson's Bay Hotel**, a more casual affair offering equally good views of the city skyline and a superb outdoor barbecue area (see page 51).

Bondi, Bronte and Coogee beaches

ⓘ *By car from the city, via Oxford St, by the Bondi and Bay Explorer, or buses Nos 321, 322, 365, 366 and 380. By rail go to Bondi Junction (Illawara Line) then take the bus (as above). For Coogee, bus Nos 372-374 and 314-315.*

Bondi Beach is by far the most famous of Sydney's many ocean beaches. Its hugely inviting stretch of sand is a prime venue for surfing, swimming and sunbathing. Behind the beach, Bondi's bustling waterfront and village offers a tourist trap of cafés, restaurants, bars, surf and souvenir shops. For years Bondi has been a popular suburb for alternative lifestylers and visiting backpackers keen to avoid the central city. It is also the place to see or be seen by all self-respecting beautiful people. If you intend swimming at Bondi note that, like every Australian beach, it is subject to dangerous rips, so always swim between the yellow and red flags, clearly visible on the beach. Watchful lifeguards, also clad in yellow and red, are on hand. Bondi Beach is the focus of wild celebrations on Christmas Day with one huge beach party, usually culminating in a mass naked dash into the sea.

To the south of Bondi Beach and best reached by a popular coastal walkway is the small oceanside suburb of **Bronte**. This little enclave offers a smaller, quieter and equally attractive beach with a number of very popular cafés frequented especially at the weekend for brunch. A little further south is **Clovelly**, which has another sheltered beach good for kids and snorkelling. Many people finish their walk at **Coogee**, which has a fine beach and bustling waterfront. Although playing second fiddle to Bondi, it is popular with those keen to stay near the beach and outside the centre.

City North → *For listings, see pages 43-65.*

North Sydney and surrounds

On the northern side of the Harbour Bridge a small stand of high-rise buildings with neon signs heralds the mainly commercial suburb of North Sydney. There is little here for the tourist to justify a special visit, but nearby, the suburb of **McMahons Point**, and more especially **Blues Point Reserve**, on the shores of Lavender Bay, offer fine city views. Another good vantage point is right below the bridge at **Milsons Point**. **Kirribilli** is a serene little suburb lying directly to the east of the bridge. **Admiralty House** and **Kirribilli House**, the Sydney residences of the governor general and the prime minister, sit overlooking the Opera House on Kirribilli Point. Both are closed to the public and are best seen from the water.

Mosman

ⓘ *By ferry from Circular Quay (Wharf 4) to Mosman Bay where buses run uphill to the commercial centre.*

Mosman has a very pleasant village feel and its well-heeled residents are rightly proud. Situated so close to the city centre, it has developed into one of the most exclusive and expensive areas of real estate in the city. However, don't let this put you off. Mosman, in unison with its equally comfy, neighbouring beachside suburb of **Balmoral**, are both great escapes by ferry from the city centre and offer some fine eateries, designer clothes shops, walks and beaches, plus one of Sydney's must-see attractions, **Taronga Zoo**.

Outback New South Wales

Some 1160 km west of Sydney, Broken Hill, or 'Silver City' as it is dubbed, is the most famous mining town in Australia, its gracious, dusty streets looking like something out of an Aussie version of Hollywood's Wild West. As well as all the obvious historical and mine-based attractions, Broken Hill is also home to a thriving arts community and numerous colourful galleries. There are tour operators to escort you to the surreal settlement of Silverton, as well as offering true outback adventures travelling to some superb regional national parks and lake systems. **Broken Hill VIC** ① *corner of Blende St and Bromide St, T8080 3560, www.visitbrokenhill.com.au, 0830-1700*, has city and regional maps, a detailed, self-guided heritage walk and trail leaflet, and organizes two-hour guided tours.

First off, pay a visit to the **Miners' Memorial** ① *T8087 1318, 0900-2200, access to memorial $2.50*, which tells the town's history. It stands atop the mullock heaps immediately to the east of the town centre. The onsite **Broken Earth Café and Restaurant** is the best place to eat in town. **The Daydream Mine** ① *20 km west of Broken Hill, signposted off Silverton Rd, T8088 5682, www.daydreammine.com.au, tours hourly 1000-1530, $20*, dating from 1882, has a walk-in mine.

Broken Hill artists create diverse works inspired by the landscapes, colours, light and perspectives of the outback. **Broken Hill Regional Art Gallery** ① *Argent St, T8080 3440, www.broken hill.net.au/bhart/main, Mon-Sun 1000-1700*, is the oldest regional gallery in NSW and has a fine mix of local and national works. The **Living Desert and Sculpture Symposium** is a hilltop collection of sandstone sculptures, 12 km northwest of the town. There are numerous tours on offer from Broken Hill, from scenic flights and 4WD to local mine tours and even camel rides. The VIC has full details.

The tiny former mining town of **Silverton**, just a short journey from Broken Hill, is pure outback, with wide, red, dusty roads and some mighty eccentric residents.

Taronga Zoo

① *T9969 2777, www.zoo.nsw.gov.au, 0900-1700, $41, children $20, concessions $23. Zoo Pass combo ticket (including ferry transfers and zoo), $48, children $23. Best reached by ferry from Circular Quay (Wharf 2), every 30 mins Mon-Fri from 0715-1845, Sat 0845-1845, Sun 0845-1745.* First opened in 1881 in the grounds of Moore Park, south of Centennial Park, before being relocated to Bradley's Head, Mosman, in 1916, Taronga contains all the usual suspects of the zoological world. It also has the huge added attraction of perhaps the best location and views of any city zoo in the world. You will almost certainly need a full day to explore the various exhibits on offer and there are plenty of events staged throughout the day to keep both adults and children entertained. The best of these is the Free Flight Bird Show, which is staged twice daily in an open-air arena overlooking the city. If you are especially interested in wildlife it pays to check out the dynamic programme of specialist public tours on offer. The Night Zoo tour after hours is popular. Taronga is built on a hill and it's worth going up to the main entrance then work your way back down to the lower gate. Or for a small additional charge on entry you can take a scenic gondola ride to the main gate.

Silverton VIC ① *2 Layard St, T8088 7566, www.silverton.org.au, 0800-1700*, can assist.

The village and landscape is so typical of the perceived Australian outback aesthetic that it has featured in numerous magazine ads and as the backdrop to films, including *Mad Max II*. Right in its heart is the famous **Silverton Hotel**, featured in the film *A Town Like Alice*, which does a good lunch, has a fine atmosphere (ask if you can 'take the test') and has places to stay. There is no public transport but most Broken Hill tour operators visit here. There is no fuel on sale.

● Where to stay
$$$$ Imperial Hotel, 88 Oxide St, T8087 7444, www.imperialfine accommodation.com. Beautifully renovated with excellent en suites or shared facilities, with a historic feel.

$ YHA Tourist Lodge, 100 Argent St, T8088 2086, brokenhill@yhansw.org.au. Deservingly popular is this friendly, family-run lodge. It offers dorms, doubles/ twins with spacious facilities, pool and bike hire. The owners are local gurus on sights and activities.

$ Silverton Hotel, T8088 5313. To this day, the hotel still plays host to Max fanatics. Good lunches, a fine atmosphere, hotel rooms and self-contained accommodation.

● Transport
Broken Hill Airport is 4 km southwest of the town via Bonanza St. A taxi, T8087 2222, to/from the airport to the city centre costs $20. **Regional Express**, T131713, www.rex.com.au, and **Qantas** offer services to Sydney and Adelaide. Long-distance coaches stop at the coach terminal, T8087 2735, beside the VIC. **Countrylink**, T132232, provides regular coach/rail services to Sydney via Dubbo. Buses stop outside the VIC on Anson St. The train station is on Crystal St, T8087 1400. **Countrylink** and **Great Southern Railways**, T132147, www.trainways.com.au, offers Sydney and Perth (via Adelaide) services twice weekly.

Balmoral, Middle Head and Bradley's Head
Balmoral Beach is one of the most popular and sheltered in the harbour. Here, more than anywhere else in the city, you can observe Sydneysiders enjoying something that is quintessentially Australian – the early morning, pre-work dip.

Balmoral Beach overlooks **Middle Harbour**, whose waters infiltrate far into the suburbs of the North Shore. On **Middle Head**, which juts out into the harbour beyond Mosman, you will find one of Sydney's best and most secluded naturist beaches – **Cobblers Beach**. The atmosphere is friendly and the crowd truly cosmopolitan, though less extrovert visitors should probably avoid the peninsula on the eastern edge of the beach. Access is via a little-known track behind the softball pitch near the end of Military Road.

You can also walk to the tip of Middle Head, where old wartime fortifications look out across North Head and the harbour entrance, or enjoy the walk to the tip of **Bradley's Head**, below the zoo, with its wonderful views of the city.

Manly

ⓘ *By ferry from Circular Quay (Wharves 2 and 3), $6.40, children $3.20, 30 mins, or the JetCat, $8.20, 15 mins. Both leave daily on a regular basis.*

Manly is by far the most visited suburb on the North Shore and is practically a self-contained holiday resort, offering an oceanside sanctuary away from the manic city centre. The heart of the community sits on the neck of the **North Head** peninsula, which guards the entrance of Sydney Harbour. **Manly Beach** is very much the main attraction. At its southern end, an attractive oceanside walkway connects Manly Beach with two smaller, quieter alternatives, **Fairy Bower Beach** and **Shelly Beach**. As you might expect, Manly comes with all the tourist trappings, including an attractive, tree-lined waterfront, fringed with cafés, restaurants and shops and a wealth of accommodation options.

Connecting Manly Beach with the ferry terminal and **Manly Cove** (on the western or harbour side) is the **Corso**, a fairly tacky pedestrian precinct lined with cheap eateries, bars and souvenir shops. Its only saving grace is the market held at its eastern end every weekend. **Oceanworld** ⓘ *T8251 7877, www.oceanworld.com.au, 1000-1730, $19, children $10, concessions $14, regular tours available, 'Swim with the sharks' $250, sharks fed on Mon, Wed and Fri at 1100*, a long-established aquarium, although looking tired, is still worth a visit if you have kids or fancy a swim with the star attractions on the aquarium's unusual 'Swim with the sharks' tour. **Manly Art Gallery and Museum** ⓘ *T9976 1420, Tue-Sun 1000-1700, free*, showcases an interesting permanent exhibition of historical items with the obvious emphasis on all things 'beach', while the gallery offers both permanent and temporary shows of contemporary art and photography. The 10-km **Manly Scenic Walkway** from Manly to Spit Bridge is an excellent scenic harbour walk, arguably the city's best. Meandering through bush and along beaches while gazing over the harbour, it's hard to believe that you are in the middle of Australia's biggest city. The walk starts from the end of West Esplanade, takes from three to four hours and is clearly signposted the whole way. Walk on a weekday if possible: Sundays can be very busy.

North Head

The tip of North Head, to the south of Manly, is well worth a look, if only to soak up the views across the harbour and out to sea. The cityscape is especially stunning at dawn. Just follow Scenic Drive to the very end. The **Quarantine Station** ⓘ *T9466 1500, www.q-station.com.au, tours Wed-Sat at 1500, Sun at 1000 and 1300, 2 hrs, from $25; Ghost Tours (can include lunch from $70 or dinner from $99) Wed-Sun 1930, 3 hrs, from $44; Family Tour Thu and Sun at 1800, 2 hrs, from $34, children $22, bookings recommended, bus No 135 from Manly wharf*, taking up a large portion of the peninsula, was used from 1832 to harbour ships known to be carrying diseases like smallpox, bubonic plague, cholera and Spanish influenza to protect the new colony from the spread of such nasties. The station closed in 1984 and is now administered by the NSW Parks and Wildlife Service. Luxury accommodation is available at the Quarantine Station and there is a good-quality restaurant.

Northern beaches

The coast north of Manly is indented by numerous bays and fine beaches that stretch 40 km to **Barrenjoey Head** at Broken Bay and the entrance to the Hawkesbury River harbour. Perhaps the most popular of these are **Narrabeen**, **Avalon** and **Whale Beach**, but there are many to choose from. Narrabeen has the added attraction of a large lake, used for sailing, canoeing and windsurfing, while Avalon and Whale Beach, further north, are smaller, quite picturesque and more sheltered. A day trip to the very tip of Barrenjoey Head is recommended and the area is complemented by **Palm Beach**, a popular weekend getaway with some fine restaurants. This is also where most of the day-to-day filming takes place for the popular Australian 'soapie' *Home and Away*. There are many water activities on offer in the area focused mainly on **Pittwater**, a large bay on the sheltered western side of the peninsula. Whether you come for a day trip or a weekend stay get hold of the free *Northern Beaches Visitors' Guide* from the Sydney VIC. The L90 bus from Wynyard goes via all the main northern beach suburbs to Palm Beach, every 30 minutes.

Sydney listings

For hotel and restaurant price codes and other relevant information, see pages 10-14.

⬤ Where to stay

Sydney has all types of accommodation to suit all budgets. Most of the major luxury hotels are located around Circular Quay, Darling Harbour and the northern CBD. Other more moderately priced hotels, motels and small boutique hotels are dotted around the southern city centre and inner suburbs. It's worth considering this option as many in the suburbs provide attractive alternatives to the busy city centre. There are plenty of backpacker hostels with most centred around Kings Cross. The CBD is best for convenience, Kings Cross is best for social activities, or beachside resorts such as Manly or Bondi for the classic Sydney lifestyle. A less obvious option is a serviced apartment in the CBD. **Medina**, T1300 633462, www.medina apartments.com.au, has several places in the city. At any time in the peak season (Oct-Apr) and especially over Christmas, the New Year and during major sporting or cultural events, pre-booking is advised for all types of accommodation. If you have not pre-booked the Rocks VIC is a good place to start.

Circular Quay and the Rocks
p23, map p26
$$$$ B&B Sydney Harbour, 140 Cumberland St, T9247 1130, www.bbsydneyharbour.com.au. Friendly B&B with a range of 10 rooms that capture

something of the building's century-plus of history without sacrificing those little luxuries. Shared and en suite. Breakfast is served in the tucked-away courtyard.
$$$$ Russell, 143A George St, T9241 3543, www.therussell.com.au. Set right in the heart of the Rocks with views of the harbour, a historic ambience and a good range of singles, en suites, standard rooms and suites. Also has an appealing rooftop garden.
$$$ Australian Heritage Hotel, 100 Cumberland St, T9247 2229, www.australian heritagehotel.com. This hotel is a good B&B with 10 comfortable doubles (shared bathrooms) and a small rooftop terrace.
$$$ Lord Nelson Pub and Hotel, corner of Kent St and Argyle St, The Rocks, T9251 4044, www.lordnelson.com.au. This historic hotel has some very pleasant and affordable en suites above the pub. The added attraction here is the home-brewed beer, food and general ambience. The pub closes fairly early at night, so noise is not usually a factor.
$$$ YHA The Rocks, 110 Cumberland St, T8272 0900, www.yha.com.au. Hugely popular given its location and its views right across Circular Quay to the Opera House and beyond. Many of the multishare and double/twin en suites have views and the rooftop deck is something many 5-star hotels in the area cannot match. It has all the regular, reliable YHA features and facilities. Limited (paid) parking near the hostel. Recommended.

City centre *p29, map p26*

At the northern edge of the CBD, fringing Circular Quay, there are reliable chain hotels that still offer a peek across the harbour. Around Haymarket the hotels become cheaper and begin to be replaced by hostels.

$$$ Capitol Square, corner of Campbell and George streets, T9211 8633, www.rydges.com. Right next door to the Capitol Theatre is this friendly boutique hotel. It has cosy en suite rooms, a good restaurant and is one of the best affordable 3-4-star hotels in the centre.

$$$ Sydney Central YHA, corner of Pitt St and Rawson Pl, T9218 9000, www.yha.com.au. Vast and very popular, next to Central Station and the main interstate bus depot, this huge heritage building has over 500 beds split into a range of dorms, doubles and twins, with some en suite. Naturally, it also offers all mod cons including, pool, sauna, café, bar, internet, mini-mart, TV rooms and employment and travel desks.

$$$ Y on the Park (YWCA), 5-11 Wentworth Av, T9285 6288, www.yhotel.com.au. Pitched somewhere between a budget hotel and a hostel it welcomes both male and female clients, has a good range of clean, modern, spacious and quiet rooms and boasts all the usual facilities. It is also well placed between the city centre and social hub of Oxford St.

$$ Alfred Park Budget Accommodation, 207 Cleveland St, Redfern, T9319 4031, www.alfredpark.com.au. A good 10-min walk south of Central Station, down Chalmers St and across Prince Alfred Park, is this cross between a budget hotel and a backpackers, offering peace and quiet. It is well kept and clean, offering tidy dorms, and spacious singles, doubles and twins. Modern facilities and free guest parking.

$$ Base Backpackers, 477 Kent St, T9267 7718, www.basebackpackers.com. Modern chain backpackers right in the heart of the city. Large, spacious and with good facilities, it has fine doubles, twins and dorms.

$$ Railway Square YHA, 8-10 Lee St, T9281 9666, railway@yhansw.org.au. An excellent, modern 280-bed YHA hostel in the station area itself, with accommodation, including some en suite doubles, and facilities in railway carriages.

$$ Wake Up, 509 Pitt St, T9288 7888, www.wakeup.com.au. Opposite Central railway station with 24-hr check-in, this is huge, but convenient, safe, clean and well run. It has nicely appointed doubles and twins, some with en suite, and a range of dorms, plus kitchen facilities, café, bar, travel desk and employment information.

Darling Harbour and Chinatown *p31, map p26*

$$$ Glasgow Arms Hotel, 527 Harris St, Ultimo, T9211 2354, www.glasgow armshotel.com.au. Good value, friendly, just on the edge of Darling Harbour, the hotel offers basic yet cosy rooms, entertaining bar and an affordable pub restaurant with a courtyard downstairs.

$$$ Pensione Hotel, 631 George St, T9265 8888, www.pensione.com.au. A no-nonsense modern hotel conveniently located on the edge of Darling Harbour. Choice of good value, European minimalist-style singles to quads, in-house restaurant/bar.

City West *p33*
Glebe

Glebe is especially popular as an alternative backpackers' venue offering a village-type atmosphere with interesting cafés, shops and pubs all within easy walking distance.

$$$$ Trickett's Luxury B&B, 270 Glebe Point Rd, T9552 1141, www.tricketts.com.au. A beautifully restored Victorian mansion, decorated with antiques and Persian rugs and offering spacious, well-appointed en suites.

$$$ Alishan International Guesthouse, 100 Glebe Point Rd, T9566 4048, www.alishan.com.au. Halfway between a small hotel and a quality hostel, this spacious, renovated Victorian mansion has spotless doubles, twins and family en suites, all with TV and fridge. Shared accommodation is also available and overall the facilities are excellent. A great value budget option, especially for couples looking for a place away from the city centre. Limited off-street parking.

$$ Glebe Village Backpackers, 256 Glebe Point Rd, T9660 8878, www.glebevillage.com. A large, working backpackers' favourite and the management works hard to maintain its sound reputation. It offers a range of dorms and a few doubles (some en suite) and is friendly, laid-back and prides itself on finding work for guests. There's an-house café, pick-ups and regular day tours to beaches and other locations.

$$ Glebe Point YHA, 262 Glebe Point Rd, T9692 8418, www.yha.com.au. A popular option away from the CBD with a nice atmosphere, offering fairly small single, double, twin and 4-bed dorms and modern facilities throughout. Barbecues on the roof are a speciality. Regular shuttle to the city and transport departure points.

City East *p35, map p37*

There is no shortage of accommodation in Kings Cross and its surrounding suburbs, with everything from the de luxe 5-star hotels to the basic and affordable hostel. Most backpackers are located along Victoria St, Orwell St or on the main drag, Darlinghurst Rd. Others are scattered in quieter locations around the main hub, especially towards Potts Point.

Kings Cross

$$$ The Barclay, 17 Bayswater Rd, T9358 6133, www.barclayhotel.com.au. Recently renovated and good value, with a touch of class. Restaurant, bar and nightclub.

$$ Funk House, 23 Darlinghurst Rd, T9358 6455, www.funkhouse.com.au. Set right on Darlinghurst Rd, this is definitely one for the younger party set. Zany artworks adorn the walls and doors. 3-4 bed dorms and double/twins all with fridge, TV and fan. Lots of freebies. Their legendary rooftop barbecues are a great place to meet others. Good job search assistance.

$$ Jolly Swagman, 27 Orwell St, T9358 6400, www.jollyswagman.com.au. Another buzzing hostel set in the heart of the action. Very professionally managed with all the usual facilities. TV, fridge and fan in most rooms. Excellent travel desk and job search assistance. Social atmosphere. 24-hr check-in, fast internet and free beer on arrival.

$$ Original Backpackers Lodge, 160-162 Victoria St, T9356 3232, www.originalbackpackers.com.au. Possibly the best hostel in Kings Cross if not the city and certainly one of the best in terms of facilities and management. The historic house is large and homely, well appointed and comfortable, offering a great range of double, twin, single, triple and dorm rooms all with TV, fridge and fans (heated in winter). There is a great open courtyard in which to socialize or enjoy a barbecue. Cable TV. The staff are always on hand to help with onward travel, job seeking or things to see and do. Book ahead.

$$ Pink House, 6-8 Barncleuth Sq, T9358 1689, www.pinkhouse.com.au. A historic mansion offering a homely feel that is lacking in many of the other Kings Cross hostels; deservingly popular, especially for those tired of the party scene. Lots of quiet corners and a shady courtyard in which to find peace of mind. Large dorms and some good doubles, cable TV and free internet.

Potts Point

$$$$ Victoria Court, 122 Victoria St, T9357 3200, www.victoria court.com.au. This is a delightful and historic boutique hotel in a quiet location. It comes with period antiques, well-appointed en suites, fireplaces and 4-poster beds. The courtyard conservatory is excellent.

$$$ De Vere Hotel, 44-46 Macleay St, T9358 1211, www.devere hotel.com.au. North, away from the mania of Kings Cross proper yet still convenient to eateries and nightlife, is one of the tidiest and best value standard hotels in the area. All rooms have a private bathroom and there are also self-contained options. Buffet breakfast.

$$ Blue Parrot, 87 Macleay St, T9356 4888, www.blueparrot.com.au. Located towards Potts Point. Modern, clean and well managed, with an attractive courtyard garden to escape the hype of the Cross and open fires in winter. Free internet.

$$ Challis Lodge, 21-23 Challis Av, T9358 5422, www.challislodge.com.au. A historic mansion, cheaper than **Victoria Court**, and therefore less salubrious, yet with a good range of singles, twins and doubles, some with en suites.

$$ Eva's, 6-8 Orwell St, T9358 2185, www.evasbackpackers.com.au. This is another clean and well-managed hostel that offers a distinctly homely feel. Arty rooms with some en suites. Rooftop space used for social barbecues and offering great views across the city.

$$ Kanga House, 141 Victoria St, T9357 7897, www.kangahouse.com.au. Offers a warm welcome and if you are lucky you may be able to secure a room with a view of the Opera House.

Darlinghurst, Surry Hills and Airport

Separated only by a river of traffic, Darlinghurst offers a fine alternative to Kings Cross. Surry Hills has few options.

$$$$ L'Otel, 114 Darlinghurst Rd, Darlinghurst, T9360 6868, www.lotel.com.au. Classy, yet given its minimalist decor perhaps not everyone's cup of tea. Ultra hip and very much a place for the modern couple. Excellent personable service and a fine restaurant attached.

$$$ Altamont, 207 Darlinghurst Rd, Darlinghurst, T9360 6000, www.altamont.com.au. Classy, traditional hotel with beautiful spacious de luxe rooms with wooden floors and fittings. Some are fantastic value.

$$$ Kirketon, 229 Darlinghurst Rd, Darlinghurst, T9332 2011, www.kirketon.com.au. Modern, chic and minimalist with a bar and restaurant.

$$ Formule 1 Motel, 5 Ross Smith Av (300 m from domestic terminal), Mascot, T8339 1840, www.formule1.com.au. Cramped but affordable motel accommodation within walking distance of the domestic terminal and international terminal transfers.

$$ Kangaroo Bakpak, 665 South Dowling St, Surry Hills, T9319 5915, www.kangaroo bakpak.com.au. A quiet backpacker option with a friendly family atmosphere. Good for longer stays.

$$ Royal Sovereign, corner of Liverpool St and Darlinghurst Rd, Darlinghurst, T9331 3672, www.darlobar.com.au. For something more traditional look no further than here. Quality refurbished rooms above the popular **Darlo** bar. Shared bathroom facilities.

Watson's Bay

$$$$ Watson's Bay, T9337 5444, www.watsonsbayhotel.com.au. Set alongside the legendary seafood restaurant (see page 51) is this fabulous boutique hotel with 32 suites, each with its own breathtaking view from the balcony. Easily reached by ferry.

Bondi and Coogee

The older, well-established beachfront hotels in Bondi look a little garish but their interiors will not disappoint, and they are only metres from the world-famous beach. There are around a dozen backpackers. Coogee is steadily growing in popularity as a viable and often cheaper alternative to Bondi Beach.

$$$$ Coogee Bay Boutique Hotel, 9 Vicar St, Coogee, T9665 0000, www.coogeebay hotel.com.au. Very pleasant, boutique-style rooms in addition to good, traditional pub-style options. Well appointed, en suite, ocean views and good value. The hotel itself is a main social focus in Coogee both day and night.

$$$$ Ravesi's, corner of Campbell Parade and Hall St, Bondi, T9365 4422, www.ravesis.com.au. Stylish and intimate with pleasant, good value 3-star standard rooms, standard suites and luxury split-level suites, most with balconies overlooking all the action. The balcony restaurant is one of the best in the area.

$$$ Bondi, 178 Campell Pde, Bondi, T9130 3271, www.hotelbondi.com.au. Traditional, with a popular public bar downstairs, a good café and a nightclub/performance space, **Zinc**, with live bands, DJs and pool competitions most nights.

$$$ Bondi Beachouse YHA, corner of Fletcher St and Dellview St, Bondi, T9365 2088, www.yha.com.au. Art deco building with great ocean views from the rooftop deck. Usual YHA reliability and full room configurations, but no en suites. Café/restaurant and, of course, the odd surfboard.

$$$ Coogee Beachside Backpackers, 178/172, Coogee Bay Rd, Coogee, T9315 8511, www.sydneybeachside.com.au. Just as good as **Surfside** (below) but smaller and with more character. There are 2 houses (Wizard of Oz and Beachside). The rooms, especially the doubles, are excellent. Good facilities, friendly staff with good work contacts. A 5-min walk to the beach. Ask about flat shares if you intend to stay long term.

$$ Lamrock Lodge Backpackers, 19 Lamrock Av, Bondi, T9130 5063, www.lamrocklodge.com. Offers clean, modern facilities and all rooms – dorm, single, twin and double – have cable TV, fridge, kitchenette and microwave. Good value.

$$ Noah's Bondi Beach Backpackers, 2 Campbell Pde, Bondi, T9365 7644, www.noahsbondibeach.com. Perched on the hill, overlooking the beach as you descend to

Bondi proper, is this large place, popular due to its position and price. As such it is certainly not the quietest. Former hotel rooms converted to dorms, twins and doubles (some with ocean view). Rooftop barbecue area offers great views.

$$ Surfside Backpackers, 186 Arden St, Coogee, T9315 7888, www.surfside backpackers.com.au. The largest of the several backpackers, beachside and very social with a solid reputation and modern facilities. 2-bedroom flats available for small groups with balcony and ocean view. They also run a sister facility at 35A Hall St, Bondi Beach, T9365 4900.

City North *p39*
North Sydney and surrounds
The quiet yet central suburb of Kirribilli, across the water from the Opera House, is an excellent place to base yourself, with a short and spectacular ferry trip to the CBD. There is very little in the way of accommodation but that is part of its charm.

$$$ Glenferrie Lodge, 12A Carabella St, T9955 1685, www.glenferrielodge.com. A vast, 70-room Victorian mansion with quality budget accommodation. The range of shared, single, twin, double, queen/king de luxe are above average with some having their own balconies. Cheap dinners are on offer nightly and there are B&B packages. Wi-Fi. Recommended.

Manly
Being a well-established resort within the city there is no shortage of accommodation in Manly. The VIC on the Forecourt beside the ferry wharf has detailed listings, maps and can help arrange bookings, T9976 1430, www.manlytourism.com.au.

$$$$ Manly Lodge Boutique Hotel, 22 Victoria Pde, T9977 8655, www.manly lodge.com.au. A homely option, popular and good value.

$$$ 101 Addison B&B, 101 Addison Rd, T9977 6216, www.bb-manly.com. For a B&B option try this historic 1-bedroom gem. Open fire, grand piano; say no more! Book well ahead.

$$ Boardrider Backpackers, 63 Corso (rear), T9977 6077, www.boardrider.com.au. New purpose-built backpackers with all the usual amenities set in the heart of the action and only metres from the ferry and beach. Dorm, twin and doubles, some with en suite.

$$ Manly Backpackers Beachside, 28 Raglan St, T9977 3411, www.manly backpackers.com.au. Well-rated and busy with some en suite doubles and small dorms.

$$ Manly Bungalow, 64 Pittwater Rd, T9977 5494, www.manlybungalow.com. Bright and sunny budget accommodation with good value double and family rooms with kitchenettes.

Northern beaches

$$ Collaroy YHA (Sydney Beachhouse), 4 Collaroy St, Collaroy Beach, T9981 1177, www.sydneybeachouse.com.au. The Hilton of Sydney backpackers offers tidy dorms, twins, doubles and family rooms (some en suite) and great facilities, including a heated pool, spacious kitchen, dining areas, TV rooms, free equipment hire and organized day trips. When it comes to facilities it deserves its reputation as one of the best budget options in the city. Book ahead. Catch the L90 or L88 bus from Central, Wynyard or QVB.

$$ Pittwater YHA, via Halls Wharf, Morning Bay, via Church Pt, T9999 5748, www.yha.com.au. A real getaway located in the Ku-ring-gai National Park and accessible only by ferry. It has dorms and a few doubles. Plenty of walking and water-based activities or simple peace and quiet. Phone for details, take all your supplies and book ahead.

🔊 Restaurants

When it comes to quality and choice there is no doubt that Sydney is on a par with any

major city in the world and with over 3000 restaurants to choose from you have to wonder where on earth to start. As a general rule you will find the best of the fine dining establishments specializing in Modern Australian cuisine in and around Circular Quay, the Rocks, the CBD and Darling Harbour, though pockets of international speciality abound, from chow mein in Chinatown to pasta in Paddington. Sydney's thriving café culture is generally centred on the suburbs of Darlinghurst, Glebe, Newtown and the eastern beaches of Bondi and Bronte.

Circular Quay and the Rocks
p23, map p26

On the eastern side of the Quay you will find mid-range and expensive options with lots of atmosphere and memorable views under the concourse of the Opera House and within 'The Toaster'.

$$ Australian Heritage Hotel, see page 43. Daily for lunch and dinner. Come here for a taste of Aussie pub life. It has a wonderful atmosphere and all the classic Australian beers. Good value and good alfresco and menu, which includes pizza, croc, emu and roo steaks.

$$ Café Sydney, Level 5, Customs House, 31 Alfred St, T9251 8683. Daily for lunch, Mon-Sat for dinner. Set high above Circular Quay at the top of Customs House, this place offers superb views and alfresco dining. The food is traditional modern Australian with a good atmosphere and occasional live jazz.

$$ The Wharf, Pier 4, Hickson Rd, Walsh Bay, T9250 1761. Lunch and dinner Mon-Sat. Off the beaten track and a firm local favourite is this option located at the end of one of the historic Walsh Bay piers. It has a great atmosphere and wonderful views of the busy harbour. Modern Australian.

$$-$ MCA Café, 140 George St, T9241 4253. Lunch Mon-Fri and breakfast and lunch Sat-Sun. At the Museum of Contemporary Art, this café is ideally located next to all the action on Circular Quay. It is a bit expensive but worth it and the seafood is excellent.

$ La Renaissance, 47 Argyle St, The Rocks, T9241 4878. Head to this patisserie for a simple lunch. Authentic French baguettes and pastries in a quiet leafy courtyard or to take away.

$ Rocks Café, T9241 2883 daily 0800-2130. A cheaper option around the back of the MCA and also good.

City centre *p29, map p26*

The sheer chaos and noise that surrounds you in the CBD is enough to put anyone off eating. A retreat to the Botanical Gardens or Hyde Park is recommended.

$$ Brooklyn Hotel, corner of George St and Grosvenor St, T9247 6744. Lunch Mon-Fri. Well known for its meat dishes, especially steak, and has plenty of inner city pub atmosphere.

$$ Pavilion on the Park, 1 Art Gallery Rd, The Domain, T9232 1322. Opposite the Art Gallery, this place is the perfect escape from the city centre, offering alfresco dining with an eclectic modern Australian menu. Perfect for lunch after a tour of the gallery.

$ Botanical Gardens Café, Mrs Macquarie Rd, T9241 2419. Daily 0830-1800. For sublime tranquillity amidst the Botanical Gardens, the bat colony might not be everybody's cup of tea but for environmentalists and botanists it's really hard to beat.

$ Casa Asturiana, 77 Liverpool St, T9264 1010. Daily for lunch and dinner. In Sydney's Spanish quarter and well known for its Spanish cuisine, tapas in particular. Lots of atmosphere and regular live music.

$ Hyde Park Café, corner of Elizabeth and Liverpool streets, T9264 8751. Daily 0700-1630. A great spot for escaping the crowds, serving breakfast, light lunches, coffee and people watching.

$ MOS Café, corner of Bridge and Phillip streets, T9241 3636. Mon-Fri 0700-2100 and Sat-Sun 0830-1700. Below the Museum of

Sydney this congenial café offers good-value Modern Australian cuisine for lunch.

$ Tearoom, on the top floor of the QVB, George St. Sun-Fri 1100-1700, Sat 1100-1500. If the shopping all gets too much escape to this gracious room where you can sink into a large comfy chair and have an enormous afternoon tea.

Darling Harbour and Chinatown
p31, map p26

$$ Coast, Roof Terrace, Cockle Bay Wharf, Darling Park, 201 Sussex St, T9267 6700. Lunch Mon-Fri and Sun, daily for dinner. Offers a fine range of Modern Australian dishes and has a formal, yet relaxed atmosphere and great views across Darling Harbour.

$ BBQ King, 18 Goulburn St, T9267 2586. Daily 1130-0200. This Sydney institution is the first place to head for if you fancy Chinese. There's nothing special about the decor or service but the food is always excellent and good value.

$ Blackbird Café, Mid Level, Cockle Bay Wharf, T9283 7385. Deservedly popular, congenial, laid back and good value with a huge selection from pasta to steak.

$ Chinta Ria – The Temple of Love, Roof Terr, Cockle Bay Wharf, 201 Sussex St, T9264 3211, www.chintaria.com. Daily for lunch and dinner. With a name like that who can resist? Great aesthetics, buzzing atmosphere with quality Malaysian cuisine.

$ Dickson House Food Court, corner of Little Hay St and Dixon St. Daily 1030-2030. Has a wealth of cheap Asian takeaways with generous meals for under $6.

$ Emperor's Garden Seafood, 96 Hay St, T9211 2135, www.emperorsgarden.com.au. Daily 0800-0100. Moving into Haymarket is one of the most reliable of the Chinatown restaurants, always bustling, offering great service and value for money.

City West *p33*
Glebe

$$ Boathouse on Blackwattle Bay, Ferry Rd, T9518 9011, www.boathouse.net.au. Tue-Sun lunch and dinner. A quality upmarket (yet informal) seafood restaurant offering refreshingly different harbour views than those sought at Circular Quay and Darling Harbour. Here you can watch the lights of Anzac Bridge or the comings and goings of Sydney's fishing fleet while tucking into the freshest seafood.

$ Badde Manors, 37 Glebe Point Rd, T9660 3797. Daily 0730 till late. Something of an institution in Glebe for many years, this student hangout can always be relied on for atmosphere and character, which is more than can be said for the service.

$ Iku Organic, 25A Glebe Point Rd, T9692 8720. Mon-Fri 1130-2100, Sat-Sun 1130-2100. The first of what is now a chain of fine vegetarian and macrobiotic vegan cafés under the Iku banner, offering a delicious array of options.

$ Nawaz Flavour of India, 142A Glebe Point Rd, T9692 0662. Quite simply Glebe's best Indian restaurant with lots of character, great service and value for money.

$ Toxteth Hotel, 345 Glebe Point Rd, T9660 2370. Daily from 1100. Modern, traditional Australian pub serving mountainous plates of good pub grub at very cheap prices.

$ Well Connected, 35 Glebe Point Rd, T9566 2655. Open 0700-2400. One of the city's first internet cafés. Laid back with a whole floor upstairs full of sofas dedicated to surfing the web. Not a bad cup of coffee either.

Newtown

$ Cinque, 261 King St, Newtown, T9519 3077. Daily 0730-late. Another popular café located next to the Dendy Cinema and a small bookshop. Great all-day breakfasts and coffee.

$ Old Fish Shop Café, 239A King St, T9519 4295. Daily 0730-2300. A charming little café and one of Newtown's best and most popular haunts, especially for breakfast and good coffee.

$ Thai Pothong, 294 King St, T9550 6277. Tue-Sun lunch, daily for dinner. On a street with more Thai restaurants than you can shake a chopstick at, this one stands head and shoulders above the rest. Good value, good choice and good service.

$ Thanh Binh, 111 King St, T9557 1175. Thu-Sun lunch, daily for dinner. Good value Vietnamese offering delicious dishes from simple noodles to venison in curry sauce.

City East *p35, map p37*
Kings Cross

As you'd expect there are a million and one fast food outlets here and other budget eateries catering for the cash-strapped backpacker and night owls.

$ Bayswater Brasserie, 32 Bayswater Rd, T9357 2177. Mon-Thu 1700-2300, Fri 1200-2300, Sat 1700-2300. A reliable choice and immensely popular for its laid-back yet classy atmosphere and imaginative Modern Australian cuisine. At the top end of this price range.

$ Café Hernandez, 60 Kings Cross Rd, T9331 2343. Great, eccentric 24-hr café serving Spanish fare, great coffee and with lots of character.

$ Govinda's, 112 Darlinghurst Rd, T9380 5155. Restaurant and cinema combo offering great value all-you-can-eat vegetarian buffet plus the movie ticket. Dinner is $19.80 and a further $10:00 for the movie/dinner package.

Woolloomooloo

The wharf has a growing reputation as one of the best places for fine dining in the city.

$$ Manta Ray, 9 The Wharf, 6 Cowper Wharf Rd, T9332 3822. Mon-Fri lunch and daily for dinner. Classy seafood restaurant. Some say one of the best in the city.

$$ Otto Italiano, 8 The Wharf, Cowper Wharf Rd, T9368 7488. Very trendy, quality

Italian with all the necessary trimmings including extrovert waiters.

$ Harry's Café de Wheels, Cowper Wharf. Sun-Thu 0700-0200, Fri-Sat till 0300. **Harry's** is something of a Sydney institution, offering the famously yummy pies with pea toppings and gravy. One is surely never enough, as the photos of satisfied customers will testify.

Darlinghurst and Surry Hills

$$ Forty One, Chifley Tower, 2 Chifley Square, T9221 2500, www.forty-one.com.au. Enjoys an international reputation for quality fine dining. Stunning views across the Botanical Gardens and harbour. Intimate yet relaxed atmosphere. Book well ahead.

$ Bar Coluzzi, 322 Victoria St, Darlinghurst, T9380 5420. Daily 0500-1900. A well-established café that consistently gets the vote as one of Sydney's best. The character, the truly cosmopolitan clientele and the coffee are the biggest draws, rather than the food.

$ Bill's Café, 433 Liverpool St, Darlinghurst, T9360 9631. Mon-Sat 0730-1500, Sun 0830-1500. One of the city's top breakfast cafés with legendary scrambled eggs. Small and at times overcrowded but that's part of the experience. Also **Bill's Surry Hills**, at 359 Crown St, Surry Hills, T9360 4762. Daily 0700-2200.

$ Le Petit Creme, 118 Darlinghurst Rd, Darlinghurst, T9361 4738. Daily from 0800. Superb little French number with all the classics, from baguettes to cavernous bowls of café au lait. Great omelettes for breakfast or lunch.

$ Longrain, 85 Commonwealth St, Surry Hills, T9280 2888. Wed-Fri and Sun 1200-1430, dinner Mon-Sat 1800-2300. Without doubt one of the best Thai restaurants in the city. Housed in a century-old warehouse space, other than its cuisine, one of its most notable features the huge wooden tables deliberately designed to encourage Asian-style banquet dining. Recommended.

$ Oh! Calcutta!, 251 Victoria St, Darlinghurst, T9360 3650. Fri lunch and Mon-Sat dinner. An award-winning Indian restaurant and by far the best in the inner east. Book ahead.

$ Una's, 340 Victoria St, Darlinghurst, T9360 6885. Daily 0730-late. Local favourite offering generous hangover-cure breakfasts and European-influenced lunches, including schnitzel and mouthwatering strudel.

Paddington

$ Indian Home Diner, 86 Oxford St, T9331 4183. You really can't go wrong here with the usual great value (if mild) Indian combo dishes and, on this occasion, a small courtyard out back.

$ Royal Hotel, 237 Glenmore Rd, T9331 2604. Lunch and dinner from 1200. One of the best choices at the increasingly popular Five Ways crossroads in Paddington. A grand old pub with gracious yet modern feel. Excellent modern Australian cuisine is served upstairs in the main restaurant or on the prized verandah. Perfect for a lazy afternoon.

Watson's Bay

$$$ Doyle's on the Beach, 11 Marine Pde, T9337 2007, www.doyles.com.au. Daily lunch and dinner. Sydney's best-known restaurant for years. It has been in the same family for generations and has an unfaltering reputation for superb seafood, atmosphere and harbour/city views, which all combine to make it a one of the best dining experiences in the city, if not Australia. If you can, book well ahead and ask for a balcony seat. Sun afternoons are especially popular and you could combine the trip with a walk around the heads. Book well ahead.

$$ Watson's Bay Hotel, 1 Military Rd, T9337 4299. Located right next door to the famous **Doyle's**, **Watson's** offers some stiff competition in the form of quality, value seafood alfresco, with lots of choice. You can even cook your own. Great for a whole afternoon, especially at the weekend.

Bondi, Bronte and Coogee

$$$-$$ Icebergs Dining Room & Bar,
1 Notts Av, Bondi Beach, T9365 9000,
www.idrb.com. Tue-Sat 1200-midnight,
Sun 1200-2200. One of the trendiest dining
spaces in the city, hanging over the beach
and attracting a glamorous crowd to its
modern Italian cuisine and sharp design.
Expensive, but one to remember.

$$ Ravesi's, corner Campbell Pde and Hall
St, Bondi Beach, T9365 4422. Daily for dinner,
Sat-Sun from 0900 for breakfast and brunch.
A well-established favourite in Bondi, offering
a combination of classy atmosphere, quality
Modern Australian cuisine and fine views of
the iconic beach.

$ Coogee Bay Hotel, corner of Coogee Bay
Rd and Arden St, T9665 0000. The most
popular spot in Coogee day or night, with
multiple bars, huge open-air eating, value
pub grub and live entertainment.

$ Jenny's, 485 Bronte Rd, T9389 7498. Daily
0700-1830. With competition on both sides,
but consistently the café of choice on the
'Bronte strip'. Favourite breakfast spot at
weekends and a great start (or finish) to the
clifftop walk between Bronte and Bondi.

City North *p39*
Manly

Manly is blessed with numerous restaurants
and cafés in a wide range.

$$ Le Kiosk, Shelly Beach, T9977 4122. Daily
lunch and dinner. Simple beach house
ambience in a beautiful setting right on the
beach. Reliable modern Australian cuisine.

$$ Manly Wharf Hotel, T9977 1266. This
fabulous redeveloped pub on the wharf is the
hottest spot in Manly in summer. Classy food
in a bustling, open space.

$ Bower, 7 Marine Pde, T9977 5451. Daily
for breakfast and lunch, Thu and some
weekends for dinner. Located right at the
end of Marine Pde with memorable views
back towards Manly Beach. Great spot
for breakfast.

$ Out of Africa, 43 East Esplanade, Manly,
T9977 0055. Daily for dinner, Thu-Sun for
lunch. Good value, authentic African cuisine
with all the expected furnishings. Seems
oddly out of place in Manly, but remains
refreshingly different.

🕐 Bars and clubs

Sydney has pubs to suit most tastes in both
the city centre and the suburbs. Most are the
traditional, street-corner Australian hotels,
but there are lots of modern, trendy
establishments, pseudo-Irish pubs and truly
historic alehouses on offer. Many pubs,
especially those along Oxford St and in Kings
Cross, attract a distinctly metrosexual
clientele. See also Entertainment, page 54, for
gay nights. For the latest in club information
and special events get hold of the free *3-D
World* magazine, available in many
backpackers, cafés or the clubs,
www.threedworld.com.au.

Circular Quay and the Rocks
p23, map p26
Bars

The best single drinking area in Sydney is
undoubtedly **The Rocks**, where history,
aesthetics, atmosphere and most importantly
darn good beer combine to guarantee a
great night out.

Australian Heritage Hotel, see page 43.
From the **Orient** negotiate the steady climb
up to Cumberland St (the steps are located
on the right, before the bridge behind the
Argyle Stores) and reward yourself with an
obligatory Australian beer. You may also like
to sample a kangaroo, emu or crocodile steak
for dinner.

Cruise, by the Passenger Terminal on the
Rocks side, and **Harbour View Hotel**, 18
Lower Fort St, are both good choices with
fine views.

Hero of Waterloo, 81 Lower Fort St,
T9252 4553. Just around the corner from
the **Nelson** is this smaller and characterful

pub that can be a bit of a squeeze but is always entertaining.

Lord Nelson, see page 43. Past Observatory Park and down to Argyle St is Sydney's oldest pub. Within its hallowed, nautically themed walls, it brews its own ales and also offers some fine pub grub and accommodation.

Mercantile, 25 George St, T9247 3570. A chaotic Irish pub, it is often busy but offers a fairly decent pint of Guinness as well as great live traditional music until late.

Opera Bar, nestled in the lower concourse just short of the Opera House. This place is outdoors and serves great bar food, has regular live music and offers a truly world-class view. Expensive but worth it.

Clubs

Basement, 29 Reiby Pl, T9251 2797, www.thebasement.com.au. Ever popular.

Jacksons on George, 176 George St, T9247 2727. A huge club spread over 4 floors with 5 bars, dining, dancing, live bands and pool, open 24 hrs.

City centre *p29, map p26*
Bars

Paddy McGuires, on the corner of George and Hay, T9212 2111. Pretty authentic Irish pub that offers pleasant surroundings in which you can actually have a decent conversation or sample a fine range of beers. Live music.

Scruffy Murphy's, on the corner of Goulburn St and George St, T9211 2002. Open well into the early hours. Popular, well-established Irish pub that always draws the crowds. It's a great place to meet people and the live bands and beers are good, but there really is very little Irish or class about it.

Scubar, corner of Rawson Pl and Rawson Lane, T9212 4244, www.scubar.com.au. Popular backpacker-oriented pub that offers cheap beer, pizzas, pool, big TV screens and popular music until late.

Clubs

Chinese Laundry and Slip Inn, 111 Sussex St, T8295 9999. Has a solid reputation and one of the largest and best clubs in Australia.

Civic Hotel, 388 Pitt St, corner of Goulburn St, T8267 3185. Though essentially a pub, cocktail bar and restaurant, this is a traditional weekend haunt for a cosmopolitan crowd who repeatedly come to enjoy old anthems and classics. Cover charge.

Orbit Bar, Level 47, Australia Sq, 264 George St, T9247 9777. Upping the tone – and altitude – considerably is this retro revolving bar (and expensive restaurant). Definitely a place to impress, and be impressed. Friendly service, great bar snacks and wonderful views.

Darling Harbour and Chinatown
p31, map p26
Bars

Cargo Bar, 52-60 The Promenade, Darling Harbour, T9262 1777. One of a few hip bars on Kings St Wharf with outdoor seating.

Clubs

Home, Cockle Bay Wharf, T9266 0600. Open 2200-0600. One of the country's largest, state-of-the-art nightclubs. Here, on 4 levels, you can get on down to house and trance. Every Sat there is a kinkidisco – the mind boggles. Cover charge.

City West *p33*

The Bank 324 King St, T8568 1988, just south of the railway station, Newtown. Always busy thanks to its dark and rambling succession of rooms and bars. It also has a great Thai restaurant in the beer garden.

Friend In Hand Pub, 58 Cowper St, Glebe, T9660 2326. 'World famous', it looks more like a venue for an international garage sale, but oozes character and also has a bar-café and Italian restaurant. Look out – the cockatoo does bite!

Kuleto's Cocktail Bar, 157 King St, Newtown, T9519 6369, www.kuletos.com.au.

Kuleto's offers something completely different, so is well worth checking out. **Toxteth Hotel**, 345 Glebe Point Rd, Glebe, T9660 2370. A far more modern, traditionally Australian affair. It is always pretty lively, has pool competitions and serves mountainous plates of good pub grub.

City East *p35, map p37*
Bars
Kings Cross is perhaps a little overrated when it come to pubs but Paddington has quite a few old traditional pubs (see below). If these are not to your taste you might like to try the more cutting-edge establishments with the music and atmosphere that the cosmopolitan and mixed gay and straight (but always trendy) clientele hold dear. Some great examples are: **Bourbon**, 24 Darlinghurst Rd, T9358 1144, www.thebourbon.com.au; **Oxford Hotel**, 134 Oxford St, T9331 3467; and **Albury Hotel**, 6 Oxford St, T9361 6555.
Coogee Bay Hotel, 9 Vicar St, Coogee, T9665 0000. Beachside hotel with multiple bars and live music.
Durty Nelly's, 9 Glenmore Rd, Paddington, T9360 4467. The smallest, best and most intimate Irish pub in the city, offering pleasant surroundings and a grand congenial jam session on Sun evenings (last orders 2330).
Hotel Bondi, 178 Campell Pde, Bondi, T9130 3271. A popular bar with live bands and a nightclub attached.
Kings Cross Hotel, 248 William St, Kings Cross, T9358 3377. In the shadow of the huge Coca Cola sign is the bizarre interior of this rowdy backpacker favourite, open well into the early hours.
Lord Dudley, 236 Jersey Rd, T9327 5399, www.lorddudley.com.au. Deep in the Paddington suburbs is this grand historic rabbit warren with a distinct UK feel and some great, if expensive, pub grub on offer.
Royal Hotel, see page 51. There's a large atmospheric public bar downstairs and a fine restaurant on the 2nd floor.

Tilbury, southeast corner of Nicholson St and Bourke St, Woolloomooloo. Attracts a good-looking crowd to its slick, open spaces. Noisy thanks to the expanses of shiny chrome and pale timber but it's always humming.
Water Bar, just inside the Wharf at Woolloomooloo. Gorgeous, dark and groovy.
Woolloomooloo Bay Hotel, 2 Bourke St, Woolloomooloo, T9357 1177. Karaoke nights and regular DJs. When you can no longer pronounce its name it's definitely time to go home!

Clubs
Paddington's Oxford St is a major focus for nightlife and the main haunt for the gay and lesbian community. Kings Cross is the main focus for travellers, particularly backpackers, but is not necessarily the best venue in town.
Arq, 16 Flinders St, Paddington, T9380 8700. It has 2 large dance floors, plenty of space and a good balcony from which to watch a friendly crowd both straight and gay.
Le Panic, 20 Bayswater Rd, Kings Cross, T9368 0763, www.lepanic.com.au. Thu-Sun from 1900. Another intimate club come cocktail bar with a must-see eclectic decor. Again it concentrates on progressive house music. Fri nights are especially good.
Sapphire Suite, 2 Kellet St, Kings Cross, T9331 0058. 2200-0500. Modern and trendy, offering a fine range of expensive cocktails, acid jazz, house and rave. Cover charge.
World, 24 Bayswater Rd, Kings Cross, T9357 7700. Modern laid-back club set in grand surrounds and offering mainly UK house music, Fri-Sat cover charge after 2200.

⊕ Entertainment

Sydney *p21, maps p22, p26 and p37*
There is always a wealth of things to entertain in Sydney. For the latest information and reviews check the *Metro* section in the Fri *Sydney Morning Herald*. *The Beat* and *Sydney City Hub* are free weeklies that are readily

available in restaurants, cafés, bars and bookshops in and around the city centre. On the net consult the websites already listed on page 23, or visit www.sydney.city search.com.au, www.whatsonsydney.com.

The usual ticket agent is **Ticketek**, City Box Offices at 50 Park St (corner Castlereagh), Mon-Fri 0900-1700, Sat 1000-1400, and Theatre Royal Sydney, MLC Centre, 108 King St, Mon-Fri 0900-1700, T132849, www.ticketek.com.au. It produces its own monthly events magazine *The Ticket*. **Ticketmaster7**, T136100, www.ticketmaster .com.au, also deals with sports events tickets.

Cinema
For listings see the *Sydney Morning Herald*. A movie ticket will cost from $17.50, children from $13. Cheaper tickets are often offered on Tue nights.

In the city centre most of the major conventional cinema complexes are to be found along George St between Town Hall and Chinatown. On Oxford St is **Chauvel**, corner of Oxford St and Oatley Rd, T9361 5398, www.chauvelcinema.net.au, which showcases more retro, foreign or fringe films. **Hayden Orpheum Cinema**, 180 Military Rd, Cremorne, T9908 4344, on the North Shore. A wonderful art deco cinema offering a fine alternative to the modern city cinemas. **IMAX Theatre**, Darling Harbour, T9281 3300, www.imax.com.au. A huge 8-storey affair showcasing 3D movies from 1000, from $20, children $15.
Moonlight Cinema, Centennial Park, www.moonlight.com.au (23 Nov-23 Feb). Old classics, take a picnic and cushions.
Open Air Cinema, Royal Botanical Gardens near Mrs Macquarie's Chair (summer only). New releases and smart deli food.

Comedy
National or international comedy acts are generally hosted by the smaller theatres, like the **Lyric** and the **Belvoir** (see Performing arts

below). A number of inner-city hotels have comedy nights once a week, including the **Roxbury Hotel**, 182 St Johns Rd, Glebe T9692 0822, and the **Marlborough Hotel**, 145 King St, Newtown, T9519 1222 (Tue), both of which are good. Other venues with more regular acts are the **Comedy Store**, Bent St, Fox Studios, T9357 1419, www.comedy store.com.au (nightly, from $12-30) and the **Laugh Garage**, B1, 60 Park St, Parramatta, T9264 1161, www.thelaughgarage.com.

Gambling
You will find that almost every traditional Australian hotel and pub in Sydney has the omnipresent rows of hyperactive pokies (slot machines), which to the uninitiated need a PhD in bankruptcy and visual literacy skills to play (whatever happened to a row of lemons or cherries?). The main focus for trying your luck in Sydney is the **Star City Casino**, 80 Pyrmont St, a coin's roll from Darling Harbour, T9777 9000, www.starcity.com.au. This vast arena has 200 gaming tables, 1500 pokies and lots of anxious faces. Open 24 hrs. Smart-casual dress mandatory.

Gay and lesbian
Sydney has a thriving gay and lesbian community that has reached legendary status through the **Mardi Gras Festival** held every Feb, which culminates in the hugely popular parade through the city on the first Sat of Mar, www.mardigras.org.au.

The main focus for social activity is Oxford St, especially at the western end between Taylor Sq and Hyde Park, while Newtown, in the inner west, is home to Sydney's lesbian scene. There are many clubs and cafés that attract a casual mix of both straight and gay. Some of the more gay-oriented bars are **Albury Hotel**, **Beauchamp Hotel** and **Oxford Hotel** on Oxford St, and the **Newtown Hotel**, 174 King St, Newtown. Some popular nightclubs for men are **Midnight Shift**, 85 Oxford St, and **Manacle**,

1 Patterson Lane, Darlinghurst, www.manacle.com.au. **DCM**, 33 Oxford St, T9267 7380, and the **Taxi Club**, 40 Flinders St, Darlinghurst, attract a mixed crowd. For more information and venues try the *Sydney Star Observer*, which is available at most gay-friendly restaurants, cafés and bookshops, especially on Oxford St. The **Bookshop**, 207 Oxford St, T9331 1103, is also a good source of information.

Live music

Australian   You will almost certainly hear the bizarre and extraordinary tones of the didgeridoo somewhere during your explorations, be it the buskers on Circular Quay or in the many souvenir shops in the city.

Folk   All the Irish pubs offer folk jam nights early in the week and live bands from Wed to Sun. For some of the best try the **Mercantile Hotel**, 25 George St, The Rocks, **Scruffy Murphy's**, corner of Goulburn St and George St, T9211 2002, **O'Malley's Hotel**, 228 William St, Kings Cross, T9357 2211. Two excellent quieter options are **Paddy McGuires**, on the corner of George and Hay, T9212 2111, and **Durty Nelly's** (the best), on Glenmore Rd off Oxford St, which is a more intimate Irish pub offering low-key jam sessions on Sun afternoons.

Jazz and blues   **Soup Plus**, 383 George St, T9299 7728, **The Basement**, 29 Reiby Pl, Circular Quay, T9251 2797, www.thebasement.com.au, and the **Harbourside Brasserie**, Pier One, The Rocks, T9252 3000, are the major local jazz venues. **Zambezi Blues Room**, 481 Kent St, behind Town Hall Sq, T9266 0200, is a fine venue and free. For daily details of jazz gigs, tune into the *Jazz Gig Guide* at 0800 on Jazz Jam, 89.7 FM Eastside Radio, Mon-Fri. For **Sydney Jazz Club** call T9719 3876, www.sydneyjazzclub.com.

Rock

The three main rock concert venues are: the massive **Acer Arena**, Homebush Bay Olympic Park, T8765 4321, www.acerarena.com.au; the 12,000-seat **Sydney Entertainment Centre**, 35 Harbour St, City, T9320 4200, www.sydentcent.com.au; and **Metro Theatre**, 624 George St, T9550 3666. Tickets for a big international band will cost $80-180.

Performing arts

Naturally the focus for the performing arts in Sydney is the **Sydney Opera House**. It offers five venues: the Concert Hall, the Opera Theatre, the Drama Theatre, the Playhouse and the Studio. The Concert Hall is the largest venue and home to the Sydney Symphony Orchestra. The Opera House is the home of Opera Australia, the Australian Ballet and the Sydney Dance Company. The Drama Theatre is a performing venue for the Sydney Theatre Company while the Playhouse is used for small-cast plays, more low-key performances, lectures and seminars. The Studio is used for contemporary music and performance. Prices and seats range from about $35-200. For details call the box office, T9250 7777, or www.soh.nsw.gov.au. See also page 24.

Belvoir Theatre, 25 Belvoir St, Surry Hills, T9699 3444, www.belvoir.com.au. A less well-known venue with a good choice.

Capitol, 13 Campbell St, T1300 136166, www.capitoltheatre.com.au. The lovingly restored **Capitol** offers a diverse range of performances.

City Recital Hall, Angel Pl, City, T8256 2222, www.cityrecitalhall.com.au. Offers a programme of regular classical music performances from around $50.

State Theatre, 49 Market St, T9022 6258, T136100, www.statetheatre.com.au. This beautiful and historic venue offers a dynamic choice of specialist and mainstream performances and cinema.

Sydney Conservatorium of Music, near the Botanical Gardens, off Macquarie St, T9351

1222, www.music.usyd.edu.au.Also hosts occasional live performances.

Sydney Entertainment Centre, 35 Harbour St, City, T9320 4200, www.sydentcent.com.au. One of the city's largest and most modern performance venues, hosting a wide range of acts, shows, fairs and sporting events.

Theatre Royal, MLC Centre, 108 King St, T136166, www.mlccentre.com.au. Noted for its musicals and plays.

Wharf Theatre, Pier 4, Hickson Rd, The Rocks, T9250 1777, www.sydneytheatre.org.au. Home of the Sydney Theatre Company.

Bangarra are a contemporary Aboriginal dance group based at Wharf 4, Walsh Bay, The Rocks, T9251 5333, www.bangarra.com.au. The **Wharf Restaurant** next door is superb for pre-performance dining.

The **Lyric Theatre** and the **Showroom**, at the Star City complex, 80 Pyrmont St, T9777 9000, offer theatre, concerts, comedy, dance and musicals. From around $40-80 for a major performance.

✿ Festivals

Sydney *p21, maps p22, p26 and p37*

Jan New Year kicks in with spectacular fireworks and celebrations that centre around The Rocks and the Harbour Bridge. Other good vantage points include Milsons Point, The Opera House and Cremorne Point.

Sydney Festival and Fringe Festival takes place through most of the month. It is a celebration of the arts including the best of Australian theatre, dance, music and visual arts and is held at many venues throughout the city. The highlights are the free open-air concerts in the Domain, including Opera in the Park and Symphony under the Stars, see www.sydneyfestival.org.au.
The 26th sees the annual **Australia Day** celebrations with the focus being a flotilla of vessels flying the flag on the harbour, www.australiaday.com.au.

Feb Without doubt the most famous Sydney event is the legendary **Gay and Lesbian Mardi Gras Festival and Parade** held throughout the month. It is an opportunity for the gay community to celebrate, entertain and shock. The highlight is a good shake of the pants and codpieces (or very lack of them) during the spectacular parade from Liverpool St to Anzac Pde (held at the end of the festival), www.mardigras.org.au.

Mar The **Royal Agricultural Easter Show** is held every Easter and now uses the state-of-the-art facilities at Olympic Park as a venue, www.eastershow.com.au.

Apr The 25th sees the annual **Anzac Day** service at the Martin Place Cenotaph and a parade down George St.

May The annual **Sydney Morning Herald Half Marathon** is a great attraction, especially when it involves crossing the Harbour Bridge, www.halfmarathon.smh.com.au. **Australian Fashion Week** celebrations showcase some of the country's top designers. There is also another fashion week in Nov to preview the best of the winter collections.

Jun Sydney Film Festival, a 2-week fest for film buffs, runs more than 150 features from 40 countries, T9318 0999, www.sydneyfilmfestival.org.

Aug Sun-Herald City to Surf, a 14-km race from Bondi Beach to the city centre, T1800 555514, www.city2surf.sunherald.com.au.

Sep Festival of the Winds at Bondi Beach is a colourful festival of kites and kite flying, while the avid sports fans fight over tickets and take several days of drinking leave for the Rugby League and Rugby Union **Grand Finals**.

Oct The weekend **Manly Jazz Festival** is a gathering of Australia's best along with some fine foreign imports. Stages located in several public arenas including the beachfront and the Corso, as well as hotels, restaurants and bars, T9977 1088.

Dec Carols by Candlelight is the main festive public celebration of song in the Domain, while the wild and wicked grab a beer glass and a patch of sand at the **Bondi Beach Christmas Party**, which usually ends up as a mass streak into the waves. Far more serious is the **Sydney to Hobart** sailing race, which departs from the inner harbour, winds allowing, every Boxing Day.

Sydney p21, maps p22, p26 and p37
Sydney can offer a superb, world-class shopping experience. The most popular shopping venues are to be found in the city centre, but many of the suburban high streets also support a wide range of interesting outlets and some colourful weekend markets.

In the city most of the large department stores, arcades, malls and specialist boutiques are to be found along **George St** and in the area around **Pitt St Mall**, **Castlereagh St** and **King St**. The suburbs of **Newtown** (King St) and **Glebe** (Glebe Point Rd) have some fascinating shops selling everything from codpieces to second-hand surfboards. **Double Bay**, **Mosman** and **Paddington** (Oxford St) are renowned for their stylish boutiques clothes shops and **The Rocks** is definitely the place to go for a didgeridoo or cuddly koala.

Art
For authentic Aboriginal art look out for the National Indigenous Arts Advocacy Association Label of Authenticity. For the best in authentic and original examples try: **Authentic Aboriginal Art Centre**, 45 Argyle St, The Rocks, T9251 4474, daily 1000-1700; **Aboriginal Dreamtime Fine Art Gallery**, Shop 8/199 George St, T9241 2953; **Coo-ee Emporium and Aboriginal Art Gallery**, Bondi, T9300 9233, www.cooeeart.com.au (by appointment); **Hogarth Galleries**, 7 Walker La, T9360 6839. Further afield try the **Boomalli Aboriginal Artists Co-operative**, 55-59 Flood St, Leichhardt, T9560 2541, www.boomalli.org.au.

There are many art galleries showcasing some of the best Australian contemporary artists with most being in The Rocks or Paddington. Try to get hold of *Art Find* brochure from one of the galleries or the Sydney VIC. **Ken Done** is one of the most famous Sydney-based artists. He has a colourful style which you will either love or hate. His main outlet is at 1 Hickson Rd, The Rocks, T9247 2740, www.kendone.com.au.

Bookshops
Dymocks is the major player with outlets throughout the city. The largest is at 424 George St, T1800 688319, www.dymocks.com.au, Mon-Wed and Fri 0900-1800, Thu 0900-2100, Sat-Sun 0900-1700.
Gould's Book Arcade, 32 King St, Newtown. The largest and most bizarre second-hand bookshop in the city, it's a 'lost world'.
Travel Bookshop, 175 Liverpool St (southern edge of Hyde Park), T9261 8200. Mon-Fri 0900-1800, Sat 1000-1700. A good source of travel information, books and maps.

Clothes
You will find all the major labels in the main central city shopping streets, arcades and department stores (see section below).
Oxford St in Paddington and also the suburbs of **Double Bay** and to a lesser extent **Chatswood** are renowned for their boutique clothes stores and Australian designer labels. Names and labels to look for include Helen Kaminski, Collette Dinnigan, Morrissey, Bare, Isogawa and Bettina Liano. For designer bargains try the **Market City** above Paddy's Markets in Haymarket. Finally, if you are looking for something different then head for **King St** in Newtown.

You'll also find all the Aussie classics such as Akubra hats, RM Williams boots and Driza-Bone oilskin coats. These are all beautifully made and well worth the money. A pair of RM's boots for example will, provided you look after them, last a lifetime.

RM Williams clothing outlets can be found at 389 George St and Shop 1-2 Chiefly Plaza, corner of Hunter St and Phillip St, www.rmwilliams.com.au.
Strand Hatters, Strand Arcade, 412 George St, T9231 6884. For Akubra hats and Driza-Bones.

Department stores and arcades
Queen Victoria Building, T9264 9209, www.qvb.com.au. Not to be missed. This vast and historic edifice has levels of retail therapy that are legendary, see also page 30. On Market St there are 3 great Sydney institutions, the characterful department stores of **Grace Bros**, T9238 9111, www.myer.com.au; **David Jones**, T9266 5544, www.davidjones.com.au; and **Gowings**, T9287 6394, www.gowings.com.au.

Food and wine
Australian Wine Centre, 1 Alfred St, Circular Quay, T9247 2755, www.australianwine centre.com. Open daily. If you are a novice or even a seasoned wine buff, before purchasing any Australian labels you might benefit from a trip here. The staff are very knowledgeable and are backed by a great collection of over 1000 wines. They also offer a worldwide delivery service.
David Jones department store, Market St, T9266 5544. For a taste of Australian foods visit the food hall in this elegant shop.
Sydney Fish Market, Pyrmont. Even if you don't like seafood a trip here is fascinating, with the stalls setting up their displays of Australia's best from 0800 (see page 33).

Handicrafts
Craft Australia Boutique, David Jones department store, Market St, 4th floor, T9266 6276. For unique Australian crafts.
Object, 417 Bourke St, Surry Hills, T9361 4511, www.object.com.au. Showcases the best in authentic Australian crafts.

The Rocks and the **weekend Rocks Market** sell a good range of souvenir products.

Jewellery
Given the fact Australia produces over 90% of the world's opals it is not surprising to find a wealth of specialist dealers. To ensure authenticity and good workmanship purchase opals only from retailers who are members of the **Australian Opal and Gem Industry Association Ltd** (AOGIA) or the **Jewellers Association of Australia**. Some of the best retailers include: **Flame Opals**, 119 George St, T9247 3446, www.flameopals .com.au, Mon-Fri 0900-1845, Sat 1000-1700, Sun 1130-1700; **Opal Minded**, 55A George St, T9247 9885, 1000-1800; and **Australian Opal Cutters**, Suite 10, 3rd floor, 295 Pitt St, T9261 2442. Pearls from the great Australian *Pinctada maxima* oyster, from gold to snow white, are also big business in Sydney and for some of the best and biggest look no further than **Bunda**, Shop 1, 488 George St , Hilton Hotel, T9261 2210.

Markets
There are plenty of weekend markets held in the inner city that offer a range of new and second-hand clothes, arts, crafts and foods.
Opera House concourse, every Sun. An uncluttered open-air market that focuses mainly on arts, crafts and souvenirs.
Paddy's Markets, Haymarket, Thu-Sun. The biggest in the city centre; fairly tacky and mildly amusing.
The Rocks Market, every Sat-Sun at the top end of George St. The most popular market. Good inner suburbs markets include:
Balmain Market at St Andrew's Church, corner of Darling St and Curtis St. Sat.
Bondi Markets, Campbell Pde. Sun.
Glebe Market, in the grounds of Glebe Public Schools, Glebe Point Rd. Sun.
Paddington Market, grounds of the church at 395 Oxford St. Sat.

Outdoor equipment

Kent St is the place to start looking for camping and outdoor equipment. **Mountain Equipment**, 491 Kent St, T9264 5888, www.mountainequipment.com and **Paddy Pallin**, No 507 Kent St, T9264 2685, www.paddypallin.com.au.

⚠ What to do

Sydney *p21, maps p22, p26 and p37*
Sydney is the venue for some of the most important major national and international sporting events in Australia. The huge success of the 2000 Olympic Games has left the city some superb sporting venues. Most are to be found at the **Sydney Olympic Park**, see page 34. Test rugby, Aussie Rules and test cricket match tickets are often very hard to come by and any attempt must be made well in advance. A ticket will cost from $50-120 for a cricket test match and $50-150 for a rugby grand final. The usual ticket agent is **Ticketek**, T132849, www.ticketek.com.au. If you cannot secure tickets or don't rate your chances obtaining a spare ticket outside the venue (often possible), joining the throngs of Sydneysiders in the city pubs can be just as enjoyable and atmospheric.

Ballooning

Cloud 9, T1300 555711, www.cloud9balloon flights.com, and **Balloon Aloft**, T1800 028568, www.balloonaloft.com, offer early morning flights over the outer suburbs or in the Hunter Valley from $269.

Cruises

There are numerous harbour cruises on offer, with most being based at Circular Quay. Trips vary from a sedate cruise on a replica of the *Bounty* to paddle steamers and fast catamarans. In recent years whales have occasionally appeared in the inner harbour, which is believed to be a sign of improving water quality. For whale-watching cruises from Sydney Harbour, check out www.whalewatching sydney.net. Thanks to the increase of whale numbers, they can guarantee sightings on their cruises, which depart from Darling Harbour and Circular Quay from late May to early Nov. Vessels include the flagship *Ocean Dreaming*, a 34-m catamaran. Trips start at around $85, T9583 1199.

Diving

Although diving is best at the Barrier Reef, if you are heading north to Queensland, NSW and Sydney have some good diving. The southern beaches, La Perouse and the Botany Bay National Park offer the best spots. There are dive shops in the city and companies offering tuition and trips, including the popular **Dive Centre**. **Dive Centre**, 10 Belgrave St, Manly, T9977 4355, and 192 Bondi Rd, Bondi, T9369 3855, www.divesydney.com. It offers shore and boat dive trips and Open Water Certificates with the latter from $395.
Pro Dive, T9255 0300, www.prodive.com.au. Offers local trips and training and stocks a good range of equipment.

Fishing

The VIC has listings of other charters based in Sydney, many of which also offer whale-watching trips Jun-Oct. Despite all the harbour activity, both the fishing and the water quality in Sydney Harbour is said to be pretty good. There are a number of fishing charters available including:
Charter One, Manly, T04-0133 2355, www.charterone.com.au. Trips range from a 3-hr jaunt from $95 to a full day, $135, with tackle hire.

Sailing

Sydney Harbour offers some of the best sailing in the world. On Boxing Day every year, at the start of the **Sydney to Hobart race**, the inner harbour becomes a patchwork of colourful spinnakers raised to the mercy of the winds.

Australian Spirit Sailing Company, T9878 0300, www.austspiritsailingco.com.au. Runs similar trips to **Sydney Mainsail** below.
Sydney by Sail, National Maritime Museum, T9280 1110, www.sydneybysail.com. Operates social day trips, introductory lessons and a 3-hr trip on the harbour from $150. The office is based below the lighthouse.
Sydney Mainsail, T9719 9077, www.sydney mainsail.com.au. Offers 3-hr trips 3 times daily with highly experienced skippers.

Scenic flights

Palm Beach Seaplanes, based in Rose Bay (eastern harbour suburbs) and Palm Beach (Pittwater), T1300 720995, www.sydneyby seaplane.com.au. A 15-min flight around the harbour costs from $160, 30 mins from $240, while a 60-min trip taking in the harbour, beaches, Ku-ring-gai National Park and Hawkesbury starts at $495. A beach picnic is $850. If you want to see the northern beaches from the air and to arrive in Palm Beach in style the one-way trip will cost you a hefty $450.

There are a number of scenic flight companies based at Bankstown Airport, T9796 2300. However, the adventurous should contact **Red Baron Scenic Flights** run by the Sydney Aerobatic School, T9791 0643, www.redbaron.com.au. It offers unforgettable aerobatic scenic harbour flights from an open cockpit Pitts Special from $440-660.

Sea kayaking

This is a great way to explore the backwaters and bays of the suburbs. The Middle Harbour, which branches off between Middle Head and Clontarf, snakes over 10 km into the lesser-known North Shore suburbs and is especially good. It offers a quiet environment and more wildlife.

Sky diving

You can test your courage sky diving in and around Sydney. Companies

include **Simply Skydive**, CM12, Mezzanine, Centrepoint, T9223 8444, www.simplyskydive.com.au, and **Sydney Skydiving Centre**, based at Bankstown Airport, T9791 9155, www.sydneyskydivers. com.au. Jumps start from about $275.

Surfing

The famous surf spots are Bondi and Manly but some of the lesser-known Sydney beaches offer better surf. Try some of the northern beaches, such as Curl Curl (home to Layne Beachley), or see what the surf report recommends.
Manly Surf School, at the **North Steyne Surf Club**, Manly Beach, T9977 6977, www.manly surfschool.com. Good value daily classes from 1100-1300, 1-10 lessons from $60-340.

Swimming

Swimming is a popular pastime. South of the Heads, the beaches at Bondi, Bronte, Clovelly and Coogee are hugely popular while to the north, Manly, Collaroy, Narrabeen, Avalon, Ocean Beach and Palm Beach are also good spots. Lifeguards patrol most beaches in summer and you are strongly advised to swim between the yellow and red flags. These are clearly staked out along the beach and placed according to conditions. Most of the city beaches also have safe, open-air, saltwater swimming pools to provide added safety, especially for children. **Bondi Icebergs pool** is a Sydney landmark but there are also quiet neighbourhood pools such the charming **McCallum Pool**, a small outdoor pool on Cremorne Point (off Milson's Road) with great views across the harbour.
Sydney Harbour Kayaks, 3/235 The Spit Rd, Mosman, T9960 4389, www.sydneyharbour kayaks.com.au. Runs guided trips and hires kayaks.

Tours

Bridge Climb, 3 Cumberland fSt, The Rocks, T8274 7777, www.bridgeclimb.com, 0700-1900. The most high-profile activity in the city is this award-winning climb. This involves the ascent of the 134-m Harbour Bridge span. The 3-hr climb can be done day or night and in most weather conditions apart from electrical storms. As well as the stunning views from the top the climb is most memorable. Although it is fairly easy going and is regularly done by the elderly, the sight and noise of the traffic below adds a special edge. You cannot take your own camera on the trip for safety reasons. Climbs during the week cost from $200, children $130, weekends $220, children $140. Twilight climbs cost from $260, children $190.

Bonza Bike Tours, T9247 8800, www.bonzabiketours.com. Increasingly popular pedal power, guided or self-guided options of 2 hrs to half day. Independent hire also available.

Harbour Islands Tours, for all island access, tour information and bookings contact the Sydney Harbour National Park Information Centre, Cadman's Cottage, 110 George St, The Rocks, T9247 5033, www.nationalparks.nsw.gov.au. Mon-Fri 0900-1630, Sat-Sun 1000-1630.

Rocks Ghost Tour, bookings (advised) can be made at the Sydney VIC, corner Argyll and Playfair streets, The Rocks, T9240 8788, or direct T1300 731971, www.ghosttours.com.au. Given the Rocks' sordid past there is plenty of material and also a child-friendly option. Tours take 2 hrs, departing at 1845 (Apr-Nov) and 1945 (Nov-Mar) and cost from $39.
Rocks Pub Tour, T1300 458437, www.therockspubtour.com. An excellent way to sample 3 of the Rocks' finest drinking establishments, 1700-1845.

Rocks Walking Tour, bookings (advised) can be made at the Sydney VIC, corner Argyll and Playfair streets, The Rocks, T9240 8788, or at the Walks Office, 23 Playfair St, T9247 6678, www.rockswalkingtours.com.au. This is the best, most entertaining and informative way to get to know this area. Tours take 90 mins,

departing Mon-Fri 1030, 1230 and 1430 and Sat-Sun 1130 and 1400. From $30, children $15, family $75.

Walking
The VIC has a number of free walking booklets including the detailed *Go Walkabout* by Sydney Ferries, *Sydney Harbour Foreshore Walks*, *Historical Sydney*, *Sydney Sculpture Walk* and the *Manly Scenic Walkway*. Another great book is *Sydney's Best Harbour and Coastal Walks* (Woodslane), sold at good bookshops.

⊖ Transport

Sydney *p21, maps p22, p26 and p37*
Air
For information and details of arrivals and departures, T9667 6065, www.sydneyairport .com.au. See also page 21.

Bus
Local The STA (**Sydney Buses**) is the principal operator with the standard buses being blue and white, the **Sydney Explorer** red and the **Bondi Explorer** blue. For information about suburban buses in Sydney, T131500, www.131500.com.au.

Standard bus fares are between $2-6.30 depending on distance and zones crossed. If you intend to travel regularly by bus, a Travel Ten ticket is recommended ($16-50.40) while further savings can be also be made with the TravelPass and Sydney Pass system (see box opposite). The Explorer buses cost $40 for the full return trip. There is an on-board commentary and you can hop on and off when you want. Both leave at regular intervals from Circular Quay. For all of the above bus fares children travel half price and there are also family concessions. Note most Explorer buses operate between 0840 and1722 only.

Drivers do not automatically stop at bus stops. If you are alone you must signal to the driver, or at night gesticulate wildly.

Ticket to ride

There are numerous popular travel pass systems in operation through the STA. The **MyMulti Day Pass** gives all-day access to Sydney's trains, buses and ferries within the suburban area from $20, children $10. Tickets can be purchased at any rail, bus or ferry sales or information outlet or on the buses themselves. **MyMulti Passes** allow unlimited, weekly, quarterly or yearly combined travel throughout designated zones or sections. A seven-day pass for the inner city, for example, costs $41, children $20. For those staying only a few days, however, the best bet is the **Sydney Pass** which offers unlimited travel on ferry and standard buses as well as the Sydney and Bondi Explorer routes and the four STA Harbour Cruises. They are sold as a three-day ($116, children $58), five-day ($152, children $76) or seven-day ($172, children $86) package. Discount, 10-trip 'TravelTen' (bus) and 'FerryTen' passes are also available and recommended, from $16 (bus) and $41 (ferry), T131500, www.131500.com.au.

Long distance Sydney Coach Terminal is in the Central Railway Station, Shop 4-7, Eddy Av, T131500 / T9281 9366, daily 0600-2230. Major interstate companies include **Greyhound** (National) T131499 (T1300 4739 46863), www.greyhound.com.au; **Murrays**, (Canberra, South NSW Coast), T132251, www.murrays.com.au; **Premier Motor Services** (national) T133410, www.premierms.com.au; and **Firefly** (Adelaide, Melbourne), T1300 730740, www.firefly express.com.au. Typical interstate services and prices 1-way from Sydney are: **Brisbane**, Greyhound, 5 daily, 20 hrs, $100; **Byron Bay**, Greyhound, 4 daily,18 hrs, $90; **Cairns**, Greyhound, 5 daily, 46 hrs, $400; **Canberra**, Greyhound, 10 daily, 5 hrs, $25; **Melbourne**, Greyhound, 5 daily, 14 hrs 20 mins, $90.

Car/campervan

Travelling by car around Sydney is a nightmare with numerous tolls, expensive parking and omnipresent parking wardens. There really is no need to see the sights by car but if you must, take lots of change. The Sydney Harbour Tunnel now has cashless tolls to improve traffic flow across the Harbour. To pay the toll, you need an electronic tag or an RTA E-Toll pass. If you use the Harbour Tunnel without a tag, register for an RTA E-Toll pass within 48 hours of your trip at myRTA.com or call T131 865. Additional fees apply for pass users. . The toll for the Harbour Bridge (Mon-Fri $4, Sat/Sun $3 southbound, free northbound) will remain payable by cash or E-Tag. **NRMA** are located at 74-76 King St, CBD, T9292 8292, T131122.

Car hire offices at the airport (Arrivals south) include **Avis**, T136333, **Budget** T132727, **Hertz** T1300 132607, **National**, T131390, **Red Spot**, T1300 668810 and **Thrifty** T136139. In the city try **Avis**, **Budget** and **Ascot** centred on or around William St, Darlinghurst. Cheaper options often include **Bayswater Rentals**, 180 William St, Kings Cross, T9360 3622, and **Dollar**, Domain Car Park, Sir John Young Cres , T9223 1444. Rates can get as low as $40 per day. Campervan hire from **Britz**, call T9667 0402, www.britz.com.au, and also **Maui**, T1300 363800, www.maui-rentals.com.

Secondhand car and campervan dealers include **Kings Cross Car Market**, Ward St Car Park, Kings Cross, T1800 808188, www.carmarket.com.au (good buying and selling), and **Travellers Auto Barn**, 177

William St, Kings Cross, T1800 674374, www.travellers-autobarn.com.au.

Cycling

The pace of cycling is perfect for sightseeing. Unfortunately the rest of the road users don't agree. Travel by bike within the city centre can be hairy to say the least. Several companies offer bike hire from about $40 per day or $200 per week, including **Inner City Cycles**, 151 Glebe Point Rd, Glebe, T9660 6605; the **Manly Cycle Centre**, 36 Pittwater Rd, Manly, T9977 1189; and **Wooly's Wheels**, 82 Oxford St, T9331 2671, www.woolyswheels.com. For general advice contact **Bicycle NSW**, Level 5, 822 George St, T9218 5400, www.bicycle nsw.org.au. For *Sydney Cycle Ways* maps and information contact the **RTA**, T9218 6816.

Ferry

A trip on one of Sydney's harbour ferries is a wonderful experience and an ideal way to see the city, as well as accessing many of the major attractions and suburbs. The principal operator is **Sydney Ferries**, which operates the 'green and golds', also the fast **JetCats** to Manly and **RiverCat** to Homebush Bay and Parramatta. Several independent companies also operate out of Circular Quay offering cruises as well as suburban transportation and water taxis. See Cruises, page 60.

Like the buses, ferry fares are priced according to zone and start at a single trip for $5.20. If you intend to travel regularly by ferry then a FerryTen ticket (from $33.50) is recommended, while further savings can also be made with the TravelPass and Sydney Pass system, see box page 63. Various travel/entry combo tickets are offered to the major harbourside sights including Taronga Zoo (Zoo Pass $48, children $23.50) and Sydney Aquarium (Aquarium Pass $33, children $17.00). Children travel half price and there are also family concessions on most fares. For ferry information T131500, www.sydneyferries

.com.au or www.sydneytransport.com.au. The main Sydney Ferries Information Centre is opposite Wharf 4, Circular Quay.

MonoRail and LightRail

MonoRail, www.metromonorail.com.au, runs in a loop around Darling Harbour and South Western CBD and provides a convenient way of getting from A to B. They run every 3-5 mins, Mon-Thu 0700-2200, Fri-Sat 0700-2400, and Sun 0800-2200. The standard fare (1 loop) is $4.90, a Day Pass costs $9.50. Children under 5 travel free and there are discounts for some major attractions.

The **LightRail** network links Central Station with Lilyfield, via a number of stops within the southwest CBD and Darling Harbour, as well as the Casino, Fish Market and Glebe. It is a 24-hr service with trains every 10-15 mins from 0600-2400 and every 30 mins from 2400-0600. There are 2 fare zones starting at a single journey at $3.40. A Day Pass with unlimited stops costs $9. Children travel at half price. For information, T8584 5288, www.metromonorail.com.au.

Taxi

Sydney's once rather dubious taxi service was given a major revamp for the 2000 Olympics and it is now much improved. Ranks are located near every railway station, at Circular Quay and numerous spots in the CBD, otherwise hail one as required. From 2200-0600 higher tariffs apply. On short journeys tipping is not expected. There are several companies including **ABC** T132522, **Combined** T133300, **Legion** T131451, **Premier** T131017 and **RSL** T132211.

Water taxis operate all over the harbour with most being based on the western edge of Circular Quay. The main operators are **Water Taxis Combined**, Circular Quay, T9555 8888, and **Yellow Water Taxis** T1300 138840.

Train

Local Sydney's 24-hr train services are a convenient way to reach the city centre and outlying areas, or to link in with bus and ferry services. Fares start at $3.20 and savings can be made with 'Off-Peak Tickets', which operate after 0900 on weekdays. Further savings can be made with the TravelPass and Sydney Pass (see box, page 63). There are coloured routes with the green/purple City Circle (Central, Town Hall, Wynyard, Circular Quay, St James and the Museum) and blue Eastern Suburbs Line (Central, Town Hall, Martin Place, Kings Cross, Edgecliff, Bondi Junction) being the most convenient. Tickets and information are available at major stations. For information about trains in Sydney, T131500, www.cityrail.info or www.131500.com.au.

Long distance All interstate and NSW state destination trains arrive and depart from the Central Railway Station on Eddy Av, just south of the city centre. There is an information booth and ticket offices on the main platform concourse. **Countrylink** are the main interstate operators running with a combination of coach and rail to all the main interstate and NSW destinations, T132232 (daily 0630-2200), www.countrylink.info. You can find a **Countrylink Travel Centre** at the railway station, T9379 3800. First class and economy fares vary so you are advised to shop around and compare prices with the various coach operators. The railway station also houses the main interstate city coach terminal (**Greyhound**) and from there, or Pitt St and George St, you can pick up regular city and suburban buses. For information T131500, www.sydneytransport.net.au. **Countrylink** operates the 'XPT' Sydney to Brisbane (12 hrs daily, overnight, from $100) and Melbourne (11 hrs, twice daily, 1 overnight, from $90).

Directory

Sydney *p21, maps p22, p26 and p37*

Banks
The major banks have ATMs. Foreign exchange is readily available on the arrivals concourse of Sydney Airport. In the city there are many outlets especially around Circular Quay and along George St.

Hospital
Prince of Wales Hospital, High St, Randwick, T9382 2222; **Royal North Shore Hospital**, Pacific Highway, St Leonard's, T9926 7111; **St Vincent's Hospital**, Victoria St, Darlinghurst, T9339 1111; **Sydney Children's Hospital**, T9382 1111.

Useful contacts
For the police, emergency T000, general enquiries T9690 4960. **City of Sydney Police Station**, 192 Day St, T9265 6499.

Around Sydney

To the west of Sydney, a mere 70 km delivers you to the fringes of some of the state's largest and most celebrated national parks, all within the Greater Blue Mountains region. Once a major barrier to the exploration of the interior, until the route west was finally opened up in the first half of the 19th century, the 'Blues' now serve as a natural wonderland; a vast playground for over one million visitors a year who come to explore the eroded valleys, gorges, bluffs and amazing limestone caves.

Even closer to home is the Ku-ring-gai Chase National Park to the north and the Royal National Park to the south, the latter tragically destroyed by the terrible bush fires that have ravaged huge swathes of the country in successive recent years. Between Ku-ring-gai and what's left of Royal National Park is the tiny Botany Bay National Park, site of Captain Cook's first landing in April 1770.

Kamay Botany Bay National Park → *For listings, see pages 77-79.*

Botany Bay holds a very special place in Australian (European) history as the site of Captain Cook's first landing, in April 1770. The landing site is near what is now Kurnell on the southern shores of Botany Bay, which along with La Perouse on the northern shore, comes under the auspices of the 458-ha Kamay Botany Bay National Park. As well as possessing highly significant historical sites for both the European and Aboriginal cultures ('Kamay' is the indigenous Gweagal people's name for the area) it presents plenty of walking opportunities and ocean views.

Within the small northern sector of the park, around **La Perouse** on the northern headland, you can take a tour of **Bare Island Fort** ⓘ *T9247 5033, guided tours Sat-Sun, $8, children $6*, built in 1885 as a defence against the perceived threat of foreign invasion. Also located on the headland is **La Perouse Museum and Visitors' Centre** ⓘ *Cable Station, Anzac Parade, T9311 3379, Wed-Sun 1000-1600, $6, children $3.30*, on the actual site of the first landing of the First Fleet in 1788. The museum explores the great historical event and the fate of French explorer the Comte de La Pérouse, as well as local Aboriginal and European heritage.

The southern sector is larger and has the best walks including the short (1 km) **Monument Track** and the more demanding **Coast Walk** to Bailey lighthouse. It also hosts the **NPWS Botany Bay National Park Discovery Centre**, a good source of park and walks information with an interesting display surrounding Cook's landing.

Royal National Park → *For listings, see pages 77-79.*

The 15,080-ha Royal National Park was the first national park in Australia, gazetted in 1879. As well as providing over 100 km of walking tracks, many taking in terrific ocean views, there are some beautiful beaches and other activities ranging from swimming to scuba diving. However, the park is subject to the constant threat of fire and more than once in the last decade the Royal has been temporarily destroyed by bush fires. The main hub of human activity is historic **Audley** at the park's northern entrance, where you will find the **NPWS Royal National Park Visitors' Centre** ① *Farnell Av, T9542 0648, 0930-1630.* **Wattamolla**, **Garie** and **Burning Palms** are three beautiful beaches and the choice of walks ranges from the 500-m (wheelchair-accessible) **Bungoona Track** to the 26-km **Coast Track** (Bundeena to Otford), which guarantees some glorious coastal views and on occasion (from June to September) the odd whale sighting. You can hire rowboats and canoes at the Audley Boatshed, near the visitors' centre, for a paddle up Kangaroo Creek. Mountain bikes are also available for hire but trail routes are limited and there is good surfing at the patrolled **Garie Beach**. Several freshwater pools also provide swimming. By car from Sydney take the Princes Highway south and follow signs for Audley (left, at Loftus on Farnell Avenue and McKell Avenue). Vehicle entry costs $11 per day.

Ku-ring-gai Chase National Park → *For listings, see pages 77-79.*

Though a few wealthy Sydney entrepreneurs might see Ku-ring-gai Chase as little more than 14,883-ha of wasted prime real estate, just 26 km north of Sydney, the rugged sandstone country that fringes the mighty Hawkesbury River, with its stunning views and rich array of native wild animals and plants, is thankfully safe from further suburban encroachment and has been since it was designated as a national park in 1894. As well as the stunning views across Pittwater and Broken Bay, the park offers some lovely bush walks, secluded beaches and regionally significant Aboriginal rock art. It is also a great place to see that much celebrated state flower, the warratah, in bloom. The highlight of the park is the **West Head Lookout**, high above the peninsula overlooking **Broken Bay** and the mouth of the **Hawkesbury River**. To the north is the beginning of the central coast and Brisbane Water National Park, while to the west is the tip of the northern beaches and the historic Barrenjoey Lighthouse. West Head is crisscrossed with walking tracks that start from West Head Road. Aboriginal rock art can be seen along the **Basin Track** – which falls to the Basin Beach campsite and the arrival/departure point of the Palm Beach ferry – and the 3.5-km **Red Hand Track** (Aboriginal Heritage Track). **Bobbin Head** at the western end of the park is a popular base for water-based activities. Here, too, is the VIC, which can supply details on walks. **NPWS Bobbin Head Information Centre** ① *Bobbin Inn, Bobbin Head Rd (western side of the park), T9472 8949, 1000-1600*, or the **Kalkari Visitors' Centre** ① *Chase Rd, between Mount Colah and Bobbin Head, T9457 9853, 0900-1700*, can supply walks, camping information and maps. By car, access is via Bobbin Head Rd, via the Pacific Highway (from the south) or from Ku-ring-Gai Chase Road via F3 Freeway (from the north). Access to the eastern side (West Head Road and West Head Lookout) is from Mona Vale Road, Northern Beaches. Vehicle entry costs $11 daily.

Blue Mountains → *For listings, see pages 77-79.*

The 'Blues', as they are affectionately known, form part of the Great Dividing Range, 70 km, or two hours, west of Sydney, and contain no less than five national parks covering a total area of 10,000 sq km. They are not really mountains at all, but a network of eroded river valleys, gorges, and bluffs, that have formed over millions of years. The result is a huge wonderland of natural features, from precipitous cliffs, to dramatic waterfalls and canyons, not to mention the most dramatic limestone caves on the continent. Once the home of the Daruk Aboriginals, the Blue Mountains were seen by the first Europeans merely as a highly inconvenient barrier to the interior and for almost a quarter of a century they remained that way, before finally being traversed in 1813 by explorers Blaxland, Wentworth and Lawson. To this day the impenetrable geography still limits transportation and essentially the same two convict-built roads and railway line completed over a century ago reach west through a string of settlements from Glenbrook to Lithgow on the other side. For decades the 'Blues' have been a favourite weekend or retirement destination for modern-day Sydney escapees, who welcome the distinctly cooler temperatures and the colourful seasons that the extra elevation creates. But superb scenery and climate aside, there are some excellent walking opportunities, as well as abseiling, canyoning and rock climbing. Given the region's popularity there are also a glut of good restaurants and a wide range of places to stay from showpiece backpackers to romantic hideaways.

Visiting the Blue Mountains
Getting there   Although public transport to and around the Blue Mountains is good you are advised to take your own vehicle or hire one, allowing you to make the most of the numerous viewpoints and sights within the region. Trains are the best way to arrive independently, leaving Sydney's Central Station (Countrylink and CityLink platforms) on the hour daily, stopping at all major towns through the Blue Mountains, T132232. The journey to Katoomba takes about two hours and costs around $30 for a day return. Numerous coach companies and hostels offer day sightseeing tours from Sydney. Some may allow overnight stops. The accredited VIC in Sydney can assist with the extensive choice and bookings. Most of the buses leave from Circular Quay.

Getting around   The route through the Blue Mountains is easily negotiable. From the west (Sydney) you take the M4 (toll), eventually crossing the Neapean River, before it forms the Great Western Highway at Glenbrook (65 km). Then you pass through Blaxland, Springwood, Faulconbridge and Woodford before arriving at Wentworth Falls. Here you reach the top of the main plateau at an average height of just above 1000 m. From Wentworth Falls the road then continues west through the northern edges of Leura and Katoomba, then north, through the heart of Blackheath and Mount Victoria. From Mount Victoria you then begin the descent to Lithgow (154 km). The rather peculiarly named Bells Line of Road provides another access point across the mountains from Windsor on the east to Mount Victoria on the Great Western Highway (77 km). Katoomba is the largest of the towns and has the best amenities. ▶ *See under the relevant destinations for further details.*

Tourist information   The main accredited VICs are in Glenbrook, Katoomba ① *Echo Point, T1300 653408, www.visitbluemountains.com.au, daily 0900-1700,* Lithgow ① *Great Western*

Highway, T6350 3230, www.tourism.lithgow.com, 0900-1700, and **Oberon** (west, near the Jenolan Caves). The main NPWS office is at the **Heritage Centre** ① *near Govetts Leap, Blackheath, T4787 8877, www.nationalparks.nsw.gov.au*. If you are approaching from the east, stop at the Glenbrook VIC and stock up with the free visitor's guide and maps. All regional centres also offer a free accommodation bookings service. The NPWS stock a wide range of books on the many walks in the national parks, as well as topographical maps.

The national parks

The Blue Mountains region contains five national parks which cover an area of 10,000 sq km, with half of that being considered 'wilderness area'. The largest, at an expansive 4876 sq km (and the second largest in the state after Kosciuszko National Park) is **Wollemi National Park**, to the north of the Bells Line of Road. It incorporates the state's most extensive officially recognized wilderness area and is very rugged and inaccessible. As well as its complex geology, topography, Aboriginal art sites and botanical features, it is also home to a rich variety of birds. Of all the parks in the region it is the one for the well-prepared modern-day explorer. There are basic NPWS campsites at Wheeny Creek, Colo Meroo, Dun's Swamp and Newnes. The main access is from Putty Road, 100 km northwest of Sydney or via Rylstone.

The most famous and accessible park is the 2470-sq-km **Blue Mountains National Park**, straddling the Great Western Highway and a string of mountain villages and towns, from Glenbrook in the east to Lithgow in the west. Only recently expanded in the 1980s, it contains natural features that range from deep canyons and forested valleys to pinnacles and waterfalls, as well as an abundance of flora and fauna. Although now receiving over one million visitors a year, much of the park remains extremely inaccessible, with over 500 sq km considered official wilderness area. Sadly, the Blue Mountains, like so many national parks in NSW, has suffered in recent years from the temporary impact of widespread bush fires. There are basic NPWS campsites at Euroka Clearing near Glenbrook, Ingar near Wentworth Falls and Perry's Lookdown near Blackheath. You can also camp anywhere within 500 m from roads and facilities. Access is from many points east and west off the Great Western Highway, or from the Bells Line of Road 70 km west of Sydney.

Next up is the beautiful 680-sq-km **Kanangra-Boyd National Park**, to the southwest of Katoomba. Fringed by the Blue Mountains National Park on all but one side it contains a similar geology and topography but is particularly famous for two natural features, the Jenolan limestone caves and the Kanangra Walls (a series of outstanding bluffs). Both are well worth visiting, with the latter considered one of the great walks in the region. There is a basic NPWS campsite at Boyd River. Access is via Mount Victoria and the Jenolan Caves 180 km west of Sydney.

To the southeast of Kanangra-Boyd and the Blue Mountains National Parks is the 860-sq-km **Nattai National Park**. It touches the region's largest body of water, Lake Burragorang, and contains the region's largest populations of eastern grey kangaroos as well as many rare plants and animals. NPWS camping near the lake. Access is 110 km south of Sydney between Warragamba Dam and Wombeyan Caves Road.

The smallest national park in the group is the 12,000-ha **Gardens of Stone National Park** north of Lithgow. Adjoining Wollemi it is most noted for its prominent and shapely limestone outcrops and sandstone escarpments. Birdlife is once again prolific. There are no campsites. Access is 30 km north of Lithgow via Mudgee Road.

Glenbrook to Wentworth Falls

Proud of its European roots and its railway heritage, the pretty village of Glenbrook, just beyond the Nepean River, acts as the unofficial gateway to the Blue Mountains. Along with Katoomba this is the main tourism administration and information centre for the Blue Mountains. **NPWS Conservation Hut** ① *Fletcher St (off Falls Rd), T4757 3827*, can provide walks information and has a small shop and café. **Glenbrook VIC** ① *off the Great Western Highway, T1300 653408, www.visitbluemountains.com.au, daily 0900-1700.*

Fringing the village, south of the highway, is the southern section of the Blue Mountains National Park and access to numerous attractions, including the **Red Hands Cave**, a fine example of Aboriginal rock art. The distinctive hand stencils made on the cave wall are thought to be over 1600 years old. You can reach the cave either by road or by foot (8 km return) from the Glenbrook Creek causeway, just beyond the park entrance. There are also shorter walks to the **Jellybean Pool** and the **Euroka Clearing**, a basic NPWS campsite and the ideal spot to see grey kangaroos, especially early or late in the day. To reach the park gate ($7 per day, walkers free), take Ross Road behind the VIC onto Burfitt Parade and then follow Bruce Road. The lookouts at **The Bluff**, at the end of Brook Road (slightly further east off Burfitt, then Grey), are also worth a look. North of the highway in Glenbrook you can also follow signs to the **Lennox Bridge**, the oldest in Australia, built by convicts in 1833.

Beyond Blaxland and Springwood is the small settlement of **Faulconbridge**, home to the **Norman Lindsay Gallery and Museum** ① *T4751 1067, www.norman lindsay.com.au, $10, children $5*. Lindsay (1879-1969) is just one of many noted artists who found the Blue Mountains conducive to their creativity and his studio remains very much the way he left it. For most, it is the stunning lookouts across **Wentworth Falls** and the **Jamieson Valley** that offer the first memorable introduction to the dramatic scenery of the Blue Mountains – assuming the weather is clear, of course. The car park is the starting point for some superb walking tracks, the best of which is the four-hour **Wentworth Pass Walk** that crosses the top of the falls and then descends precariously down to the valley floor. Then, if that were not enough, the track skirts the cliff base, through rainforest, before climbing back up via the dramatic **Valley of the Waters** gorge to the **Conservation Hut** (see above). From there it's an easy walk back to the car park. Another excellent walk is the five-hour **National Pass Walk** that follows a cutting halfway up the cliff, carved out in the 1890s. Both walks involve steep sections around cliff edges and laddered sections, but if you have a head for heights either one is highly recommended. Give yourself plenty of time and make sure you get maps from the Conservation Hut before you set out.

For something less demanding, try the **Den Fenella Track**, which will take you to some good lookouts, then you can return or preferably keep going (west) to the Conservation Hut along the **Overcliff Track**. Better still, is the magical **Undercliff Track** to **Princes Rock Lookout**.

Leura

Although the pretty village of Leura plays second fiddle to Katoomba, the two essentially merge into one. Possessing a distinct air of elegance, the residents of Leura are proud of their village and in particular their gardens. **Everglades Gardens** ① *37 Everglades Av, T4784 1938, www.evergladesgardens.info, 1000-1700, $8, concessions $6, children $4*, provide the best horticultural showpiece and have done since the early 1930s. **Leuralla and NSW Toy and Railway Museum** ① *36 Olympian Pde, T4784 1169, www.toyandrailwaymuseum.com.au, 1000-1700, $10, children $2*, is well worth a look, for kids and parents alike. There are several walks and lookouts around the cliff fringes in Leura with the best being the short 500-m walk to the aptly named **Sublime Lookout**, offering arguably the best view of the Jamieson Valley and Mount Solitary. Follow signs from Gladstone Road, west of the Mall.

Katoomba → See map, page 72.

Considered the capital of the Blue Mountains, the erstwhile mining town of Katoomba offers an interesting mix of old and new and a truly cosmopolitan ambience. As well as the wealth of amenities and activities based in the town, many come here simply to see the classic picture-postcard view of the Blue Mountains from the famous **Three Sisters lookout**. The steady stream of tourist traffic flows down Katoomba's main drag towards **Echo Point** to enjoy this view. It is little wonder the place is so popular. Built precariously 170 m above the valley floor, the lookout seems to defy gravity. Dawn and sunset are the best times to visit. From the lookout it is possible to walk around to the stacks and descend the taxing **Giant Stairway Walk** (30 minutes) to the valley floor. From there you join the **Federal Pass Track**, back through the forest below the cliffs to the **Katoomba Cascades** and **Orphan Rock** (a lone pillar that became separated from the nearby cliff over many centuries of erosion). From Orphan Rock it is a short walk to a choice of exits: the hard option, on foot, up the 1000-step Furbers Steps, or for the less adventurous, the Scenic Railway, see below. Give yourself three hours.

Katoomba presents many other excellent walking options, including the **Narrow Neck Plateau** (variable times) and the **Ruined Castle** (12 km, seven hours). The latter starts from the base of the Scenic Railway and can be made as part of an extended overnight trip to the summit of Mount Solitary. It's recommended, but go prepared. The **Grand Canyon** walk (5 km, four hours) from Neates Glen, Evans Lookout Road, Blackheath, is also a cracker.

West of Echo Point the junction of Cliff Drive and Violet Street will deliver you to the highly commercial **Scenic World** ⓘ *T4782 0200, www.scenicworld.com.au, 0900-1700, Railway Skyway and Cableway $28, Skyway $16*, with its unusual scenic transportations. The **Scenic Railway** option takes you on an exhilarating descent to the valley floor; on what is reputed to be the world's steepest 'inclined funicular railway'. At the bottom you can then take a boardwalk through the forest to see an old coal mine with an audiovisual display and bronze sculpture. In contrast, the **Scenic Skyway** provides a more sedate bird's-eye view of the valley floor and the surrounding cliffs. The last, and most recent, of the trio, is the **Scenic Cableway** that takes you on a 545-m ride into – or out of – the World Heritage-listed rainforest of the Jamison Valley. Once at the bottom, you can take the Scenic Walkway to the base of the Scenic Railway. In all, there are just under 3 km of elevated boardwalk, 380 m of which is accessible by wheelchair. If you survive that there is also a cinema showing a Blue Mountains documentary on demand and a revolving restaurant.

Maxvision Edge Cinema ⓘ *225 Great Western Highway, T4782 8900, www.edge cinema.com.au, from 1020, from $14.50*, with its six-storey, 18-m high, 24-m wide screen, is worth visiting for its precipitous film of the Blue Mountains, *The Edge*.

Medlow Bath, Blackheath and Megalong Valley

From Katoomba the Great Western Highway heads north through the pretty villages of Medlow Bath, Blackheath and Mount Victoria. Although not as commercial as their bustling neighbour, all provide excellent accommodation, restaurants and are fringed

Katoomba

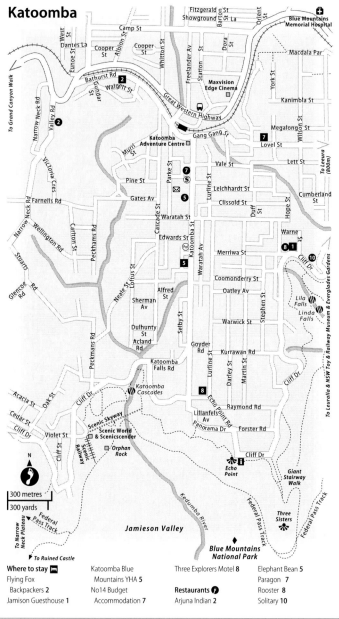

Where to stay 🛏

Flying Fox
  Backpackers **2**
Jamison Guesthouse **1**

Katoomba Blue
  Mountains YHA **5**
No14 Budget
  Accommodation **7**

Three Explorers Motel **8**

Restaurants 🍴
Arjuna Indian **2**

Elephant Bean **5**
Paragon **7**
Rooster **8**
Solitary **10**

both north and south by equally stunning views and excellent walks. To the east is the easily accessible **Megalong Valley**, particularly well known for its horse trekking, with **Grose Valley** to the west. **Evans** and **Govetts Leap Lookouts**, east of Blackheath, provide the best easily accessible viewpoints, but there are also some lesser-known spots well worth a visit.

In **Medlow Bath** is the historic **Hydro Majestic Hotel**, built in 1903 and the longest building in Australia at the time. Though a hotel in its own right, its original function was as a sanatorium, offering all manner of health therapies, from the sublime – mud baths and spas – to the ridiculous – strict abstinence from alcohol. At the time the rarefied air in the Blue Mountains was hailed as a cure-all for city ills and people flocked to the Hydro. Today, although the mud baths (and thankfully the prohibition) have gone, the hotel still provides fine accommodation and a great spot for afternoon tea.

Blackheath is a sleepy little village with a lovely atmosphere, enhanced in autumn when the trees take on their golden hues. There are two lookouts well worth visiting. The first, **Evans Lookout**, is accessed east along Evans Lookout Road and provides the first of many viewpoints across the huge and dramatic expanse of the Grose Valley. One of the best walks in the region, which we recommend, the **Grand Canyon Trail**, departs from Neates Glen, off Evans Lookout Road (5 km, five hours). From there you descend through the rainforest and follow Greaves Creek through moss-covered rock tunnels and overhangs, before climbing back up to Evans Lookout. The other lookout, **Govetts Leap**, is a stunner and has the added attraction of the **Bridal Veil Falls**, the highest (but not necessarily the most dramatic), in the Blue Mountains. Just before the lookout car park is the **NPWS Heritage Centre** ① *T4787 8877, www.npws.nsw.gov.au, 0900-1630*, which is worth a visit and can provide walking information, maps, guide and gifts. **Fairfax Heritage Track**, built to accommodate wheelchairs, links the centre with the lookout. From Govetts Leap you can walk either north to reach Pulpit Rock or south to Evans Lookout via the falls.

Although Govetts and Evans are both stunning, three other superb lookouts await your viewing pleasure and can be accessed from Blackheath. These are often missed, but no less spectacular. The first, **Pulpit Rock**, can be reached by foot from Govetts (2.5 km, 1½ hrs) or better still, by 2WD via (unsealed) Hat Hill Road. The lookout, which sits on the summit of a rock pinnacle, is accessed from the car park by a short 500-m walk. From the same car park then continue north to **Anvil Rock**, being sure not to miss the other short track to the bizarre geology of the wind-eroded cave. Perry Lookdown is 1 km before Anvil Rock and a path from there descends into the valley to connect with some demanding walking trails. Also well worth a visit is the aptly named **Hanging Rock**, which will, on first sight, take your breath away. Watch your footing and do not attempt to climb to the point, as tempting as it may be. It is also a favourite abseiling spot. Like all the other lookouts on the southern fringe of the Grose Valley, sunrise is by far the best time to visit. The rock can be reached along a rough, unsealed track (Ridgewell Road), on the right, just beyond Blackheath heading north. It is best suited to 4WD but if you don't have your own transport most local 4WD tours go there.

Megalong Valley, accessed on Megalong Valley Road, west of Blackheath town centre, provides a pleasant scenic drive and is one of the most accessible and most developed of the wilderness Blue Mountains valleys. **Megalong Australian Heritage Centre** ① *T4787 8188, www.megalong.cc, 0800-1730*, offers a whole range of activities from horse trekking and 4WD adventures, to livestock shows.

Canberra: Australia's capital city

Derived from the Aboriginal word *Kamberra* (meeting place), Australia's capital is, sadly, one of the most underrated cities in the world. It lacks intimacy and is too modern to have developed a sense of history, but, if you can ignore the negative publicity, it's actually a pleasant place and offers a great deal to see and do. A sightseeing bus tour is a good way of experiencing the sights, particularly if you are short of time. Cycling is also a great way to get around, with many cycleways. An efficient bus service runs throughout the city and to the airport. Contact the VIC ① *330 Northbourne Av, 3 km north of the centre, T1300 554 114 / T6205 0044, www.canberra tourism.com.au, Mon-Fri 0900-1700, Sat-Sun 0900-1600*, for more details and maps.

If you're short of time don't miss the National Museum, the New Parliament Building and the National Capital Exhibition, all of which are neatly contained within the National Triangle, or Parliamentary Triangle. Although the temptation is to head straight for the Triangle's crowning glory, the New Parliament Building, start your tour instead at the **National Capital Exhibition** ① *Regatta Point, Commonwealth Park, T6272 2900, www.nationalcapital.gov.au, 0900-1700, free*, which imaginatively outlines the fascinating history of the nation's capital from its indigenous links to today's intriguing landscaped metropolis. The views across Lake Burley Griffin are memorable.

Completed in 1988, **New Parliament House** ① *T6277 5399, www.aph.gov.au, 0900-1700, guided tours every 30 mins from 0900*, is the architectural showpiece of Canberra and one of Australia's great man-made wonders, like Sydney's Opera House and Harbour Bridge. Where else in the world is there such a building with its lawn on the roof? Once you have trampled all over it and taken in the angles, perspectives and views you can then turn to the interior. Along with more fascinating architecture the interior hosts precious Australian art and craft, including Arthur Boyd's impressive *Shoalhaven Tapestry*. When Parliament is sitting, access is allowed to

Lithgow

Lithgow marks the western boundary of the Blue Mountains and was founded in 1827 by explorer Hamilton Hume. An industrial town and Australia's first producer of steel, its main tourist attraction is the remarkable Zig Zag Railway (see below), 10 km east in Clarence, as well as a scattering of historical buildings. The town also acts as the gateway to the Jenolan Caves and Kanangra-Boyd National Park to the south and the wilderness Wollemi National Park, to the north. Wollemi is one of the largest and the most inaccessible wilderness areas in NSW, a fact that was highlighted in no uncertain terms in 1994 with the discovery of the Wollemi Pine, a species that once flourished over sixty million years ago. The exact location of the small stand of trees is kept secret.

There are two fairly low-key museums in the town. **State Mine and Heritage Park and Railway** and **Lithgow Small Arms Museum**. **Eskbank House Museum** is a Georgian homestead built in 1842, complete with period furnishings and Lithgow pottery. The VIC

'Question Time' in the House of Representatives and begins at 1400. Tickets are free; make bookings through the Sergeant of Arms office. Facing Lake Burley Griffin, in the heart of the National Triangle, is the Old Parliament House completed in 1927, hub of the nation's political life until the New Parliament House took over in 1988. Immediately outside is the Aboriginal Tent Embassy that serves as a pertinent reminder that the Aboriginal people of Australia were living here for tens of thousands of years before the first acre of land was ever purchased. Sitting proudly on the shores of Lake Burley Griffin, the National Museum of Australia ① *Lawson Crescent, T6208 5000, www.nma.gov.au, 0900-1700, free (admission charge to some specialist displays)*, is superb, with a range of exciting displays and themed galleries that convey all things 'Aussie', all beautifully designed and presented.

⊖ Where to stay

The VIC has listings and a bookings service, T1300 554 114, www.visitcanberra.com.au. **$$$ Kurrajong**, 8 National Circuit, Barton, T6234 4444, www.hotel kurrajong.com.au.

One of the capital's best boutique hotels. It is well positioned between the lively suburb of Manuka and the National Triangle.
$$-$ Canberra City YHA, 7 Akuna St, T6248 9155, www.canberracity accommodation.com.au. The best budget option, costing more than your average hostel but worth it. Kitchen, bar, pool and spa.

⊖ Transport

The international airport, T6209 3336, www.canberraairport.com.au, is 8 km east of the centre via Morshead Drive. **QantasLink**, **Virgin Blue**, **Tiger Airways** and **Regional Express** fly to/from Sydney, Brisbane and Melbourne. Long-distance coaches stop at the Jolimont Tourist Centre, 65 Northbourne Av, Civic T02-6211 8545. **Greyhound** and **Premier Motor Services** have services to Sydney, Brisbane and Melbourne. The train station is in Kingston suburb, 6 km south of the centre, off Cunningham St, T6257 1576. **Countrylink**, T132232, runs regular daily services to/from Sydney and Melbourne (train/coach).

can supply town maps and accommodation listings. Of far more natural and historic appeal are the derelict villages of **Newnes** and **Glen Davis**, to the north of Lithgow, between the scenic Gardens of Stone National Park and the western fringe of the Wollemi National Park. Both were once thriving villages supporting a population of thousands that worked in the two large oil-shale refineries during the early 1900s. South of Newnes an added attraction is the old 400-m rail tunnel that was once part of a busy line that connected the shale plants with Clarence Station. Now left dark and forbidding, the tunnel is the silent home of glow worms (gnat larvae), which light up its walls like a galaxy of stars. All along the unsealed roads to both Newnes and Glen Davis look out for the prolific birdlife.

In **Clarence**, 10 km east of Lithgow, you will find the **Zig Zag Railway** ① *T6351 4826, www.zigzagrailway.com.au, $28, concessions $22, children $14 (return)*, a masterpiece of engineering originally built between 1866 and 1869. Operated commercially up until

1910 as a supply route to Sydney it now serves as a tourist attraction with lovingly restored steam trains making the nostalgic 8-km (1½ hours) journey from Clarence to Bottom Points (near CityRail's Zig Zag Station). They leave Clarence on Wednesdays and at the weekend at 1100, 1300 and 1500. On other weekdays the less exciting motorized trains take over and leave at the same time. Request drop off if you are arriving by CityRail from Sydney/Katoomba at the Zig Zag Station.

Jenolan Caves

① T6359 3911, www.jenolancaves.org.au, the main caves can only be visited by guided tour, daily from 1000-2000. Cave combo tickets from $28-$40. Caving adventure tours are also an option, costing from $75-$200.

The Jenolan Caves, on the northern fringe of the Kanangra-Boyd National Park, south of Lithgow, comprise nine major (and 300 in total) limestone caves considered to be amongst the most spectacular in the southern hemisphere. After over 160 years of exploration and development – since their discovery in 1838 by pastoralist James Whalan – the main caves are now well geared up for your viewing pleasure with a network of paths and electric lighting to guide the way and to highlight the bizarre subterranean features. As well as guided cave tours, some other caves have been set aside for adventure caving, and above ground, there is a network of pleasant bush trails. If you are short of time the **Lucas Cave** and **Temple of Baal Cave** are generally recommended. The **Chiefly Cave** is the most historic and along with the **Imperial Cave** it has partial wheelchair access. The **River Cave** is said to be one of the most demanding. On your arrival at the caves you immediately encounter the **Grand Arch**, a 60-m wide, 24-m high cavern that was once used for camping and even live entertainment to the flicker of firelight. Nearby, the historic and congenial **Caves House** has been welcoming visitors since 1898 (see Where to stay below).

Bells Line of Road

Bells Line of Road is named after Archibald Bell, who discovered the 'second' route through the Blue Mountains to Lithgow from Sydney, in 1823, at the age of 19. Starting just west of Richmond in the east, then climbing the plateau to fringe the northern rim of the Grose Valley, it provides a quieter, more sedate, scenic trip across the Great Divide. Just beyond the village of Bilpin, west of Richmond, the huge basalt outcrop of Mount Tomah (1000 m) begins to dominate the scene and supports the 28-ha cool-climate annexe of the **Sydney Botanical Gardens (Mount Tomah)** ① T4567 3000, 1000-1600, $5.50, children $4.40. Opened in 1987, the garden's rich volcanic soils nurture over 10,000 species, including a huge quantity of tree ferns and rhododendrons. Although the gardens are well worth visiting in their own right, it is the views, the short walks and the restaurant that make it extra special. Just beyond Mount Tomah (right) is the **Walls Lookout**, with its expansive views across the Grose Valley. It requires a one-hour return walk from the Pierces Pass Track car park but the effort is well worth it. Back on the Bells Line of Road and just a few kilometres further west is the junction (north, 8 km) to the pretty village of **Mount Wilson** which is famous for its English-style open gardens. These include **Linfield Park** and **Nooroo**. Also of interest is the **Cathedral of Ferns** at the northern end of the village. The **Wynnes** and **Du Faurs Lookouts** can also be reached from Mount Wilson and are signposted, east and west of the village centre.

Around Sydney listings

For hotel and restaurant price codes and other relevant information, see pages 10-14.

Ku-ring-gai Chase National Park *p67*
$$ Pittwater YHA, T9999 5748, pittwater@yhansw.org.au. Take the ferry from Church Point to this great place.

Blue Mountains *p68, Katoomba map p72*
Leura has many excellent historic B&Bs and self-contained cottages and Katoomba has plenty of choice. Wentworth also has plenty of good B&Bs. If you prefer something a bit quieter, the villages north of Katoomba – Medlow Bath, Blackheath and Mount Victoria – all provide some excellent accommodation. There are plenty of places to stay in and around Jenolan. Prices are higher at weekends and you are advised to book ahead at any time of year, especially winter.
$$$$ Glenella Guesthouse, 56 Govetts Leap Rd, Medlow Bath, T4787 8352, www.glenellabluemountainshotel.com.au. Well known and surprisingly affordable, historic guesthouse, with a reputable restaurant attached, plus all the comforts including sauna, open fires and cable TV.
$$$$ Imperial, 1 Station St, Mount Victoria, T4787 1878, www.hotel imperial.com.au. Reputedly the oldest tourist hotel in Australia. Beautifully restored, it is a fine place to soak up the history and offers a wide range of well-appointed rooms from the traditional to the 4-poster with double spa. Breakfast included, good restaurant, bar and live entertainment at the weekends.
$$$$ Jemby-Rinjah Eco Lodge, 336 Evans Lookout Rd, Medlow Bath, T4787 7622, www.jembyrinjah lodge.com.au. 1- or 2-bedroom, self-contained, modern cabins (one with a Japanese hot tub) and log fires, all

in a beautiful bush setting close to the lookout and walks. Dinner and bed and breakfast packages are also available.
$$$$ Jenolan Caves Resort, Jenolan Caves, T1300 763311, www.jenolancaves.com. Grand, with a wealth of facilities, this resort has the renowned Caves House. It offers a range of rooms and suites, plus self-contained cottages with a restaurant, bistro, bar and a host of activities.
$$$ Blackheath Caravan Park, Prince Edward St, Blackheath, T4787 8101. In a quiet suburban bush setting within walking distance of the village. Onsite vans, powered and non-powered sites, barbecue and kiosk, but no camp kitchen.
$$$ Jamison Guesthouse, 48 Merriwa St, Katoomba, T4782 1206, www.jamisonhouse .com.au. One of the many fine historic B&Bs, lodges and self-contained cottages in and around Katoomba. This one is long-established and large with plenty of old world European-style charm, period decor, en suites, a guest lounge with log fire and a popular French restaurant attached (see below). Close to all amenities.
$$$ Jenolan Cabins, Porcupine Hill, 42 Edith Rd, Jenolan Caves, T6335 6239, www.jenolancabins.com.au. Self-contained cabins sleep 6 with 1 queen size and bunks. The owners also operate local tours.
$$$ Katoomba Blue Mountains YHA, 207 Katoomba St, Katoomba, T4782 1416, bluemountains@yhansw.org.au. Beautifully renovated art deco building. A showpiece hostel for the YHA and fast developing a reputation as one of its best. It's modern, spacious, friendly and has good facilities. Trips arranged, also bike hire and internet.
$$$ Three Explorers Motel, 197 Lurline St, Katoomba, T4782 1733, www.3explorers. com.au. For a motel option try this recommended and unconventional option. They also offer a 2-bedroom cottage.

$$ Flying Fox Backpackers,
190 Bathurst St, Katoomba, T02-4782 4226,
www.theflyingfox.com.au. Long-established
and sociable, spacious dorms and great bush
camping. Good advice on local activities and
transport to walking tracks.

$$ No14 Budget Accommodation,
14 Lovel St, Katoomba, T4782 7104,
www.bluemts.com.au/no14. Another fine
alternative, providing a peaceful, relaxed
atmosphere in a old former guesthouse with
double, twin, single and family rooms. Polished
floors and an open fire add to the atmosphere.

🍽 Restaurants

Blue Mountains *p68, Katoomba map p72*
Katoomba and the Blue Mountains generally
pride themselves in offering some classy
restaurants and fine cuisine. Book ahead for
the expensive places.

$$$ Silk's Brasserie, 128 The Mall, Leura,
T4784 2534. Daily for lunch and dinner (book
ahead). One of the many fine restaurants and
cafés in Leura, this one offers fine modern
Australian cuisine.

$$$ Solitary, 90 Cliff Dr, Katoomba, T4782
1164. Lunch Sat-Sun and public/school
holidays and dinner Tue-Sat. A classy award
winner with a fine reputation offering
imaginative modern Australian cuisine and
fine views across the Jamieson Valley.

$$ Arjuna Indian, 16 Valley Rd, Katoomba,
T4782 4662. Thu-Mon at 1800 (book ahead).
The best Indian restaurant in the region and
the views are almost as hot as the curry.

$$ Rooster, Jamieson Guesthouse, 48
Merriwa St, Katoomba, T4782 1206. Daily for
dinner and for lunch Sat-Sun. An old favourite
that serves good value French-influenced
cuisine, with fine views to boot. Also very
good accommodation.

$$ Vulcans, 33 Govetts Leap Rd, Blackheath,
T4787 6899. Fri-Sun for lunch and dinner.
Another well-known Blackheath institution;
the only drawback is the limited opening.

$ Elephant Bean, 159 Katoomba St,
Katoomba, T4782 4620. Wed-Mon
0800-1500. A fine café especially for lunch.
$ Paragon, 65 Katoomba St, Katoomba,
T4782 2928. Daily 0800-1700. If you have a
sweet tooth you just cannot afford to miss
out on this art deco Katoomba institution.

🏔 What to do

Blue Mountains *p68, Katoomba map p72*
All based in Katoomba unless stated
otherwise. See the VIC for full listings.
Australian School of Mountaineering,
166 Katoomba St, T4782 2014,
www.asmguides.com. Hardcore professional
rock climbing and bush craft trips, plus others.
Blue Mountains Adventure Company, 84a
Bathurst Rd, T4782 1271, www.bmac .com.au.
A well-established local company with a fine
reputation, range of affordable options from
abseiling to mountain biking.
**Blue Mountains Explorer Double-decker
Bus**, T4782 1866, www.explorerbus.com.au.
A local service with 30 stops around
Katoomba and Leura, hourly between 0945
and 1645. An unlimited jump-on/off day pass
costs $36, concessions $30, children $18.
Blue Mountain Horseriding Adventures,
T4787 8188, www.bluemountainshorse
riding.com.au. Based in the Megalong Valley
west of Katoomba, offers hour/half/full and
multi day horse rides from $50.
Getabout 4WD Adventures, T8822 5656,
www.getabout.com.au. Professional day and
multi-day 4WD tours (Blue Mountains day
tour $685) with a tag-along options allowing
you to take your own vehicle.
High 'N' Wild, 3/5 Katoomba St, T4782 6224,
www.high-n-wild.com.au. Abseiling, canyoning,
rock climbing and mountain biking.
Tread Lightly Eco-Tours, 100 Great Western
Highway, Medlow Bath, T4788 1229,
www.treadlightly.com.au. Very clued-up and
eco-friendly, great bushwalking and 4WD
tours throughout the region from $135.

Trolley Tours, 285 Main St, 1800-801577. A 29-stop historic trolley bus tour around the sights of Katoomba and Leura. All-day travel pass, daily 1015-1615, $20.

⊖ Transport

Kamay Botany Bay National Park *p66*
Access to the northern sector is via Anzac Parade. **Sydney Buses**, T131500, runs regular daily buses from Railway Sq (No 393) or Circular Quay (No 394) in Sydney's CBD. To get to the southern sector by car, follow Princes Highway south, turn left on to The Boulevarde, and then follow Captain Cook Drive. Vehicle entry to the park costs $11. By train from Sydney's Central Station, take **CityRail**, T131500, to Cronulla (Illawarra line), then **Kurnell Bus**, T9523 4047, No 987.

Royal National Park *p67*
By **train** take **CityRail** (Illawarra line) from Central Station to Loftus (4 km from Audley), Engadine, Heathcote, Waterfall or Otford. You can also alight at Cronulla and take the short crossing by ferry to Bundeena at the park's northeastern corner, T9523 2990, www.cronullaferries.com.au, from $5.70, children $2.85.

Ku-ring-gai Chase National Park *p67*
The nearest public transport (western side) by train is with **CityRail**, T131500 (Northern Line), from Central Station to Berowa, Mount Ku-ring-gai and Mount Colah, then walk to Bobbin Head (3-6 km). A better option is to catch a bus (No L90) to Palm Beach (eastern side) then the ferry to Basin Beach. Ferries also run to Bobbin Head (see page 67).

Blue Mountains *p68, Katoomba map p72*
Katoomba train station is off Main St, at the northern end of Katoomba St. Trains leave Sydney's Central Station on a regular basis. **Countrylink**, T132232, offers daily services to/from Sydney hourly. **CityRail**, T131500,

with **Fantastic Aussie Tours**, T4782 1866, also offer a number of rail/coach tour options with Blue MountainsLink, operating Mon-Fri and Blue Mountains ExplorerLink, operating daily. Prices include return transport and a tour on arrival in Katoomba. **Greyhound** has coaches on the westbound run from Sydney to Dubbo, stopping behind the train station near Gearin Hotel, Great Western Highway. **Blue Mountains Bus Co**, T4751 1077, www.bmbc.com.au. Operates a standard Hail 'n' Ride service around Katoomba, **Leura** and Wentworth Falls. Mon-Fri 0745-2025, Sat 0800-1530, Sun 0915-1530, from $2. **Katoomba Radio Cabs**, Katoomba, T4782 1311. Operates a 24-hr taxi service between **Mount Victoria** and **Wentworth Falls**.

Medlow Bath, **Blackheath** and **Mount Victoria** are all on the main local bus/train routes to/from Katoomba. The train station is in the centre of town off the Great Western Highway and on Station St.

Lithgow is on the main local and westbound bus/train route to/from Katoomba and Sydney. See above for details of tours and services. The train station is on Main St, **Countrylink** and **CityRail**, both offer regular daily services east and west.

There is no public transport to the **Jenolan Caves**, but tour operators in Katoomba and Sydney run tours. A day tour to the caves will cost about $120 exclusive of caves tour, $150 with a cave inspection and around $200 with a cave inspection and a spot of adventure caving. The VICs in Katoomba or Sydney have full details. See What to do, page 78.

❶ Directory

Katoomba *p71, map p72*
Banks Most bank branches with ATMs are located along Katoomba St. **Hospital Blue Mountains District Hospital**, Great Western Highway (1 km east of the town centre), T4784 6500.

South Coast NSW

Few visitors have any idea that the little corner of southern NSW is just as beautiful as anywhere else in the state. Overshadowed by Sydney and the north coast, it has pretty much been left alone. But the south coast has over 35 national parks and nature reserves; more than any other region in the state and most are above the waterline. The south coast also has its fair share of beautiful unspoiled beaches and stunning coastal scenery. South of Wollongong and Kiama the coast is split into three quite distinct regions: the Shoalhaven Coast which extends from Nowra to Batemans Bay; the Eurobodalla Coast which stretches from Batemans Bay to Narooma; and the Sapphire Coast which idles its way to the Victorian border.

Wollongong and around → *For listings, see pages 87-92.*

Wollongong is a very attractive place, despite the stark industrial landscapes of Port Kembla to the south, and without doubt its greatest assets are its beaches, its harbour (with its historic lighthouse) and behind that, **Flagstaff Point** headland and the **Wollongong Foreshore Park**. Either side of Flagstaff Point over 17 patrolled beaches stretch from the Royal National Park in the north to Bass Point in the south, all providing excellent opportunities for sunbathers, swimmers and surfies. Wollongong serves as the gateway to the Illawarra region, an area renowned for its dramatic coastline and rugged mountain backdrop. It is also the first main stop along the 140-km 'Grand Pacific Drive' that encompasses some of the state's finest and most unspoilt coastline.

In the heart of the city the **Wollongong City Gallery** ① *corner of Kembla St and Burelli St, T4228 7500, www.wollongongcitygallery.com, Tue-Fri 1000-1700, Sat-Sun 1200-1600, free*, is definitely worth a visit. Considered one of the best and one of the largest regional galleries in NSW, it offers a wide range of media and an exciting programme of local, regional and interstate exhibitions. For train enthusiasts the **Cockatoo Run** ① *T1300 653801, www.3801limited.com.au, runs to Robertson every 2nd Sunday of the month and Kiama every 3rd Sunday, from $50, children $40, lunch an extra $25, bookings required*, is a scenic mountain railway that climbs through the Illawarra Ranges from Wollongong to Robertson in the Southern Highlands. Extended tours throughout the state are also on offer. South of the city centre, in the suburb of Berkeley, is Wollongong's unique attraction, the **Nan Tien Buddhist Temple** ① *Berkeley Rd, T4272 0600, www.nan tien.org.au, Tue-Sun 0900-1700, $4, also offers vegetarian lunches for $12 per person*. This is the Southern Hemisphere's largest Buddhist temple open to visitors and offers a varied programme of weekend workshops and accommodation, see Where to stay, page 87.

Public transport to the temple is with Premier Illawarra Bus Company (No 34) from Marine Drive. Wollongong offers some excellent surfing with the best breaks on **North Beach**, just north of Flagstaff Point, and **Bulli Beach**, 12 km north of the centre. There are plenty of places to hire equipment; see What to do, page 90. Find local information at the new **VIC** ① *Southern Gateway Centre, Princes Hwy, Bulli Tops, T4267 5910, www.southerngatewaycentre.com.au, Mon-Fri 0900-1700, Sat 0900-1600, Sun 1000-1600.*

The **Illawarra Ranges**, flanking Wollongong inland, have some excellent viewpoints that are well worth seeing, such as the **Mount Keira Lookout** in the Illawarra Escarpment State Recreation Area (left on Clive Bissell Road), and the **Bulli Lookout** (right), both off Highway 1 (Ousley Road), just north of the city. There are numerous fine beaches north of the city. **Bulli Beach** is perhaps the best, but it is a case of taking your pick, all the way from the city centre to **Otford** at the southern edge of the **Royal National Park**. Another great local attraction just to the south of the city, and beyond Port Kembla, is **Lake Illawarra**. Essentially a saltwater harbour, sheltered from the ocean by a narrow strip of land, it provides a haven for a wide range of water sports, from sailing to kayaking.

Kiama and Berry → *For listings, see pages 87-92.*

Just to the south of Lake Illawarra, the pretty coastal town of Kiama is the first of many that are encountered on the journey between Wollongong and the Victorian border. The centre of activity revolves around **Blowhole Point**, crowned by its 1887 lighthouse. During a good southeasterly, the surging waves can plough into the blowhole with awesome power, creating a thunderous roar and spout of mist, as if issued from some angry subterranean dragon. To the north of Blowhole Point is **Pheasant Point**, with its rock pool, and north again is **Bombo Beach**, a favourite amongst the local surf set. **VIC** ① *Blowhole Point Rd, T4232 3322, www.kiama.com.au, open 0900-1700.*

South, beyond the Mount Pleasant Lookout on the Princes Highway, is **Werri Beach**, which is a good one for surfing, then via Crooked River Drive, the headland villages of **Gerringong** and **Gerroa**. At Gerroa, the **Crooked River Winery** ① *11 Willow Vale Rd, 9 km south of Kiama, T4234 0975*, can provide a congenial stop with the added bonus of a fine café and coastal views. From the **Kingsford Smith Lookout** in Gerroa – which pays tribute to Australia's most famous aviator – it is hard to resist the temptation to explore the vast swathe of **Seven Mile Beach**, which beckons from below the rooftops. Inland, via the little village of **Jamberoo**, 10 km away, is the **Minnamurra Rainforest**, part of the **Budderoo National Park**. The popular **NPWS Minnamurra Rainforest Centre** ① *T4236 0469, www.nationalparks.nsw.gov.au, 0900-1700, $11 vehicle entry, café and shop*, is signposted off Jamberoo Mountain Road, heading west, acts as a base for explorations of the forest and the Minnamurra Falls.

Roughly halfway between Kiama and Nowra is the delightful little village of **Berry**, which is well worth a stretch of the legs to take a closer look. Almost impossible to miss is the bizarre façade and interior of the **Great Southern Hotel Motel**, 95 Queen Street. Not only is there a small fleet of rowboats on the roof and a signpost laden with markers to all conceivable destinations, there's also, next door, a bottle shop completely decked in shiny hubcaps. But it doesn't end there. Inside, the bar is decked with a wide array of objects including a centrepiece First World War torpedo set proudly above the pool table. During the great Pacific nuclear testing controversy in the mid-1990s, the said torpedo was actually rammed at admirable speed into the gates of the French Embassy in Canberra atop a VW Beetle. There are plenty of good cafés and restaurants along Berry's main drag.

Shoalhaven coast → *For listings, see pages 87-92.*

Beyond Berry you reach the Shoalhaven River and the twin towns of **Bomaderry** and **Nowra**. From here you are entering the south coast proper and an area known as Shoalhaven, which extends from Nowra to **Batemans Bay**. Although the town of Nowra is a fairly unremarkable introduction to the south coast, just to the east and especially around Jervis Bay and beyond, its true magic begins to be revealed, with some of the best beaches and national parks in the state. If you have time you may also like to consider some Tourist Drives inland to Kangaroo Valley and the Morton National park (Fitzroy Falls) or others that explore the coast in more detail. The VIC can provide all the details. Nowra is home to the **Shoalhaven VIC** ⓘ *corner of Princes Highway and Pleasant Way, T4421 0778, www.shoalhaven.nsw.gov.au, 0900-1630*, as well as the **NPWS office** ⓘ *55 Graham St, Nowra, T4423 2170*.

Paringa and Nowra Park, to the west of Nowra, fringes the riverbank and offers a riverside walk that takes in the 46-m **Hanging Rock Lookout** and a number of climbing sites. There are also river cruises.

Jervis Bay and around
Jervis Bay is a deep, sheltered bay that sits neatly in the embrace of the Beecroft Peninsula to the north and the exquisite Booderee National Park to the south. It is blessed with stunning coastal scenery, beautiful white beaches, a marine park with world-class dive sites and even a resident pod of over 60 playful dolphins, all of which combine to earn it the quiet reputation as the jewel of the NSW South Coast. Local information is available from **Huskisson Trading Post** ⓘ *1 Tomerong St, Huskisson, T4441 5241, www.tourism jervisbay.com.au, 0900-1700*.

The old shipbuilding town of **Huskisson** (known as 'Husky') and its neighbour **Vincentia** are the two main settlements on Jervis Bay and form the gateway to the bay's water-based activities. The diving in the **Jervis Bay Marine Park** in particular is said to be second only to the Great Barrier Reef and is well known for its marine variety and water clarity. A few companies offer activities like whale and dolphin watching, see page 90.

Booderee National Park ⓘ *day fee (including and per car) costs $10 and camping fees (from $10-$20) must be paid on top of that, so if you intend staying overnight it does add up*, formerly known as the Jervis Bay National Park, takes up almost the entire southern headland of Jervis Bay and is, without doubt, one of the most attractive coastal national parks in NSW. Owned and administered by a collaboration of Parks Australia and the Wreck Bay Aboriginal Community, it offers a wealth of fine, secluded beaches, bush walks, stunning coastal scenery and a rich array of wildlife. Not to be missed are **Green Patch Beach**, the further flung **Cave Beach**, a good surf spot, and **Summercloud Bay**. The walking track to **Steamers Beach** (2.3 km) is also recommended although there are many fine options to choose from. Another unique attraction in the park is the 80-ha **Booderee Botanic Gardens** ⓘ *Mon-Fri 0800-1600, Sat-Sun 1000-1700, free with park entry fee*, created in 1952 as an annexe of the Australian National Botanic Gardens in Canberra.

There are over 1600 species centred on the small freshwater Lake McKenzie, with most being coastal plants more suited to the local climate. There are a number of short walks and nature trails. The **VIC** ① *Village Rd, T4443 0977, www.booderee.np.gov.au, 0900-1600*, at the park entrance, can supply detailed information about the park, its attractions, walks, amenities and its scattering of great campsites. Provisions can be bought at the general store ① *0700-2100, or 1900 outside school holidays*, in Jervis Bay Village, off Jervis Bay Road, which is within the park boundary.

Murramarang National Park

① *Day-use vehicle entry costs $11, pedestrians free. Access to Pebbly Beach is via Mt Agony Rd (unsealed) right of the Princes Highway 10 km north of Batemans Bay. Depot Beach and Durras North are accessed via North Durras Rd off Mt Agony Rd. Pretty Beach and the Murramarang Aboriginal Area are accessed via Bawley Point and Kioloa on Murramarang Rd (sealed) off the Princes Highway 16 km south of Ulladulla.*

The 11,978-ha Murramarang National Park is most famous for its tame and extremely laid-back population of eastern grey kangaroos. Here they not only frequent the campsites and the foreshore but on occasion are even said to cool off in the surf. The park is a superb mix of forest and coastal habitat that offers a host of activities from swimming, surfing and walking to simple socializing with the resident marsupials. Of the beaches and campsites, **Pebbly Beach** and **Depot beach** are the most popular spots, but **Durras North**, south of Depot Beach and Pretty Beach to the north, is also great. There is a network of coast and forest walks available including the popular 'Discovery Trail' off North Durras Road, which skirts the edge of **Durras Lake**. There is also a fine coastal track connecting Pretty Beach with Pebbly Beach.

Eurobodalla Coast → *For listings, see pages 87-92.*

The Eurobodalla coastal region stretches from Batemans Bay in the north to Narooma in the south. The bustling seaside resort of **Batemans Bay** provides an ideal stopover along the coastal Princes Highway. Most of the Bay's beaches are located southeast of the town centre and if you have time it is worth heading that way. Tomakin and Broulee offer the best surf and fishing sites and jet skis can be hired on Coriggan's Beach. On the river you can take a leisurely three-hour cruise upstream to the historic riverside village of Nelligen. The area offers some excellent sea kayaking. There are numerous excellent dive sites around the Bay. See What to do, page 90, for details. Just off the Princes Highway near the town centre is the very helpful **VIC** ① *T4472 6900, www.naturecoast-tourism.com.au, 0900-1700*.

Nestled on a headland in the glistening embrace of the Wagonga River Inlet and surrounded by rocky beaches, national parks and the odd accessible island, **Narooma** has all the beauty and potential activities for which the south coast is famous. The biggest attraction is **Montague Island**, about 8 km offshore. Officially declared a nature reserve and administered by the National Parks and Wildlife Service, Montague has an interesting Aboriginal and European history and is crowned by a historic lighthouse built in 1881. But perhaps its greatest appeal are the colonies of fur seals and seabirds – including about 10,000 pairs of fairy penguins – that make the island home. Between October and December humpback whales can also be seen on their annual migration. There are tours of the island, see page 90.

Back on the mainland the immediate coastline has some interesting features including **Australia Rock**, which as the name suggests, looks like the outline of Australia. It is however not the rock that plays with the imagination but a hole in its middle. Access is via Bar Rock Road beyond the golf course, at the river mouth on Wagonga Head. Further south **Glasshouse Rocks** is another interesting geological formation. On the western side of town the Wagonga Inlet offers fishing and river cruises (see page 90). The **VIC** ① *off Princes Highway, T4476 2881, www.naturecoast-tourism.com.au, 0900-1700*, is at the northern end of town.

Sapphire Coast → *For listings, see pages 87-92.*

From Narooma to the Victorian border is a region known as the Sapphire Coast. Just south of Narooma, in the shadow of Gulaga Mountain, are the quaint and historic villages of **Central Tilba** and **Tilba Tilba** with a population of around 100. Now classified by the National Trust, they boast many historic cottages and also offer some of the South Coast's best cafés and arts and crafts outlets. Ask for a self-guided heritage leaflet from the VIC in Narooma. They can also provide listings for numerous cosy B&Bs in and around the two villages. **Tilba Valley Wines Vineyard** ① *off the Princes Highway, 5 km north of Tilba Tilba, T4473 7308, www.tilbavalleywines.com, open from 1000*, was established in 1978 and produces Shiraz, Semillon and Chardonnay. It offers tastings and has a small tavern-like restaurant.

Next along are the villages of **Bega** and **Tathra**. Bega's biggest tourist attraction is its famous **cheese factory** ① *Lagoon St, T6491 7762, www.begacheese.com.au, 0900-1700, free*. To the north and west of Bega is the 79,459-ha **Wadbilliga National Park**, a wilderness region of rugged escarpment and wild rivers. Along the road to the **Brogo River Dam** you can stay at **Fernmark Inn**, a perfect base from which to explore the park's rivers, perhaps best done by canoe (see page 90). From Bega you can then head straight for Merimbula or take a diversion to the coastal village of **Tathra**, where you can laze on the beach or explore the **Bournda National Park**. The 10-km Kangarutha Track from Tathra South to Wallagoot Lake is recommended. The **VIC** ① *at Bega Cheese Factory (see above), T6491 7645*, has information and listings.

Merimbula serves as the capital of the Sapphire Coast and receives most of its tourist traffic. Surrounded by fine beaches and bisected by Merimbula Lake (which is actually a saltwater inlet), it offers plenty to see and do, with **Main Beach**, south of the lake, being the most popular for swimming and body boarding. The lake itself is a great venue for boating, windsurfing and fishing. The surrounding coast also offers some good diving and is the happy home of a resident pod of dolphins. From September to December migrating whales join the party making cruising the town's speciality. On the northern bank of Merimbula Lake is the **VIC** ① *2 Beach St, T6495 1129, www.marimbulatourism.com.au, 0900-1700*, which has full details of diving, horse trekking and scenic flights; see also page 90. The **NPWS** ① *corner of Sapphire Coast and Merimbula Drive, T6495 5000, 0830-1630*, has a great Discovery Centre, offering parks and regional walks information, natural history displays, maps and gifts.

Kosciuszko National Park

At over 600,000 ha, the Kosciuszko National Park is the largest in New South Wales and certainly one of the most beautiful. Home to the continent's highest peak, the 2228-m Mount Kosciuszko, the famous Snowy River and the country's best skiing and snowboarding resorts, the park also offers a plethora of year-round mountain activities, such as hiking, mountain biking, whitewater rafting, horse trekking and fishing. And with much of the park being wilderness, it also offers sanctuary to many rare native plants and animals. Jindabyne, at the eastern fringe of the park, is the main satellite town for the skiing and snowboarding resorts and has a huge range of accommodation and restaurants. It also hosts the NPWS Snowy Region Visitors' Centre, ① *just off Kosciuszko Rd, T6450 5600, www.environment.nsw.gov.au, 0830-1700.*

The best of the skiing and snowboarding resorts is Thredbo, set in a beautiful river valley, overlooked by the Crackenback Mountain Range. For a full list of the many activity and accommodation options, visit the excellent VIC ① *6 Friday Drive, T1300 020 589 / T6459 4100, www.thredbo.com.au, winter 0800-1800, summer 0900-1600.* Things don't grind to a halt after the snow disappears. In summer Thredbo becomes an alpine walking centre and the Valley Chairlift stays open, offering walkers the shortest route to the summit of Mount Kosciuszko.

⊖ Transport

Countrylink has daily coach services to Jindabyne from Sydney, while **V-Line** has services from Melbourne. To get to the ski fields, the 8-km long Skitube at Bullock's Flat, 20 km east of Jindabyne (Alpine Way), connects Thredbo Valley with Perisher Blue Resort and the summit of Blue Cow Mountain. It operates daily in winter on the hour from 0900-1500. A shuttle bus service runs between Jindabyne and Thredbo.

Ben Boyd National Park → *For listings, see page 89.*

Sheer wilderness, beautiful coastal scenery, sublime walks, strange, colourful geological features, great campsites and even a remote lighthouse all combine to make the Ben Boyd National Park one of the best coastal parks in NSW. The 9490-ha park straddles Twofold Bay and the fishing village of Eden.

Visiting Ben Boyd National Park

Access to the park is off Princes Highway (signposted). Roads within the park are both sealed and unsealed. Unsealed sections are badly rutted, but negotiable by 2WD when dry. Day-use vehicle entry to the park costs $6. NPWS office in Merimbula (see above) can provide detailed information on the park, its walks and its campsites.

Around the park

In the northern section of the park, the principal feature is **The Pinnacles**, a conglomerate of white and orange, sand and clay that has eroded into strange pinnacle formations over many thousands of years. They can be reached on a short 500-m-circuit walk from the car park off the 2 km Haycock Road, which is partly sealed and signposted off the Princes Highway. To the north, at the end of Edrom Road (16 km, signposted off the Princes Highway), is **Boyd's Tower**, which though very grand, never served its intended purpose as a lighthouse. Below the tower a clearing looks down to clear azure waters and the strange volcanic convolutions of the red coastal rocks. Another diversion off Edrom Road, to the west, takes you to the remains of the **Davidson Whaling Station**, created in 1818 and the longest-running shore-based station in Australia, ceasing operations in 1930. Further south off Edrom Road an unsealed, badly rutted road leads to the delightful and wildlife-rich **Bittangabee campsite** (15 km, then 5 km on the left), see page 89.

Back on the main track the Disaster Bay Lookout is worth a look before the track terminates at the 'must-see' **Green Cape Light Station** (21 km). Surrounding by strange, rust-coloured rocks, pounded by surf and home to laid-back kangaroos, it is a wonderful place to find some solitude. **City Rock**, accessed down a short badly rutted track, off the lighthouse road, is signposted also well worth seeing. The wave action against the rock platform is dramatic and a favourite haunt for sea eagles. The superb but demanding (30 km) **'Light to Light' Walking Track** connects the Green Cape Light Station with Boyd's Tower, passing the **Bittangabee** and **Saltwater Creek** campsites along the way. It is one of the best and most remote coastal walks in NSW.

South Coast NSW listings

For hotel and restaurant price codes and other
relevant information, see pages 10-14.

▲ Where to stay

Wollongong and around *p80*
$$ Keiraview Wollongong YHA, 75-79
Keira St, T4229 1132, www.yha.com.au. The
city's best backpackers with modern facilities,
dorms, doubles and singles, most en suite,
parking and internet.
$$ Pilgrim Lodge, at the Nan Tien Buddhist
Temple, Berkeley Rd, Berkeley, T4272 0500,
www.nantien.org.au. For something
completely different, this offers comfortable,
modern en suite doubles, triples and family
rooms, with meals if required. Specialist
meditation weekend packages.

Kiama and Berry *p81*
$$$$ Bellawongarah at Berry B&B, 869
Kangaroo Valley Rd, Bellawongarah, T4464
1999, www.accommodation-berry.com.au.
Country home and cottage in an elevated
bush setting only 10 mins from Berry.
A former 1868 church now serves as a
self-contained cottage, while the spacious,
contemporary 3-storey house has 2 rooms
with a shared bathroom and a loft suite with
double spa bathroom. Wonderfully peaceful
and a good change from coastal
accommodation. 2-night minimum stay.
$$$$ Easts Van Park (Big 4), Ocean St, Easts
Beach, Kiama, T4232 2124, www.eastvan
parks.com.au. A spacious beachside motor
park with above average facilities.
$$$ Berry Hotel, 120 Queen St, Berry,
T4464 1011, www.berryhotel.com.au.
Good-value pub-stay rooms and an
award-winning restaurant.

Shoalhaven Coast *p82*
$$$$ Rest Point Garden Village, Browns
Rd (5 km south of Shoalhaven), T4421 6856,
www.nowracaravanpark.com.au. The most

modern motor park in the area with a range
of accommodation including powered and
non-powered sites.

Jervis Bay
$$$$ Paperbark Lodge and Camp,
605 Woollamia Rd, T4441 6066,
info@paperbarkcamp.com.au. An excellent
eco-tourist set-up in a quiet bush setting
with luxury en suite tent units, outdoor
camp fire, good onsite restaurant (see
Restaurants below), tours and activities.
Book ahead.
There's also a scattering of upmarket
B&Bs, motels, pub-hotels, budget
and motor park options in and around
Huskisson, including:
$$$ Huskisson Beach Tourist Resort,
Beach St, Huskisson, T1300 733027,
www.huskissonbeachtouristresort.com.au.
$$ Jervis Bay Backpackers, Owen St, T0402
109 912, www.jervisbaybackpackers.com.au.
Centrally located, small but perfectly adequate.

Booderee National Park
All the campsites have groups of tame
kangaroos and rosellas. Campsites of various
sizes range in price from $10-20 for 5. Note
the camping fee does not include vehicle
entry ($10) so that does add extra cost, but it
is well worth it! For bookings, T4443 0977,
www.deh.gov.au/parks/booderee. Book well
ahead during public holidays.
There are good campsites with hot
showers at **Green Patch**, while **Bristol Point**,
with similar facilities, is designed for groups.
Camping with cold showers is available at
Cave Beach (there is a 250-m walk to the
site from the car park).

Murramarang National Park
$$$$ Depot Beach, T4478 6582. Cabins,
powered and non-powered sites with
modern facilities.

$$$$ Eco-Point Murramarang Resort, Banyandah St, South Durras, T4478 6355, www.murramarangresort.com.au. A top spot and although not in the park itself it has its own tame kangaroos and some sublime coastal scenery. Luxury cabins, en suite/standard powered and non-powered sites, pool, bar/restaurant, camp kitchen, activities and canoe and bike hire.

$$ Pretty Beach, T4457 2019. Powered and non-powered sites with similar facilities.

$ NPWS campsite, Pebbly Beach, T4478 6023, www.nationalparks.nsw.gov.au. Good facilities, with hot showers and fire sites. A warden collects fees daily. It's often busy so it's wise to book ahead.

Eurobodalla Coast *p83*
The VIC in Batemans Bay has full accommodation listings. There are several other motor parks located beachside along Beach Rd southeast of the centre as well as the one mentioned below. In Narooma there are plenty of standard motels for which the VIC has full listings. There are also a couple of options out of town that are worth the trip.

Batemans Bay
$$$$ Big 4 Batemans Bay Beach Resort, 51 Beach Rd, T4472 4541. Five-star beachside holiday park with full facilities.

$$$$ Bridge Motel, 29 Clyde St (200 m west of the bridge), T4472 6344. Well-placed motel accommodation.

$$$$ Comfort Inn Lincoln Downs, Princes Highway (on the right just beyond the bridge heading north), T4478 9200, www.lincolndowns.com.au. Excellent hotel with full facilities .

$$$ Shady Willows Holiday Park, Old Princes Highway, corner of South St, T4472 4972, www.shadywillows.com.au. Backpackers and those in campervans should head here. It incorporates a YHA with dorm or onsite caravans for couples, fully equipped kitchen, pool, internet, bike hire.

$ The best places for camping are the NPWS sites in the kangaroo-infested Murramarang National Park (see above).

Narooma
$$$$ Big 4 Island View Beach Resort, Princes Highway (5 km south of the town centre), T4476 2600, www.islandview.com.au. Convenient position with full motor park facilities including camp kitchen and internet.

$$$$ Mystery Bay Cottages, 121 Mystery Bay Rd, Mystery Bay, 3 km off Princes Highway, 10 km south of Narooma, T4473 7431, www.mysterybaycottages.com. A good self-contained option in a rural setting close to the beach.

$$$ Priory at Bingie, Priory Lane, Bingie, 26 km north, T4473 8881, www.bingie.com. This delightful B&B is in a stylish modern home, offering 3 good double rooms, plenty of peace and quiet, an art gallery/workshop and great ocean views.

Sapphire Coast *p84*
There are plenty of motels and self-contained apartments in Merimbula. The VIC can supply full details.

$$$$ Merimbula Beach Holiday Park, Short Point Beach, east on Short Point, Merimbula, T6499 8999, www.merimbula beachholidaypark.com.au. One of the best-placed motor parks for peace and quiet, facilities and beach access. Camp kitchen.

$$$ Fernmark Inn, 610 Warrigal Range Rd, Brogo, T6492 7136, www.fernmark.com.au. Worldly themed en suites, health treatments and fine cuisine, this place makes a good base to explore the surrounding area. Recommended.

$$ Wandarrah Lodge YHA, 8 Marine Pde, Merimbula, T6495 3503, www.wandarrah lodge.com. au. Excellent and purpose built, providing modern en suite dorms, double and family rooms, a well-equipped kitchen, 2 lounges, internet, free breakfast.

NPWS camping, Hobart Beach, off Sapphire Coast Drive, south of Tathra, T6495 5000.

Ben Boyd National Park *p85*
$$$ Wonboyn Lake Resort, 1 Oyster Lane, 19 km off Princes Highway, T6496 9162, www.wonboynlakeresort.com.au.
Self-contained en suite cabins, shop, spa and restaurant.
$$$ Wonboyn Cabins and Caravan Park, Wonboyn Rd (33 km south of Eden), T6496 9131, www.wonboyncabins.com.au. Onsite vans, powered and non-powered sites.
$ Saltwater Creek and **Bittangabee Bay**, T6495 5000. Basic (but delightful) camping. Self-registration, fees apply. Book well ahead.
There is also modern, self-contained accommodation available in the **lighthouse**, T6495 5000, fscr@environment.nsw.gov.au.

🍴 Restaurants

Wollongong and around *p80*
$$$ Aqua, 17/54-58 Cliff Rd, T4225 9888. Daily for breakfast, lunch and dinner. A fine seafood and Modern Australian option with a classy ambience and wide-ranging menu clearly giving its neighbour some competition.
$$$ Beach House, 16 Cliff Rd, T4228 5410. Lunch and dinner daily from 1200. A well-established seafood restaurant. Recommended.
$$$ Harbourfront, 2 Endeavour Drive, T4227 2999. Lunch and dinner daily from 1200, breakfast Thu-Sun. Quality seafood with views to match.
$$ Lagoon Seafood, Stuart Park, corner George Hanley Drive and Kembla St, North Wollongong, T4226 1677. Daily 1000-0200. Local favourite which overlooks Wollongong Beach.
Keira St is good for cheap eats, including:
$ Food World Gourmet Café, 148 Keira St, T4225 9655. Great value Chinese.

Kiama and Berry *p81*
There are plenty of cafés and affordable eateries in Kiama with most located along Terralong St and Collins St or beside the harbour.
$$$ Cargo's, on the Wharf, T4233 2771. Daily for lunch and dinner.
$$ Chachi's Italian, The Terraces, T4233 1144. Closed Tue.
$$ Manning Street Deli, 14 Manning St, T4232 4030. Daily for breakfast and lunch. Best bet for coffee and light meals.
$$ Ritzy Gritz New Mexican Grill, 40 Collins St, T4232 1853. Daily. Affordable option, locally popular and colourful.
There are many good cafés and restaurants along Berry's main drag, and if the pub food in the **Southern Hotel** is not sufficient, then try the award-winning **Coach House** in the Berry Hotel.

Shoalhaven Coast *p82*
In the centre of Nowra, Kinghorne St is the main drag and best place to browse menus.
$$$ Boatshed, 10 Wharf Rd, south bank below the bridge, T4421 2419. Tue-Sat from 1800. For fine dining it's hard to beat.

Jervis Bay
$$$ Gunyah Restaurant, Paperbark Camp (see page 87, daily for dinner). For fine dining (out of town). Recommended.
$ Husky Pub, Owen St. No-nonsense, good value pub food.

Eurobodalla Coast *p83*
Batemans Bay
$$$ On the Pier, Old Punt Rd, just north and west of the bridge, T4472 6405. Lunch and dinner, closed Mon. This one can always be relied on for excellent seafood as well as classy Modern Australian.
$ Boatshed, Clyde St, T4421 2419. For fresh fish and chips with the seagulls on the waterfront.

Sapphire Coast *p84*

Market St and Beach St in Merimbula have numerous affordable cafés and restaurants.

$$ Wharf, overlooking the inlet at Merimbula Aquarium, Lake St, T6495 4446. Daily for lunch and Wed-Sat for dinner. Locally recommended.

⚠ What to do

Wollongong and around *p80*

Boat Shed, Windang, near the harbour entrance, T4296 2015. Rents boats, canoes and kayaks for Lake Illawarra.

Just Cruisin' Motorcycle Tours, T4294 2598, www.justcruisintours.com.au. Cruise the Illawarra and surrounds on a chauffeured Harley, from $90 per hour.

Skydive the Beach, T4225 8444, www.skydivethebeach.com.au. From $285 (cheaper for groups).

Sydney Hang Gliding Centre, T4294 4294, www.hanggliding.com.au. Trips around Stanwell Park and the Illawarra Ranges north of Wollongong, 30 mins from $245. It is also the base for Australian champion Tony Armstrong, T04-1793 9200, www.hangglide oz.com.au, who will take you up tandem, from $220.

Shoalhaven Coast *p82*
Jervis Bay

Huskisson has several companies offering whale (Jun-Nov) and dolphin watching (year round) as well as standard bay or twilight barbecue cruises of 2-3 hrs from $30-$65:

Dolphin Explorer, 62 Owen St, T4441 5455.

Dolphin Watch, 50 Owen St (main drag), T4441 6311, www.dolphinwatch.com.au.

Jervis Bay Kayak Co, T4441 7157, www.jervisbaykayaks.com. Excellent half/full/weekend and multi-day sea kayaking trips in Jervis Bay or further afield from $100. Independent hire also available.

Pro Dive, 64 Owen St, T4441 5255, www.divejervisbay.com.au. This is a very knowledgeable, professional operation offering a range of diving options and courses. Bike hire also available.

Eurobodalla Coast *p83*
Batemans Bay

You can take a leisurely 3-hr cruise to the historic riverside village of Nelligen (30 mins stopover) on the locally built *Merinda*, at 1100, from $30, children $15 (lunch options available), T4472 4052.

Bay and Beyond Sea Kayaks, T4478 7777, www.bayandbeyond.com.au. Good half or full day and river and lake tours, from $55-110.

National Diving Academy, 5/33 Orient St, T4472 9930. Access, trips and gear hire.

Narooma

Island Charters, Bluewater Drive, T4476 8080, www.islandchartersnarooma.com. Independent sightseeing, fishing or dive charters from $65, Montague Island from $75, children $55.

NPWS, book at the VIC. 4-hr guided tour of Montague Island at 0930 and a 3½-hr evening tour at dusk. All tours are weather permitting and numbers are limited, from $130, children $99. Tours depart from the town wharf on Blue Water Drive. Also offers 1- to 2-night island accommodation packages, T0407 909111.

The knowledgeable crew aboard the 90-year-old **Wagonga Princess**, T4476 2665, www.wagongainletcruises.com, offer 3-hr cruises up the river with an emphasis on wildlife and history. Departs 1300 daily in summer and Sun, Wed and Fri off season, from $33.

Sapphire Coast *p84*
Merimbula and around

Brogo Wilderness Canoes, T6492 7328, www.brogocanoes.com.au. Trips (including overnight camping), half day $25.

Cycle 'n' Surf, 1B Marine Parade, Merimbula, T6495 2171. Hires bikes, surf/body boards and fishing tackle.

Merimbula Marina, T6495 1686,
www.merimbulamarina.com. Whale
watching from $40, 2-hr dolphin cruise from
$25, children $10. Fishing charters of 1-3 hrs
at a very reasonable $35-55.
Ocean Wilderness Kayaking, T6495 3669.
Quality ocean and lake trips, half-day to
overnight, from $125. Whale sightings are
possible from late Sep to late Nov.
Sapphire Eco-Tours, T6494 0283,
www.sapphirecoastecotours.com.au (or
book at the VIC). Ideal opportunity for
visitors with hire cars to explore the region's
rich and varied national parks aboard a
14-seater 4WD OKA vehicle. Half or full
day trips.
Sinbad Cruises, Merimbula, T6495 1686,
www.merimbulamarina.com/sinbad.html.
Cruises on the Pambula River and Pambula
Lake with afternoon tea ($20), lunch ($25) or
dinner ($40).

Eden
Cat Balou Cruises, Eden, T0427-962027,
www.catbalou.com.au. Whale-watching
cruises (late Sep to late Nov) from $40 and
year round 2-hr sightseeing trips along the
Ben Boyd National Park (Twofold Bay)
coastline, from $30, children $17.

Transport

Wollongong and around p80
Murray's, T132251, www.murrays.com.au.
Daily service to **Canberra** and **Narooma** via
Batemans Bay, from $26. Long-distance
coaches stop at the Wollongong City Coach
Terminal, corner of Keira St and Campbell
streets, T4226 1022. Open Mon-Fri
0745-1730, Sat 0745-1415. **Greyhound**,
T131499, and **Premier Motor Services**,
T133410, offer daily services to **Sydney**
(Brisbane) and **Canberra** (Melbourne) via the
Princes Highway.
   Taxi: **Wollongong Radio Cabs**, T4229 9311.
   The train station is west of the city centre
at the end of Burrelli St and Station St.

CityRail offers regular daily services to/from
Sydney to **Bomaderry** where the line ends.

Kiama and Berry p81
Kiama Coachlines, T4232 3466, operates
services from the Bong Bong Rd train station
to the **Minnamurra Rainforest**, daily at
1005. Long-distance coaches stop in the
centre of town on Terralong St, or at the
Bombo Railway Station, 1.5 km north.
Premier and **Greyhound** both offer daily
services between **Canberra** (Melbourne) and
Sydney (Brisbane).
   Bike hire is available with **Kiama Cycles
and Sports**, 27 Collins St, T4232 3005.
   Taxi T4464 1181.
   The train station is off Bong Bong Rd in
the centre of town. **CityRail**, T131500, offers
regular daily services from **Sydney**.

Shoalhaven Coast p82
In **Nowra** numerous long-distance coach
and local bus companies base their
operations at the bus terminal on Stewart Pl.
Premier and **Greyhound** offer daily services
between **Canberra** (Melbourne) and
Sydney (Brisbane). Nowra Coaches, T4423
5244, operates regular daily bus services
between **Nowra**, **Huskisson**, **Vincentia** and
Wreck Bay.
   Taxi T4421 0333.
   Bomaderry train station is the end of the
line from Sydney. **CityRail**, T131500, offers
daily services via **Kiama** and **Wollongong**.
   For bike hire contact **Pro Dive**, see page 90.
   Access to **Booderee National Park** is via
Jervis Bay Rd off Princes Highway and south
of Huskisson and Vincentia.

Eurobodalla Coast p83
Batemans Bay
Long-distance coaches stop outside the
Promenade Plaza on Orient St or the Post
Office on Clyde St. **Premier**, **Greyhound** and
Priors, T4472 4040, run daily services
between **Canberra** (Melbourne) and

Sydney (Brisbane). **Murray's**, T132251, also runs services to **Canberra**, north to **Nowra** and south to **Narooma**. The VIC or **Travelscene**, Shop 6, 8 Orient St, T4472 5086, assists with bookings.

Narooma

Long-distance coaches stop in the town centre on Princes Highway, with services between **Canberra** (Melbourne) and **Sydney** (Brisbane). **Murray's** also offers services to **Canberra** and north to **Nowra**.

Sapphire Coast *p84*

From Merimbula, **Deane's Buslines**, T6299 3722, www.deanesbuslines.com.au, runs local daily services to **Bega**, **Eden** and **Pambula**. Long-distance coaches stop at the Ampol Service Station in the town centre. **Premier** and **Greyhound** offer daily services between **Melbourne** and **Sydney** (Brisbane). **V-Line**, T136196, operates additional services to **Melbourne**.

Contents

Footprint features

Central & North Coast NSW

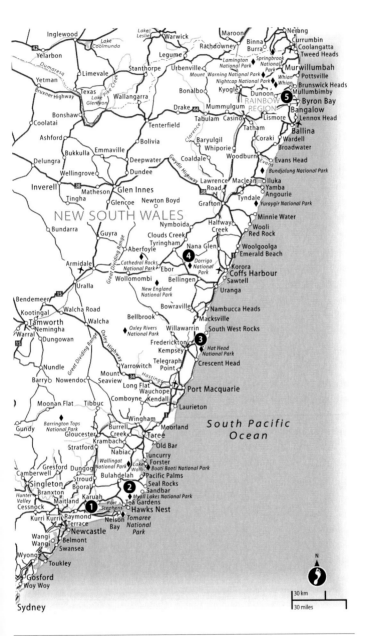

Sydney to Port Macquarie

With the lure of Byron Bay to the north, few take the time to explore the coast and national parks between Sydney and Port Macquarie. But to do so is to miss out on some of the best coastal scenery in the state. Myall Lakes National Park offers a superb diversion, and a couple of days exploring the beaches and lakes is highly recommended. Just inland are the vineyards of Hunter Valley, a name synonymous with fine wines and world-class vineyards – a little piece of Australia that conjures up images of mist-covered valleys and rolling hills, clothed in a patchwork of grape-laden vines. Although not necessarily producing the best wines in Australia, this is one of the best venues in the country to learn something of the process or sample that classic vineyard ambience and enjoy the congenial conviviality of fine wine, fine food and fine accommodation. To the north are the high and secluded river valleys of the Barrington Tops National Park, an area renowned for its unpredictable climate and diverse wildlife, while back on the coast is Nelson Bay, an ideal stopover on the route north and gateway to the beautiful Tomaree Peninsula.

Newcastle and the Hunter Valley → *For listings, see pages 104-111.*

As one of the most industrialized cities in Australia – with a main drag and a city centre mall as inspiring as a bowl of week-old porridge – Newcastle has limited tourist appeal. It is mostly used as a base from which to visit the Lower Hunter Valley, home to dozens of wineries, which provide one of the finest 'winery' experiences in the world. From Newcastle, the Hunter River becomes increasingly scenic, with rolling hills draped in vineyards backed by wilderness forest, given over to the vast Wollemi (pronounced 'Wollem eye') National Park.

Visiting Newcastle and the Hunter Valley
Getting there and around The nearest main airport to Hunter Valley is at Newcastle. Shuttles ferry people to and from the airport to the Valley. There are plenty of coaches and tours from Sydney, Newcastle and Port Stephens and trains arrive at Maitland and Scone. From Newcastle there are regular coach and train connections with the main surrounding cities and tourist centres, with frequent daily services from Sydney and Port Stephens.
➺ *See Transport, page 109.*

Don't miss ...

Numbers relate to numbers on map on page 94.

Tourist information Hunter Valley (Wine Country Tourism) VIC ① *455 Wine Country Drive (4 km north of the town centre), T4990 0900, www.winecountry.com.au, Mon-Thu 0900-1730, Fri 1800, Sat 1700, Sun 1600*, is the principal centre, well set up with a café and winemaking display. It provides detailed and objective vineyard information as well as accommodation and tour bookings. You are strongly advised to pick up the free detailed maps from the VIC. **Newcastle VIC** ① *361 Hunter St, opposite the Civic Rail Station, T4974 2999, www.visitnewcastle.com.au, Mon-Fri 0900-1700, Sat-Sun 1000-1500*.

Newcastle

Newcastle grew from its humble beginnings as a penal colony to become one of the largest coal ports in the world, shipping vast amounts of the black stuff from the productive Hunter Valley fields. Major steel production followed, until its rapid decline in the late 20th century. To add insult to injury, in 1989 the city suffered Australia's worst earthquake in modern times. Despite this, the city still boasts some very fine and gracious historical buildings, including the 1892 **Christ Church Cathedral**, the 1890 **Courthouse** and several classics on and around Hunter and Watt streets such as the **post office** (1903), **railway station** (1878) and **Customs House** (1877).

The **Newcastle Regional Art Gallery** ① *Laman St*, is worthy of investigation, while history buffs will enjoy the newly renovated **Maritime and Military Museum** ① *T4929 3066, www.fortscratchley.org.au, Wed-Mon 1000-1600, entry fee, full site tours from $12, tunnel tour $10*. Serving as the city's main museum, Fort Scratchley has been extensively redeveloped in recent years and not surprisingly places a special emphasis on the town's military history as well as its infamous earthquake. The fort itself was first established in 1882 and at the risk of making it sound like the local McDonalds it houses an impressive range of 'muzzle loaders' from a 20-pounder to the full 80-pounder. It's enough to work up quite an appetite.

The beaches on the eastern fringe of the city are superb and well known for their excellent surfing, swimming (patrolled in summer) and fishing, while 6 km inland the 180-ha **Blackbutt Reserve** ① *daily 0900-1700, free*, is an excellent nature reserve that presents a fine opportunity to see wild koala. By car there are four main entrances into Blackbutt Reserve. These include off Carnley Avenue (Blackbutt Picnic Area), Freyberg Street (Richley Reserve), Queens Road and Lookout Road. Buses (Nos 317 and 224) pass by Orchardtown Road and Lookout Road.

A vine romance

With so many vineyards, choosing which to visit can be tough. There are many tours on offer, but for those with little prior knowledge it is advisable to mix some of the large, long-established wineries and labels with the smaller boutique affairs. Although many of the biggest names are well worth a visit, you will find a more, relaxed and personalized service at the smaller establishments. Also be aware that almost every vineyard has received some award or another and this is not necessarily a sign that one is better than the next. The following wineries are recommended and often considered the must-sees but it is by no means a comprehensive list.

Of the large long-established vineyards (over a century old), **Tyrells**, www.tyrrells.com.au, **Draytons**, www.draytonswines.com.au and **Tullochs**, www.tulloch.com.au. (all in Pokolbin) are recommended, providing fine wine and insight into the actual wine-making process. Tyrells also has especially nice aesthetics. **Lindemans**, www.lindemans.com, **McGuigans**, www.mcguiganwines.com.au (again in Pokolbin), and **Wyndhams**, www.wyndhamestate.com (Branxton), are three of the largest and most well-known labels in the region, offering fine vintages and a broad range of facilities. McGuigans and Wyndhams also offer guided tours. Of the smaller boutique wineries, **Oakvale**, www.oakvalewines.com.au, **Tamburlaine**, www.tamburlaine.com.au, and **Pepper Tree** – with its classy restaurant and former convent guesthouse added attractions – are also recommended. All are located in Pokolbin. Then, for a fine view as well as vintage, head for the **Audrey Wilkinson Vineyard**, DeBeyers Road, Pokolbin, www.audrey wilkinson.com.au, or **De Luliis**, Lot 21, Broke Road, www.dewine.com.au, with its lookout tower. The VICs have details.

Given the fact that copious wine tasting and responsible driving do not mix, organized tours are by far the best way to tour the vineyards. All day jump-on-jump-off services are also available around the main vineyards. Another fine alternative is to visit the various vineyards by bike. For details of the various tours on offer, see page 108.

Hunter Valley

This is really two distinct regions, the Lower Hunter Valley and Upper Hunter Valley, with the vast majority of the vineyards (over 80) in the lower region. The Hunter River and the New England Highway bisect both. The Lower Hunter Valley encompasses the area from Newcastle through Maitland to Singleton, with Cessnock to the south considered the 'capital' of the Lower Hunter Valley's vineyards, which are concentrated in a few square kilometres to the northwest. Though the region's true heritage lies below the ground, in the form of coal, it is vineyards that dominate the economy these days, producing mainly Shiraz, Semillons and Chardonnays. They range from large-scale producers and internationally recognized labels to low-key boutiques. Despite the sheer number, the emphasis in the Hunter Valley is definitely on quality rather than quantity. Though the vineyards are all comprehensively signposted around Cessnock, you are strongly advised to pick up the free detailed maps from the VIC. See also box above.

For many, their first introduction to the great wine growing region is the drab and disappointing former mining town of **Cessnock**. Head north and west, however, and things improve as you reach the vineyard communities of **Pokolbin**, **Broke** and **Rothbury**.

Nelson Bay and around → *For listings, see pages 104-111.*

Nelson Bay is the recognized capital of an area known as **Port Stephens**, a name loosely used to describe both the natural harbour (Port Stephens) and the string of foreshore communities that fringe its southern arm. Nelson Bay is fast developing into a prime New South Wales coastal holiday destination and provides an ideal first base or stopover from Sydney. Other than the stunningly beautiful views from Tomaree National Park and from Tomaree Heads across the harbour to Tea Gardens and Hawks Nest, there are an ever-increasing number of activities on offer in the area, from dolphin watching to camel rides.

Visiting Nelson Bay
Getting there The nearest airport is at Newcastle (Williamtown), 30 km away, with regular connections to main centres. Coaches serve Nelson Bay from Sydney direct or connect with interstate services in Newcastle. ▸▸ *See Transport, page 109.*

Getting around Nelson Bay is small enough to navigate on foot. Local regional buses connect the town with surrounding attractions of Port Stephens.

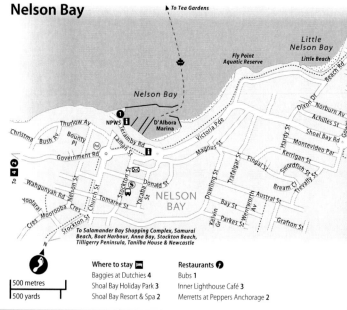

Nelson Bay

Where to stay	Restaurants
Baggies at Dutchies **4**	Bubs **1**
Shoal Bay Holiday Park **3**	Inner Lighthouse Café **3**
Shoal Bay Resort & Spa **2**	Merretts at Peppers Anchorage **2**

Tourist information Port Stephens VIC ⓘ *Victoria Pde, T4980 6900, www.port stephens.org.au, Mon-Fri 0900-1700, Sat-Sun 0900-1600*, has a guide. NPWS ⓘ *12B Teramby Rd (Marina Complex), T4984 8200, hunter@npws.nsw.gov.au*, has national parks and camping information.

Places in Nelson Bay and around

Even if you do nothing else around the Nelson Bay area except laze about on its pretty beaches, do climb to the summit of **Tomaree Head**, at the far east end of Shoal Bay, which is particularly spectacular at sunrise or sunset. The views that reward the 30-minute strenuous ascent are truly memorable.

The best beaches in the area are to be found fringing the national park, east and south of Nelson Bay. To the east, **Shoal Bay** is closest to all amenities while farther east still, within the national park boundary, **Zenith Beach**, **Wreck Beach** and **Box Beach** all provide great surfing, solitude and scenery. Two kilometres south of Shoal Bay the glorious beach that fringes **Fingal Bay** connects Point Stephens with the mainland. You can access the headland and its fine walking tracks at low tide. South of Fingal Bay, though not connected to it by road, **One Mile Beach** is a regional gem while **Samurai Beach**, just north of that, is the local naturist beach. West of One Mile Beach **Boat Harbour** gives way to **Anna Bay** which forms the northern terminus of **Stockton Beach**, stretching for over 30 km all the way down to Newcastle. It's well worth a visit simply to see the endless sweep of dunes. If you have 4WD you can 'let rip' but a permit must be obtained from the Council (or the VIC). See also What to do, page 108.

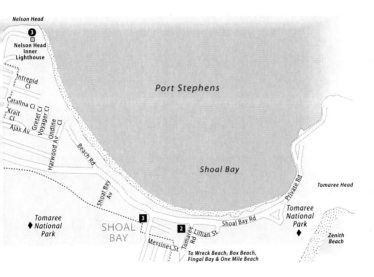

There is a healthy suburban population of **koalas** in the region and the best places to see them are the fringes of Tomaree National Park or wooded areas of the Tilligerry Peninsula (via Lemon Tree Passage Road, off Nelson Bay Road, 30 km south of Nelson Bay). There are guided walks, see What to do, page 108. While you are in the area you may also be tempted to visit **Tanilba House** ① *Caswell Corner, Tanilba, T4982 4866, Wed, Sat-Sun 1030-1630, admission charge*, one of the oldest homesteads in Australia, built by convicts in 1831. Closer to Nelson Bay is the **Nelson Head Inner Lighthouse**, *T4984 9758, 1000-1600*, set just above Little Bay, 1.5 km east of the town centre, with guided tours, great views and a small café. Little Bay is also a great place to see pelicans as they wait patiently for fishermen's handouts late in the day.

Barrington Tops National Park

① *NPWS office, 59 Church St, Gloucester, T6538 5300, gloucester@npws.nsw.gov.au, Mon-Fri 0830-1700, is the nearest to the park. There is also an office in Nelson Bay.*

The 40,453-ha Barrington Tops National Park encompasses a 25-km long plateau extending between a series of extinct volcanic peaks in the Mount Royal Ranges, north of the Hunter Valley. Rising to a height of 1577 m at Polblue Mountain, the plateau forms one of the highest points on the Great Dividing Range and contains a diverse range of habitats, from rainforest to alpine meadows, with many waterfalls and glorious views. The high elevation also results in unpredictable weather year round and an annual rainfall of over 2 m, with sub-zero temperatures and snow in winter. Given its geographical position, the park hosts a diverse range of species including lyrebirds, bandicoots and spotted-tailed quolls. At the very least you are almost certain to encounter kangaroos as well as small squadrons of elegant and very vocal black cockatoos.

The scenery and wildlife alone make a day trip well worthwhile, but given the many excellent B&Bs, campsites, walks and activities available you may well be tempted to extend your stay. The Great Lakes VIC in Forster (see page 103) handles Barrington Tops information. Look out for the free brochure, *Barrington Tops World Heritage Area*, and also visit www.barringtons.com.au. If you have your own transport there are various routes. From the south and east, the park and the two main fringing communities of Dungog and Gloucester are best reached from Bucketts Way Road (Highway 2) which heads northwest off the Pacific Highway 33 km north of Newcastle. Alternatively, the northern sector of the park (and Gloucester) can be accessed west off the Pacific Highway at Nabiac, 160 km north of Newcastle. If you have 2WD and your time is limited, the drive up the Gloucester River Valley to Gloucester Tops is recommended. Take the Gloucester Tops Road off Bucketts Way Road, 10 km south of Gloucester. The climb to the plateau begins at the Gloucester River Camping Area (see Where to stay, page 106). The northern sector of the park offers a more extensive 78-km scenic drive (mostly unsealed) from Gloucester to Scone via Scone Road and then Barrington Tops Road, west of Gloucester. Sadly, the best views from Carey's Peak and its surrounding campsites can only be reached by 4WD south off Forest Road, just west of the Devils Hole Camping Area. The southern sector of the park is accessed 40 km northwest of Dungog, via Salisbury and the Williams River Valley Road.

Myall Lakes National Park → *For listings, see pages 104-111.*

Myall Lakes National Park, or Great Lakes as it is known, combines beautiful coastal scenery with a patchwork of inland lakes, waterways and forest to create one of the best-loved eco-playgrounds in NSW. Just four hours north of Sydney, the only drawback is its inevitable popularity during holidays and weekends. However, given the sheer scale of the area (21,367 ha), of which half is water, there is always somewhere to escape the crowds. The main settlements fringing the national park are Tea Gardens and Hawks Nest on the northeastern shores of Port Stephens, Bulahdelah on the Pacific Highway to the northwest and the popular surf spots of Bluey's Beach and Pacific Palms to the north. If you have at least two days to spend here, the route below, from Tea Gardens in the south to Pacific Palms in the north, or vice versa, is recommended. A day fee per vehicle of $7 applies to the park.

Visiting Myall Lakes National Park

Getting there Myall is best explored by car though there are regional bus services between Taree and Sydney. ›› *See Transport, page 109.*

Getting around For navigation, whether on foot, by car or paddle, the *Great Lakes District Map* ($10) is not only recommended but essential. Copies can be bought in the VIC. There are daily local bus services around the area, paddleboat hire and houseboat hire.

Tourist information Great Lakes VIC in Forster serves as the region's main centre. Local VICs are in **Tea Gardens** ⓘ *209 Myall St, T4997 0749, 1000-1600*; **Bulahdelah** ⓘ *corner of Pacific Highway and Crawford St, T4997 4981, www.greatlakes.org.au, Mon-Fri 0900-1700, Sat-Sun 0900-1500*, and **Pacific Palms** ⓘ *Boomerang Drive, Bluey's Beach, T6554 0123, 1000-1600*. All can provide NPWS information; the nearest NPWS office is in Nelson Bay. Also see www.greatlakes.org.au.

Tea Gardens and Hawks Nest

The little-known but fast-developing coastal settlements of Tea Gardens and Hawks Nest, on the northeastern shores of Port Stephens, serve not only as excellent holiday destinations in themselves but as the main southern gateway to the Myall Lakes National Park. Straddling the Myall River and surrounded by beautiful beaches, headlands, coastal wetlands and forest, these twin towns offer a wealth of activities from surfing to koala spotting, though most people come here simply to escape the crowds, relax and enjoy the beautiful scenery and laid-back atmosphere.

The place to be is **Bennetts** (Ocean Beach) at the southeastern end of Hawks Nest. From there you can access the **Yaccaba Walk** (3 km return) to the summit of the Yaccaba Headland, affording some memorable views across the mouth of Port Stephens and the numerous offshore islands. To reach Bennetts Beach, cross the bridge from Tea Gardens on Kingfisher Avenue, turn right on Mungo Brush Road, then left to the end of Booner Street. The bridge connecting the two towns is often called 'The Singing Bridge' because of its tendency to 'sing' in strong winds.

Another excellent but far more demanding walk is the **Mungo Track** that follows the Myall River through coastal forest to the **Mungo Brush Campsite** (15 km one way). It starts on the left, off Mungo Brush Road, 600 m past the national park boundary. The detailed booklet, *Walkers' Guide to The Mungo Track*, breaks the entire walk into sections with additional alternatives and is available from the VIC Tea Gardens, NPWS or Hawks Nest Real Estate on Tuloa Avenue. Look out for koalas along the way, especially late in the day. Dolphin-watching cruises, diving, golf, fishing charters and boat, sea kayak, canoe and surf ski hire are all readily available in the twin towns. Tea Gardens VIC (see Tourist information above) has full listings.

Hawks Nest to Bulahdelah

From Hawks Nest, Mungo Brush Road heads north, parallel with the Myall River, to meet the southern boundary of the Myall National Park (4.5 km). From there the road remains sealed and cuts through the littoral rainforest and coastal heath for 15 km to the Mungo Brush Campsite beside the Bombah Broadwater, the second largest of the Great Lakes.

Before reaching Mungo Brush consider stopping and walking the short distance east to the long swathe of deserted beach. **Dark Point**, about 5 km north of the southern boundary at Robinson's Crossing, is an interesting rocky outcrop and the only significant feature along this 44 km of beach between Hawks Nest and Seal Rocks. It is an interesting spot and the site of a midden (ancient refuse tip) used by the Worimi Aboriginal peoples for centuries before invading European cedar cutters displaced them. This particular example is thought to be at least 2000 years old. Lying tantalizingly offshore is **Broughton Island**, which is accessible by day trip from Nelson Bay.

From Mungo Brush the road skirts the northern shores of **Bombah Broadwater**, turning inland past increasingly thick stands of paperbark trees to reach the Bombah Point ferry crossing which – provided there is enough water – runs daily every half an hour from 0800 to 1800. There is a small fee. **Bombah Point** is dominated by the large yet unobtrusive **EcoPoint Myall Shores Resort**. On the same road, 10 km from Bulahdelah, are the **Bombah Point Eco Cottages**. See page 106 for details.

Bulahdelah, Seal Rocks and Sanbar

From Bombah Point 16 km of partly sealed roads takes you to the small community of **Bulahdelah** and the Pacific Highway. Bulahdelah has a helpful VIC and is the main venue for houseboat hire for the region. Four kilometres north of Bulahdelah, the Lakes Way – the main sealed access road through the Great Lakes region – heads east, eventually skirting Myall Lake, the largest of the lakes. Before reaching the lake, however, you may consider the short diversion 5 km north along **Stoney Creek Road**. Some 38 km into the southern fringe of the Bulahdelah State Forest, along Wang Wauk Forest Drive, is the **Grandis**, a towering 76-m flooded gum reputed to be the highest tree in NSW.

Back on the Lakes Way, between Myall Lake and Smiths Lake, Seal Rocks Road (unsealed) heads 11 km southeast to reach the coast and the pretty beachside settlement of **Seal Rocks**. The residents of this sublime little piece of wilderness know all too well that it is the jewel in the Myall and do not really want to advertise the fact. There is a superb beach and short rainforest and headland walks; the 2-km stroll to the **Sugarloaf Point Lighthouse** past the **Seal Rocks Blowhole** is well worth it. The views from the lighthouse (no public access to the interior) are excellent and Lighthouse Beach to the south is more than inviting. Seal Rocks lie just offshore and serve as a favourite regional dive site (they are home to numerous grey nurse sharks). Since 1875 there have been 20 shipwrecks, with the *SS Catterthun* being one of the nation's worst with the loss of 55 lives.

Back on the Lakes Way, just before **Smiths Lake**, look out for signs to the **Wallingat National Park**. If it is a fine day, an exploration (4WD and map required) of the forest is recommended, with the steep climb to **Whoota Whoota Lookout** providing fine views north over the lakes and coast.

Sandbar, 1 km past the turn off to Smiths Lake village, is also a sight for sore eyes. Here you'll find some excellent, quiet beaches (500-m walk), good birdwatching along the sandbar that holds the lake back from the sea and many lakeside activities based at the delightful caravan park.

Pacific Palms and Bluey's Beach

Four kilometres north of Smiths Lake is the small community of **Pacific Palms** fringing the southern shores of Lake Wallis. Two kilometres east are the delightful little communities of **Bluey's Beach**, **Boomerang Beach** and **Elizabeth Beach**. While Pacific Palms boasts its lakeside charms and activities, Bluey's and its associates are something of a local surfing mecca. Bluey's Beach itself is idyllic and further north, beyond Boomerang Point, Boomerang Beach is only marginally less attractive. Further north, the rather unfortunately named Pimply Rock and Charlotte Head give way to **Elizabeth Beach**, which is an absolute stunner.

Forster-Tuncurry and around → *For listings, see pages 104-111.*

The twin coastal towns of Forster-Tuncurry, which straddle Wallis Lake and the Cape Hawke Harbour, are a favourite domestic holiday destination forming the northern fringe of the park and providing the northern gateway to the superb Great Lakes Region. Although the towns themselves have some fine beaches and numerous water-based activities, it is the lakes, beaches and forests of the Booti Booti and Myall Lakes National Parks to the south that keep visitors coming back. As one of the most appealing coastal regions between Sydney and Byron Bay, a few days here are highly recommended. For all the necessary amenities Forster is the place to stay but there are some superb alternatives in the national park and coastal villages to the south; see Myall Lakes National Park, page 101.

Visiting Forster-Tuncurry

The **Great Lakes VIC** ① *beside the river on Little St, Forster, T6554 8799, www.greatlakes.org.au, daily 0900-1700*, serves Forster-Tuncurry and the Great Lakes (Myall) Region as far south as Tea Gardens and Hawks Nest. To find your way around the twin towns and region ask for the free *Cartoscope Great Lakes Region Map*. The Great Lakes District Map ($12) is recommended if you intend to explore the Myall Lakes and National Park fully. The VIC also supplies NPWS camping and national parks information.
▸▸ *See Transport, page 109.*

Places in Forster-Tuncurry

Many short-term visitors find ample satisfaction on Forster Beach, which sits at the mouth of the Hawke Harbour Inlet, just north of Forster's main drag, Head Street, but better beaches await your attention further east. **Pebbly Beach**, only a short walk along the coast from Forster Beach (or alternatively accessed by car, just beyond the junction of Head Street and MacIntosh Street), is a great spot for families and despite the name does possess some sand. At the western end of town, **One Mile Beach** is the town's true favourite, offering great views and good surfing at its northern end. It is best accessed via Boundary Street, south off Head Street/Bennetts Head Road, then east down Strand Street. **Bennetts Head**, at the terminus of Bennetts Head Road, also provides good views south along One Mile Beach, north to Halliday's Point and straight down into almost unbelievably clear waters.

If you can drag yourself away from the town beaches, the **Booti Booti National Park**, straddling the Lakes Way and the distinctly svelte strip of terra firma between Lake Wallis and the ocean, is well worth investigating. At the park's northern fringe, head east along Minor Road (just south of Forster, off the Lakes Way) and climb to the top of **Cape Hawke** where there is a lookout tower (40 minutes return). **McBride's Beach** sits in almost perfect isolation below and is one of those beaches that instantly has you mesmerized. It is as good as it looks and the ideal place to escape for the day, provided you are up for the 20-minute walk from the parking area just west of the lookout car park. To the south **Seven Mile Beach** stretches to **Booti Hill**, **The Ruins** and **Charlotte Head**. The Ruins has a good NPWS campsite and the southern edge of the park offers some excellent walks, with the 7-km track from The Ruins to Elizabeth Beach being recommended. **Elizabeth Beach** is another regional gem that has the habit of detaining all who visit – sometimes for days! On the western side of Lakes Way, **Wallis Lake** provides saltwater swimming, fishing, boating and numerous picnic sites.

Sydney to Port Macquarie listings

For hotel and restaurant price codes and other relevant information, see pages 10-14.

◎ Where to stay

Newcastle and Hunter Valley *p95*
Newcastle has a wide range to suit all budgets and is a good venue to base yourself to enjoy the laid-back beach culture while still within range of the Hunter Valley. There are dozens of B&Bs, guesthouses, self-contained cottages and restaurants set amongst the vineyards of Hunter Valley, mainly around Pokolbin and Rothbury. If you are on a budget or searching for a bargain, aim to stay midweek, when accommodation is cheaper. In and around Cessnock you will find operators have to offer lower rates due to the huge competition in and around the vineyards. Contact the Hunter Valley (Wine Country Tourism) VIC, see page 96.

$$$$ Casuarina Restaurant and Country Inn, 1014 Hermitage Rd, Pokolbin, T4998 7888, www.casuarinainn.com.au. One of several world-class establishments combining fine accommodation with fine dining. It offers 9 beautifully appointed, themed suites from the 'French Bordello' to the 'British Empire'.
$$$$ Newcastle Backpackers, 42 & 44 Denison St, Newcastle, T4969 3436, www.backpackersnewcastle.com.au. Traditional home-style hostel with excellent welcoming and helpful hosts. Well located and with the added plus of a heated pool. Free pick-ups from bus or train.
$$$$ Peppers Guest House, Ekerts Rd, Pokolbin, T4993 8999, www.peppers.com.au. 48 de luxe rooms, suites and a private homestead. All beautifully appointed and with a tariff to match. The homestead has all the usual extras, including pool, spa and the

obligatory open fire. The in-house **Chez Pok Restaurant**, see page 107, is widely regarded as one of the best restaurants in the area.

$$$ Hunter Country Lodge, 1476 Wine Country Drive, North Rothbury, T4938 1744, www.huntercountrylodge.com.au. A quirky motel/restaurant combo with log cabin-style rooms. **Shakey Tables** restaurant, page 107, is equally quirky and adds to the attraction.

$$$ Hunter Valley YHA, 100 Wine Country Drive, Nulkaba (near Cessnock), T4991 3278, www.yha.com.au. A purpose-built hostel set on 26 acres in the heart of vineyard country. Offers spacious dorms, doubles and twins (some en suite). Sauna, pool, outdoor barbecue and wood-fired pizza oven. It also offers its own wine tours and bike hire.

$$$ Newcastle Beach YHA, 30 Pacific St, Newcastle, T4925 3544, www.yha.com.au. Housed in a gracious heritage building, complete with chandeliers, ballroom, large open fireplaces and leather armchairs. Deservingly popular, it offers numerous spacious dorms and doubles and the odd family and single room. Also on offer is internet, free use of surf/boogie boards. An added attraction is the weekly all-you-can-eat barbecues and pizza nights. Parking (metered) can be a problem during the day.

$$ Cessnock Hotel, 234 Wollombi Rd, Cessnock, T4990 1002, www.huntervalley hotels.com.au. Traditional town hotel-cum-pub with 18 comfy rooms and a popular bistro. Good value and a fine chance to meet the locals.

Nelson Bay and around *p98, map p98*
There is plenty of choice in and around Nelson Bay, from resorts and modern self-contained apartment blocks to tidy B&Bs and koala-infested hostels.

$$$$ Baggies at Dutchies,
9 Burbong St, Nelson Bay, T4984 9570, www.dutchies.com.au. Very tidy, self-contained apartments with both standard units and a de luxe unit with good deck views across the harbour and a spa.

$$$$ Shoal Bay Holiday Park,
Shoal Bay Rd, T4984 3411, shoalbay@ beachsideholidays.com.au. Excellent beachside, modern and friendly motor park. It is close to all amenities and offers the full range of accommodation options, including camping. Great camp kitchen.

$$$$ Shoal Bay Resort and Spa, Shoal Bay Rd, T4981 1555, www.shoalbayresort.com.au. Enjoying a solid reputation, this resort has apartments, suites, family and standard rooms (all en suite) with B&B or half board, pool, à la carte, casual dining and a top-quality day spa. Located overlooking the bay and near to all amenities.

$$ Samurai Beach Bungalows, corner of Frost Rd and Robert Connell Close, approach from Nelson Bay Rd, Anna Bay, T4982 1921, samurai@nelsonbay.com. This eco-friendly YHA affiliate is recommended. Although on the bus route, it is some distance from Nelson Bay (5 km) but its position amidst bush at the edge of the Tomaree National Park gives it a more relaxed atmosphere. Accommodation options range from dorm to en suite double bungalows (with TV and mini kitchen). The general facilities are also excellent. Free sand, surf and boogie board hire, bike hire and pick-ups. Recommended.

Barrington Tops National Park *p100*
The local VICs have full accommodation listings including the numerous quaint B&Bs that surround the park. The NPWS can also supply details of the many campsites.

$$$$ Barringtons Country Retreat, 1941 Chichester Dam Rd, 23 km north of Dungog, T4995 9269, www.thebarringtons.com.au. A popular bush resort offering comfortable lodges, à la carte (BYO) restaurant, pool, spa and organized activities such as horse riding.

$$$$ Salisbury Lodges T4995 3285, www.salisburylodges.com.au. On the southern slopes of the national park about 40 km northwest of Dungog, this establishment gets consistently good reviews. Peaceful, good facilities with spas and log fires in 3 lodges, a de luxe spa room and very cute cabin. Also in-house restaurant.

$ Gloucester River Camping Area, Gloucester Tops Rd, T6538 5300. Fine riverside spot at the park boundary and comes complete with tame kangaroos but no showers. No bookings required.

Myall Lakes National Park *p101*
$$$$ Bombah Point Eco Cottages, 10 km from Bulahdelah on the same road as **Eco Point Myall Shores Resort** (see below), Bombah Point, T4997 4401, www.bombah.com.au. Consists of 6 very classy, self-contained, modern eco-friendly cottages in a peaceful setting. Very popular, so book ahead.

$$$$ EcoPoint Myall Shores Resort, Bombah Point, T4997 4495, www.eco point.com.au. Provides a range of accommodation from luxury waterfront villas, en suite cabins and budget bungalows to shady powered and non-powered sites. There is also a small licensed restaurant, café/bar, fuel, a small store, boat and canoe hire.

$$$$ Sandbar Caravan Park, 3434 The Lakes Way, Sandbar, T6554 4095, sandbar@paspaley.com.au. This lakeside park offers self-contained cabins, powered and non-powered sites, barbecue, kiosk, fuel, canoe and bike hire and a 9-hole golf course.

$$$ Bluey's by the Beach, 186 Boomerang Dr, Pacific Palms, T6554 0665, www.blueys bythebeach.com.au. A good motel option with 9 tidy units, an outdoor pool and spa, all within a short stroll from the beach.

$$$ BreakFree Moby's Beachside Retreat, Redgum Rd (off Boomerang Drive), Pacific Palms, T1800 655322, www.breakfree mobys.com.au. Boutique-style, contemporary 1- to 3- bedroom villas, with a smart restaurant, pool and spa. Also convenient for surf beaches.

$$$ Seal Rocks Camping Reserve, Kinka Rd, Seal Rocks, T4997 6164, www.sealrocks campingreserve.com.au. Out of the 3

campsites in and around Seal Rocks, this has the best facilities. It overlooks the main beach and offers a handful of self-contained cabins, powered and non-powered sites.

Forster-Tuncurry and around *p103*
$$$$ Forster Beach Caravan Park, Reserve Rd, T1800 240632, www.forsterbeachcaravan.com.au. Centrally placed park right beside the Harbour Inlet and Forster Beach, within walking distance of Forster town centre. It has a good range of cabins and barbecues but lacks privacy.

$$$$ Tokelau guesthouse, 2 Manning St, T6557 5157, www.tokelau.com.au. Opposite the bridge on the north bank (Tuncurry). Historic and beautifully renovated heritage home offering 2 cosy en suites, with spa or a traditional clawfoot bath.

$$ Lanis Holiday Island, 33 Lakes Way (near Bright St Intersection), T6554 6273, www.toptouristparks.com.au. Holiday park with good facilities located on the banks of Wallis Lake and boasting its own 25 ha bushland island for tent sites. There are spas in the self-contained cabins, en suite powered sites, pools and Wi-Fi.

$ NPWS Ruins campsite, beneath Booti Hill at what is known as the 'Green Cathedral' about 20 km south, T6591 0300. The best bet out of town. Great position, beach or lakeside, with good coastal and forest walks. Self-registration, hot showers, but no fires allowed.

🍴 Restaurants

Newcastle and Hunter Valley *p97*
The main venues for fine dining in Newcastle are Queens Wharf and the Promenade beside the river, while Beaumont St in the suburb of Hamilton has the widest selection of lively and affordable cafés and pubs. In the Lower Hunter Valley the best restaurants are mostly found in the hotels of the vineyards. You can expect to pay more for a meal here (most often with a main between $25-35), but the quality almost always makes up for it. Book well in advance.

$$$ Chez Pok at Peppers Guest House ,
Ekerts Rd, T4998 7596, www.peppers.com.au.
Daily for breakfast, lunch and dinner. Popular,
top-class restaurant, offering local fare with a
French, Asian and Italian edge.
Booking essential.

$$$ Scratchley's, 200 Wharf Rd, on the
Promenade, Newcastle, T4929 1111,
www.scratchleys.com.au. Mon-Sat 1130 for
lunch and 1730 for dinner, and open all day
Sunday from 1130. Something of a
regional institution over the last decade
combining excellent cuisine – mainly seafood
and steak – with great views across the river.
Again, book ahead.

$$ The Cellar Restaurant, Broke Rd,
Pokolbin, T4998 7584, www.the-cellar-
restaurant.com.au. Daily for lunch, Mon-Sat
for dinner. Highly regarded.

$$ Queens Wharf Brewery, 150 Wharf Rd,
Newcastle, T4929 6333. Located on the city's
foreshore this is one of its most popular
hotels, with good food and live
entertainment on Sun afternoons.

$$ Shakey Tables, Hunter Country Lodge,
220 Cessnock-Branxton Rd, North Rothbury,
T4938 1744, www.shakeytables.com.au. Daily
for dinner and Sun from 1230. An unusual and
colourfully decorated place for a tasty meal.

$$-$ Kent Hotel, 59 Beaumont St, Newcastle,
T4961 3303. One of many traditional and often
historic pubs in the city, which can provide
quality, quantity and good value. This hotel
also hosts live gigs most evenings.

Nelson Bay and around *p98, map p98*
Most of Nelson Bay's eateries are to be
found in the D'Albora Marina Complex on
Victoria Pde.

$$$ Merretts at Peppers Anchorage,
Corlette Point Rd, Corlette, T4984 0352. Daily
for breakfast, lunch and dinner. This is a fine
dining, award-winning option. It's fully
licensed, has a varied traditional Australian
menu and comes recommended, especially
for seafood or set lunches.

$ Bubs, 1 Teramby St (just west of D'Albora
Marina Complex), Nelson Bay, T4984 3917.
Daily 1100-1800. Good fish and chips.

$ Inner Lighthouse Café, Nelson Head,
above Little Beach, T4984 2505. Daily 1000-
1600. A decent café with great harbour views.
For something different consider the dinner
cruise options with **Moonshadow**, from $65,
see What to do, page 108

Myall Lakes National Park *p101*
$$ Oyster Hut, Marine Pde, Tea Gardens,
T4997 0579. This is the place to sample local
fare, such as fresh, locally harvested oysters.

Forster-Tuncurry and around *p103*
Other than the fish and chip shops at **$ Beach
St Seafoods** 1 Wallis St, you will find more
value seafood and pub grub at the popular
$ Lakes and Ocean Hotel, 10 Little St, T6555
6005. Across the bridge, the **$ Fisherman**'s
Co-operative on the riverbank (right, heading
north) is also a good bet.

$$ Bella Bellissimo, Memorial Drive, T6555
6411. Good value Italian dining, friendly
family atmosphere. Lake views.

$ Paradise Café, 51 Little St, T6554 7017.
Tues-Sun 0800-1600. A regular award winner
set overlooking Wallis Lake and one that
seems to maintain its good reputation
beyond just the location.

⚙ Festivals

Newcastle and Hunter Valley *p97*
The highlight of the busy events calendar is
the wonderfully hedonistic and convivial
Lovedale Long Lunch, held over a weekend
every **May** where several top wineries and
chefs combine with music and art,
www.lovedalelonglunch.com.au.
Other top events include the **Jazz in the
Vines Festival**, www.jazzinthevines.com.au;
Opera in the Vines and the **Newcastle
Mattara and Maritime Festival**,
www.mattarafestival.org.au, all held
in **Oct**.

Newcastle and Hunter Valley *p97*

Harbour cruises

Moonshadow, T4984 9388, www.moonshadow.com.au. Modern catamaran company offering lunch and dinner cruises, dolphin watching 1-3 hrs from $26, children $13.50.

Nova Cruises, T0400-381787, www.nova cruises.com.au. Whale watching or harbour cruises and Hunter Valley tours. All entertaining and good value. Whale watching cruises Wed, Sat and Sun 1000 from $60, children $35.

Hot air balloon tours

Balloon Aloft, Rothbury, T4991 1955, www.balloonaloft.com. From around $299.

Hunter Valley Hot Air Ballooning, T1800 818191, www.huntervalleyhotair ballooning.com.au.

Wine tours

If you have the time, the best way to experience the area's delights is to splash out on 3 days of relaxation, vineyard tours, fine dining and a stay at one of its many cosy B&Bs. However, for most a day tour taking in about 5 wineries with numerous tastings and the purchase of 1 or 2 bottles of their favourite vintage will have to suffice. There are numerous tour operators offering a whole host of options and modes of transport, from the conventional coaches and mini-vans to horse-drawn carriages and bikes. Most of the smaller operators will pick you up from your hotel and many can arrange lunch or dinner.

Hunter Valley Cadillac Tours, T4966 4059, www.cadillactours.com.au. Tours in restored classic Cadillac convertibles.

Hunter Valley Classic Carriages, T4991 3655, www.huntervalley classiccarriages.com.au. More horse, less power, half day from $50, full $85.

Hunter Valley Cycling, T0418-281480, www.huntervalleycycling.com.au. For traditional pedal power, from $30.

Vineyard Shuttle Service, T4991 3655, www.vineyardshuttle.com.au. Local mini-van firm offering flexibility and good value, from $42.

Nelson Bay and around *p98, map p98*

The VIC has a comprehensive list of daily tours and excursions and can assist with bookings. The main activities are cruising with dolphin, whale-watching and island trips, 4WD and horse trekking excursions to the vast Stockton Bight sand dunes as well as diving and fishing. Tour schedules are reduced in winter.

Diving

Pro Dive, D'Albora Marina, Teramby Rd, T4981 4331, www.prodivenelsonbay.com, and **Feet First**, T4984 2092, www.feetfirst dive.com.au, both offer local dive and snorkelling trips in the Fly Point Aquatic Reserve, 1 km east of the town centre.

Dolphin and whale watching

Dolphin watching (year round) and whale watching (Jun-Nov) are top of the agenda, with numerous vessels operating.

Imagine, T4984 9000, www.imagine cruises.com.au. Comfortable and less crowded cruises of 1½-4 hrs on a sail catamaran. Options include dolphin swimming, from $30-229. Recommended.

Moonshadow, Shop 3, 35 Stockton St, T4984 9388, www.moonshadow.com.au. The biggest operator with the largest, fastest and most comfortable vessels (Supercats). They offer daily cruises from 1½-4 hrs in search of sea mammals (1030, 1330 and 1530 from $26/$60), 7-hr trips to Broughton Island off the Myall Coast (Tue-Thu and Sun 1000 from $75) and twilight dinner and entertainment trips around the port, from 1900, $65.

6WD, 4WD, quad bike and horse trekking tours

Stockton Beach, south of Nelson Bay, with its incredible dune habitat and wrecks, provides a major playground for 4WD and quad bike tours, as well as horse trekking.

Moonshadow 4WD Tours, T4984 4760, www.moonshadow4wd.com.au. Standard 4WDs, a 6X6 and sand-boarding shuttles, 1-3 hrs, from $23-78. Their extended 3-hr trip takes in the *Sygna* shipwreck and 'Tin City', a hidden ramshackle settlement, threatened by the encroaching sand.

Johno's Getaways Beach Fishing, T0412688873, johno@nelsonbay.com. Dune adventures with fishing as the main activity.

Quad Bike King, T4919 0088, www.quadbikeking.com.au. As the name suggests, quad-bike tours of the dunes with sand-tobogganing, 2 hrs from $75. A great all-weather activity.

Rambling Sands Horse Treks, Janet Pde, off Nelson Bay Rd, Salt Ash, T4982 6391. Bush and dune treks of 1½-2 hrs, from $80.

Sahara Trails Horse Riding and Farmstay, T4981 9077,

www.saharatrails.com. 1-2 hr bush, coast and beach rides from $50-120. Stay and ride packages are also an option.

Sea kayaking

Blue Water Sea Kayaking, T0405-033518, www.kayakingportstephens.com.au. Guided day or sunset trips suitable for beginners and for the more experienced. Tours start from 1 hr, $25, and they offer pick-ups.

Surfing

Surfing lessons are available with ex-pro **Port Stephens Learn to Surf** at Fingal Bay, T0401-214455, www.portstephens learntosurf.com. Group 2 hrs from $50, private $70, 3-day $135.

Forster-Tuncurry and around *p103*
Boat tours

All manner of watercraft, from barbecue boats to canoes, can be hired along the waterfront.

Dive Forster Cruises, Fisherman's Wharf, T6554 7478, www.diveforster.com.au. Swimming with dolphins. Tours, from $70, $45 non-swimmers, children $25.

Tikki Boatshed, 15 Little St, T6554 6321, opposite the VIC.

Diving

There are several excellent dive sites in the region including Seal Rocks, the *SS Satara* wreck dive, Bennetts Head and the Pinnacles, which are all well known for their grey nurse sharks. There are several local dive operators including **Forster Dive Centre**, 11-13 Little St, T6555 4477, www.forsterdive centre.com.au, and **Action Divers**, Shop 4, 1-5 Manning St, Tuncurry, T6555 4053, www.actiondivers.com.au.

⊖ Transport

Newcastle and Hunter Valley *p95*
Air

Newcastle Airport, T4928 9800, www.newcastleairport.com.au, is 24 km north of the city centre. **Jet Star**, T131538, www.jetstar.com.au; **Qantas Link**, T131313, www.qantas.com.au; **Regional Express**, T131713, www.rex.com.au; and **Virgin Blue**, T136789, www.virginblue.com.au, offer regional services from Sydney and other destinations.

   Port Stephens Coaches, T4982 2940, www.pscoaches.com.au, stops off at the Williamtown (Newcastle) Airport ($6.60) while **Happy Cabby**, T4976 3991, www.happycabby.com, offers transfers to and from **Newcastle** and **Sydney** from $35.

   Cessnock-based **Vineyard Shuttle Service**, T4991 3655, operates shuttle services from the airport to **Hunter Valley** accommodation.

Bus and ferry

Local Newcastle Bus and Ferry, T131500, www.newcastlebuses.info, provides local bus and ferry services. Fares start at $3.30 and allow an hour's unlimited travel with an all-day pass costing $9.80. Bus/ferry and train/bus/ferry passes are available.

Ferry Services, T131500, link central **Newcastle** (Queens Wharf) with **Stockton** Mon-Sat 0515-2400, Sun 0830-2200, one way $3, tickets on board. **Rover Coaches**, 231 Vincent St, Cessnock, T4990 1699, www.rovercoaches.com.au, runs services between **Newcastle** and **Cessnock** as well as an all-day jump-on-jump-off service around the vineyards from $40.

Long distance Coaches stop next to the train station in Newcastle. **Greyhound**, T131499, runs daily **Sydney** and north/southbound services. They stop at all major towns along the **New England Highway**. Countrylink Travel Centre (see under Train below) acts as a booking agent. Port Stephens Coaches, T4982 2940, www.pscoaches.com, also provides daily services to **Sydney** and **Port Stephens**, while **Rover Coaches**, T4990 1699, www.rovercoaches.com.au, covers the **Hunter Valley**. If you intend to pass through the Great Lakes Region and Myall National Park, **Busways**, T4997 4788, runs a daily regional bus service between **Taree** and **Sydney** via **Forster-Tuncurry**, **Bluey's Beach**, **Hawks Nest** and **Newcastle**.

Taxi

If you want to avoid driving between your accommodation and restaurant **Vineyard Shuttle Service**, T4991 3655, in Cessnock, offers local transfers or call a conventional taxi, T4990 1111. **Newcastle Taxis** T133300.

Train

The main train station is located at the far end of Hunter St. **Cityrail**, T131500, has regular daily services to **Sydney**. Countrylink, T132232, has a travel centre at the station (daily 0900-1700) and luggage storage. Note state-wide service connections are from Broadmeadow, 5 mins west. The nearest train station for Hunter Valley is Maitland, which links with **Newcastle** and **Sydney**'s Cityrail, T131500. **Countrylink**, T132232, offers state-wide services to **Queensland** via **Scone**.

Nelson Bay and around *p98, map p98*
Air

The nearest airport is close to Newcastle (Williamtown), 30 km south (see page 98).

Bus

Local Port Stephen's Coaches, T4982 2940, www.pscoaches.com, has regular bus services between the airport and Port Stephens and local bus services.

Long distance Coaches stop on Stockton St in Nelson Bay. **Port Stephens Coaches**, Local above, serves Nelson Bay from Sydney direct. Another alternative is to use the more frequent Newcastle-bound services (see above), then catch the regular daily service from Newcastle to Nelson Bay. If you intend to pass through the **Great Lakes Region** and **Myall National Park**, Busways, T4983 1560, www.busways.com.au, has daily services between **Taree** and Sydney via **Tuncurry-Forster**, **Bluey's Beach**, **Hawks Nest** and **Newcastle**.

Car

Car hire from **Avis**, Newcastle Airport, T136333.

Ferry

Ferry services, T4126 2117, link **Nelson Bay** with **Tea Gardens**, 4 times daily from Nelson Bay, return $25, children $12.

Train

Train services to **Newcastle** with onward bus connections.

Barrington Tops National Park *p100*

Bus

The only way to access the park by public transport is with the **Forster Bus Service** (No 308), T6554 6431, www.forsterbus.com.au, which accesses **Gloucester**, Mon-Fri, from **Forster-Tuncurry**.

Myall Lakes National Park *p101*

Bus

Busways, T4983 1560, and **Forster Bus Service**, T6554 6431, operate daily local bus services around **Tea Gardens** and **Hawks Nest** and south as far as **Pacific Palms**, **Bluey's Beach** and **Smith Lake** (Mon-Fri). Busways also runs regional bus services between **Taree** and **Sydney** via **Forster-Tuncurry**, **Bluey's Beach**, **Hawks Nest** and **Newcastle**.

Ferry

Port Stephens Ferry Services, T4126 2117, links **Nelson Bay** with **Tea Gardens**, daily (from Nelson Bay 0830, 1200, 1530 and 1630), return $25, children $12. Boat hire in **Tea Gardens** and **Hawks Nest**.

Forster-Tuncurry and around *p103*

Bus

Forster Bus Service, T6554 6431, www.forsterbus.com.au, operates daily local bus services around the twin towns Mon-Fri. Long-distance buses stop outside the VIC on Little St. The VIC also acts as a booking agent.

Greyhound, T131499, services from **Sydney** or **Port Macquarie**. Busways, T4983 1560, www.busways .com.au, also offers services between **Taree** and **Sydney** via **Tuncurry**, **Forster**, **Bluey's Beach**, **Hawks Nest** and **Newcastle**.

Train

The nearest train station is at Taree. Countrylink, T132232, offers daily services north and south. **Busways** (see above) or **Eggins Coaches**, Taree, T65522700, provide links between the train station and Forster.

❶ Directory

Newcastle and Hunter Valley *p95*

Banks Most of the major banks with ATMs can be found along the Hunter St Mall in Newcastle. **Useful numbers Police**, corner of Church and Watt streets, T4929 0999.

Nelson Bay and around *p98, map p98*

Banks Most of the major branches with ATMs are to be found along Stockton or Magnus St, Nelson Bay. **Police** Government Rd, Nelson Bay, T4981 1244.

Myall Lakes National Park *p101*

The main amenities such as **post offices**, **service stations** and **supermarkets** can be found on Marine Dr in Tea Gardens, Mungo Brush Rd and Booner St in Hawks Nest and Boomerang Drive in Bluey's Beach.

Port Macquarie to Byron Bay

There are some great stops on this route. Port Macquarie itself is often unfairly overlooked. The fast developing coastal town of South West Rocks near Smoky Cape and the sublime coastal Hat Head National Park are relaxing places to explore. For many the main destination on the north NSW coast is laid-back Byron Bay, which is usually the last port of call before crossing the state border. It's well worth diverting inland, however, especially to the arty village of Bellingen, a pleasant stop on the way to the Dorrigo and New England National Parks, both of which offer some superb views and bush walks.

Port Macquarie → *For listings, see pages 128-140.*

Officially declared as possessing the best year-round climate in Australia and blessed with a glut of superb beaches, engaging historic sites, wildlife-rich suburban nature reserves and water-based activities, the former penal colony of Port Macquarie is rightfully recognized as one of the best holiday destinations to be found anywhere in NSW. Due perhaps to more domestically oriented advertising, or simply the 6 km of road between the town and the Pacific Highway, it seems the vast majority of international travellers miss Port Macquarie completely as they charge northwards towards more high-profile destinations such as Byron Bay. But if you make the effort and short detour, you will not be disappointed.

Arriving in Port Macquarie
Getting there Port Macquarie is 10 km east of the Pacific Highway along the Oxley Highway. The airport is 3 km away. Long-distance buses serve the town and there is a train station 18 km away with connecting buses to the town centre. ▶▶ *See Transport, page 138.*

Tourist information There is a **VIC** ① *The Glasshouse, corner of Clarence St and Hay St, T6581 8000, www.portmacquarieinfo.com.au, Mon-Fri 0830-1700, Sat-Sun 0900-1600.* **NPWS** ① *152 Horton St, T6586 8300, midnorthcoast.region@environment.nsw.gov.au, Mon-Fri 0900-1630.*

Places in in Port Macquarie
Allman Hill on Stewart Street is home to the settlement's first cemetery (where the gravestones reveal the hardships and life expectancies). Nearby is Gaol Point Lookout, site of the first gaol, now offering pleasant views across the harbour and Town Beach. If you would like to quietly search the heavens, visit the **Observatory** ① *Rotary Park on William St, www.pmobs.org.au, viewing nights Wed and Sun 1930 EST, 2015 DST, $8, children $7.* On the eastern side of Rotary Park is Town Beach, the most convenient for

Port Macquarie

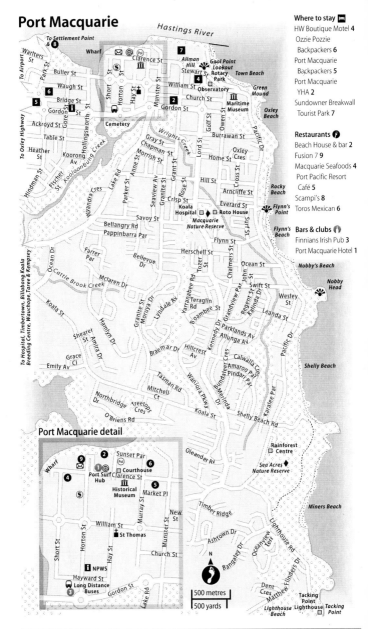

Hastings River

To Settlement Point & 🚤 8

Wharf

Warlters St
Park St
Buller St
Waugh St
Bridge St
Gordon St
Ackroyd St
Table St
Heather St
Short St
Horton St
Hay St
Clarence St
Gore St
Hollingsworth St
Munster St

Allman Hill Stewart St
Gaol Point Lookout
Rotary Park
Town Beach

William St
Observatory
Church St
Gordon St
Green Mound
Maritime Museum
Oxley Beach

To Airport
To Oxley Highway

Cemetery

Fischer St
Koolaonbung Creek
Koorong Av
Hindman St
Wyandra Cres
Lake Rd
Parker St
Anne St
Seaview Av
Granite St
Grant St
Crisp St
Rose St
Savoy St
Bellangry Rd
Pappinbarra Par

Gray St
Chapman St
Morrish St
Wrights Creek
Lord St
Home St
Hill St
Golf St
Owen St
Burrawan St
Oxley Cres
Cross St
Arncliffe St
Everard St
Pacific Dr
Rocky Beach
Flynn's Point

Koala Hospital
Roto House
Macquarie Nature Reserve

Flynn St
Flynn's Beach

To Hospital, Timbertown, Billabong Koala Breeding Centre, Wauchope, Taree & Kempsey

Ocean Dr
Cattle Brook Creek
Koala St
Shearer St
Hamlyn Dr
Amira Dr
Grace Cl
Emily Av
Farrer Par
Bellevue Dr
Mclaren Dr
Granite St
Morua Dr
Lyndale Av
Braemar Dr
Tasman Rd
Mitchell Ct
Northbridge Dr
Treetops Cres
O'Briens Rd

Herschell St
Tozer St
Chalmers St
Ocean St
Yarranabee Rd
Teraglin Rd
Boambee St
Kennedy Dr
Hillcrest Av
Grandview Par
St John St
Regent St
Swift St
Kalinda St
Leanda St
Wesley St
Parklands Av
Allunga Av
Calwalla Cres
Amaroo Par
Pindarri Par
Bundarra Cres
Melinda Cres
Waniora Pkwy
Koala St
Shelly Beach Rd
Karatel Par
Pacific Dr

Nobby's Beach
Nobby Head
Shelly Beach

Oleander Av
Rainforest Centre
Sea Acres Nature Reserve
Timber Ridge
New St
Munster St
Ashtown Dr
Bangalay Dr
N
Miners Beach
Oceanview Terr
Lighthouse Rd
Matthew Flinders Dr
Dent Cres
Tacking Point
Lighthouse Beach
Lighthouse
Tacking Point

Port Macquarie detail

Sunset Par
Wharf
Courthouse
Port Surf Hub
Clarence St
Historical Museum
Market Pl
William St
St Thomas
Murray St
Munster St
Church St
Short St
Horton St
Hay St
NPWS
Hayward St
Long Distance Buses
Gordon St
Lake Rd

500 metres
500 yards

Where to stay 🛏
HW Boutique Motel **4**
Ozzie Pozzie
  Backpackers **6**
Port Macquarie
  Backpackers **5**
Port Macquarie
  YHA **2**
Sundowner Breakwall
  Tourist Park **7**

Restaurants 🍴
Beach House & bar **2**
Fusion 7 **9**
Macquarie Seafoods **4**
Port Pacific Resort
  Café **5**
Scampi's **8**
Toros Mexican **6**

Bars & clubs 🍸
Finnians Irish Pub **3**
Port Macquarie Hotel **1**

swimming with good surfing at the northern end. South of here, the **Maritime Museum** ⓘ *6 William St, T6583 4505, daily 1000-1600, $4, children $2*, is worth a look for a delve into the coast's history.

The 1869 **Courthouse** ⓘ *corner of Clarence St and Hay St, T6584 1818, Mon-Sat 1000-1500, $2*, served the community for over a century and has been refurbished faithfully. Across the road is the **Historical Museum** ⓘ *$5*, housed in a former convict-built store (1835) and containing 14 rooms of historical artefacts.

St Thomas's Church ⓘ *corner of Hay St and William St, T6584 1033, Tue-Fri 0930-1200 and 1400-1600, donation welcome*, is the fifth oldest Anglican Church still in use in Australia, built by convict labour in the late 1820s. Its most interesting feature actually lies buried beneath one of the pews, in the form of one Captain Rolland – the port's former gaol supervisor – who died from sunstroke. He was buried inside to avoid his body being dug up by vengeful convicts.

A healthy suburban population of koalas lives in the area's nature reserves and parks and numerous roadside signs are testament to this. In town, one of the best places to spot a wild koala is in Sea Acres Nature Reserve (see below), but if you have no joy there is always the **Koala Hospital** ⓘ *Lord St, T6584 2399, www.koalahospital.org.au, daily, donation welcome*, in the Macquarie Nature Reserve. Although you cannot see any sick marsupials, some of the pre-released critters are usually on display. Feeding takes place daily at 1500 and 1630. There's also the **Billabong Koala Breeding Centre** ⓘ *61 Billabong Drive, 10 km from the town centre, T6585 1260, www.billabongkoala.com.au, 0900-1700. $18, children $11*, which not only provides copious koala patting (1030, 1330 and 1530) but also the usual array of Australian natives such as wallabies, wombats and rainbow lorikeets in 2.5ha of landscaped gardens, with a café, barbecue and picnic areas. Step back in time with a visit to **Timbertown Wauchope** ⓘ *Oxley Highway, west of Wauchope, T6586 1940, www.timbertown.com.au, about 20 mins' drive west of Port Macquarie, daily 0930-1530, $5, children $3, family $12*, where you can ride the steam train, watch the bullock team display, observe the timber craftsmen at work and smell the coals of the blacksmith's fire.

The beaches that fringe the western suburbs of the town from the Hastings River mouth south to Tacking Point and beyond are simply superb, offering excellent swimming, fishing, surfing, walks and views. Whale-watching tours operate from June to November; prices start from $40 per person. For further details, contact **Greater Port Macquarie VIC** ⓘ *T1300 303155*. North of the town, the great swathe of **North Beach**, stretching 15 km to Point Plomer, fringed by the diverse coastal habitats of Limeburners Creek Nature Reserve, provides almost total solitude. South, beyond Green Mound, Oxley Beach and Rocky Beach are less accessible. Beyond those, Flynn's Beach and Nobby's Beach are two other favourite spots with great views and good swimming as well as fossicking and snorkelling on the extensive rock platforms.

South of Nobby Head the coastal fringe gives way to Shelly Beach and the 72-ha coastal **Sea Acres Nature Reserve** ⓘ *T6582 2930, 0900-1630, $6, children $3, under 7s free, family $15*, one of the best places in town to spot wild koalas (particularly in the late afternoon). This sublime piece of rainforest is preserved with a 1.3 km boardwalk providing the ideal viewpoint. The boardwalk starts and finishes at the Rainforest Centre, which itself houses an interesting range of displays, a café and shop. Guided tours are available and recommended. Then it is on to Miners Beach, reached by coastal paths from the same car park. This is a favourite spot for naturists. At the terminus of Lighthouse Road is Tacking Point, named by Matthew Flinders in 1802, and the pocket-sized Tacking Point Lighthouse built in 1879. From there you are afforded great views south along Lighthouse Beach towards Bonny Hills and North Brother Hill.

South West Rocks and Hat Head → *For listings, see pages 128-140.*

South West Rocks is the best-kept secret on the NSW north coast. It has everything that Byron Bay has, except the footprints. Long swathes of golden sand, great fishing and swimming, a cliff-top lighthouse, stunning views and a superb local national park – Hat Head – combine to make South West Rocks the ideal place to get away from it all for a few days. Here, you can watch dolphins surfing rather than people. South West Rocks is best reached and explored using your own transport.

Visiting South West Rocks

South West Rocks Visitors' Centre ① *1 Ocean Av, T6566 7099, www.kempsey.nsw.gov.au, 0900-1700.* **Kempsey VIC** ① *South Kempsey Park, off Pacific Highway, Kempsey, T6563 1555, www.kempsey.midcoast.com.au, daily,* is a good source of information. They have NPWS national parks information. ▸▸ *See Transport, page 138.*

Places in South West Rocks

South West Rocks sits at the southern bank of the Macleay River mouth and the western end of Trail Bay, where the colourful, wave-eroded rocks that earned the village its name form the perfect playground for swimmers and snorkellers. At the eastern end of Trial Bay the charming settlement of **Arakoon** fringes the Arakoon State Recreation Area and Laggers Point, site of the pink granite monolith of **Trial Bay Gaol** ① *T6566 6168, 0900-1700, $8,* built in 1886 and now housing a small museum that offers an insight into the torrid existence of its former inmates. Trial Bay was named after *The Trial*, a vessel that was stolen by former convicts and wrecked in the bay in 1816. Several other vessels with more conventional crews were wrecked in Trial Bay in the 1970s. A few rusting remnants still reach out from their sandy graves. At the terminus of Wilson Street, at the western end of Arakoon, is **Little Bay**, with its sublime, people-free beach. The car park also provides access to the **Graves Monument walking track** (2 km return) which provides memorable views back across Trial Bay and the Trial Bay Gaol. **Gap Beach**, accessed a little further south, is another fine spot, especially for the more adventurous surfer. South of Arakoon (3 km), Lighthouse Road provides access to the northern fringe of the **Hat Head National Park**, **Smoky Beach** and the **Smoky Cape Lighthouse**. The 1891 lighthouse is one of the tallest and oldest in NSW and provides stunning views south to Crescent Head and north down to the beckoning solitude of North Smoky Beach.

South of South West Rocks, accessed via Hat Head Village Road and Kinchela, the small village and headland of **Hat Head** sits in the heart of the national park separating the long swathes of Smoky Beach north and Killick Beach to the south. The village has a caravan park, limited amenities and walking access to Hat Hill, Korogoro Point, Connor's Beach and the Hungry Hill Rest Area.

Bellingen and Dorrigo National Park → *For listings, see pages 128-140.*

Away from the coast, sitting neatly on the banks of the Bellinger River in the heart of the Bellinger Valley, is the pleasant country village of Bellingen, renowned for its artistic and alternative community, its markets, music festivals and laid-back ambience. Simple relaxation or country walks are the name of the game for travellers here, before they continue further inland to explore the superb national parks of Dorrigo (see page 117), and Oxley and New England (see page 117), or resume the relentless journey northwards up the coast. The village has its own nickname used affectionately by the locals – Bello.

Visiting Bellingen and Dorrigo National Park
Getting there   There are no long-distance connections to Bellingen – you must travel to Nambucca Heads or Urunga and then get a connection. ▸▸ *For transport details for Dorrigo National Park, see page 138.*

Tourist information   Bellingen Shire VIC ① *T6655 5711, www.bellingen.com, Mon-Sat 0900-1700, Sun 1000-1400*, is beside the Pacific Highway in Urunga, just south of the Bellingen turn-off. Ask for a free street map of the town. In Bellingen itself you will find the **Waterfall Way VIC** ① *29 Hyde St, T6655 1522, www.waterfallway.com, T6655 5711, www.bellingen.com, Mon-Sat 0900-1700, Sun 1000-1400*. Further afield the **Dorrigo VIC** ① *Hickory St, T6657 2486, www.dorrigo.com.au, 1000-1600*, offers local listings. Ask for a free street map. **NPWS Dorrigo National Park Rainforest Centre** ① *Dome Rd, T6657 2309, www.nationalparks.nsw.gov.au*, supplies details on national parks, walks and other local information.

Bellingen
Bellingen's peaceful tree-lined streets are lined with some obvious heritage buildings, many of which are protected by the National Trust. The small **Bellingen Museum** ① *Civic Sq, Hyde St, T6655 0289, Mon and Wed-Fri 1000-1200*, contains a low-key collection of photos and artefacts from the mid-1800s. The **Old Butter Factory** ① *Doepel Lane, 0930 to 1700*, on the western approach to the village, and the unmistakable **Yellow Shed** ① *2 Hyde St, 0930 to 1700*, are the two main arts and crafts outlets in the village, selling everything from opals to wind chimes. The Old Butter Factory also has a café and offers a range of relaxation and healing therapies including iridology, massage and a flotation tank. The colourful **Bellingen craft and produce market** is considered one of the best in the region and is held in the local park on the third Saturday of the month. The village also hosts a top quality **Jazz Festival** ① *www.bellingenjazzfestival.com.au*, in mid-August, and the equally popular **Global Carnival** ① *www.globalcarnival.com*, which is an entertaining celebration of world music held in the first week in October.

Nature lovers should take a look at the large (and smelly) flying fox (fruit bat) colony on **Bellingen Island** (which is now no longer an island) beside the river, within easy walking distance of the village. The best place to see the bats is from the Bellingen Caravan Park on Dowle Street (cross the Bridge off Hyde, on to Hammond then turn right into Dowle), while the best time is around dusk when they depart to find food. But even during the day it is an impressive sight indeed as they hang like a thousand fuzzy Christmas decorations from almost every tree.

New England and Cathedral Rocks national parks

The 71,207 ha New England National Park is breathtaking. What makes it so special is not only its sense of wilderness and rich biodiversity, but its stunning vistas, Point Lookout being the most popular and accessible viewpoint, and truly memorable. Do not venture here expecting to see those views automatically however. What adds an atmospheric and unpredictable edge to this viewpoint is its height, which, at over 1564 m, often results in a shroud of mist or worse still, sheets of rain. It really can be a glorious day in Armidale and along the coast and yet Point Lookout is like Edinburgh Castle in midwinter. Still, if you can afford a couple of days, the camping, the views and the varied walks around Point Lookout (2.5 km to a full day) are well worthwhile.

Just north of Point Lookout Road, Round Mountain Road (8 km) ventures into the heart of Cathedral Rock National Park. The main feature here is the magnificent granite tors – Cathedral Rocks – and in spring, vivid displays of wild flowers. The 6-km Cathedral Rock Track from the Barokee Rest Area is a circular route with a 200-m diversion to the Rocks.

The VIC and NPWS offices in Armidale and the Dorrigo Rainforest Centre ① T6657 2309, www.environment.nsw.gov.au, stock the relevant leaflets and information surrounding the parks, their walks, camping and self-contained accommodation. To reach the New England and Cathedral Rocks National Parks, Point Lookout Road is unsealed and accessed (signposted) off Waterfall Way, 5 km south of the Waterfall Way/Guyra Road Junction (3 km west of Ebor). It is then 11 km to the park boundary and a further 3 km to Point Lookout.

Dorrigo and Dorrigo National Park

Provided the weather is kind and the clouds do not blind you, you are in for a scenic treat here. Even the **Dorrigo National Park Rainforest Visitors Centre** ① T6657 2309, 0900-1700, has amazing views. Sitting right at the edge of the escarpment, the view across the forested slopes and across the Bellinger Valley towards the coast is even better from the slightly shaky 100-m **Skywalk** that projects like a jetty out across the rainforest canopy. From its end you can survey the glorious scene and listen to the strange and distant calls of elusive rainforest birds. You may also see the odd python curled up in a branch or right next to the handrail. The visitor centre itself has some good interpretative displays and a small café. The main office and shop can provide the necessary detail on the excellent rainforest walks (ranging from 400 m to 5 km) that begin from the centre and descend in to the very different world beneath the forest canopy.

From the Rainforest Centre it is then a short, scenic 10-km drive along the edge of the escarpment to the **Never Never Picnic Area**, which is a fine network of rainforest walks, including the 5.5-km **Rosewood Creek Track** to **Cedar Falls**, the 4.8-km **Casuarina Falls Track** and the 6.4-km **Blackbutt (escarpment edge) Track**. Before heading into Dorrigo township itself, it is worth taking the short 2-km drive to **Griffith's Lookout** for its memorable views across the Bellinger Valley. The road to the lookout is signposted about 1 km south of Dome Road off the Waterfall Way. Just north of Dorrigo (1.5 km), the **Dangar Falls** may prove a disappointment after long dry periods but after rain can become a thunderous torrent of floodwaters.

Coffs Harbour → *For listings, see pages 128-140.*

Roughly halfway between Sydney and Brisbane and the only spot on the NSW coast where the Great Dividing Range meets the sea, Coffs Harbour is a favourite domestic holiday resort and the main commercial centre for the northern NSW coast. Surrounded by rolling hills draped in lush banana plantations and pretty beaches, it's a fine spot to kick back for a couple of days.

The main activities in town are centred around the attractive marina where regular fishing, whale- and dolphin-watching cruises are on offer, together with highly popular

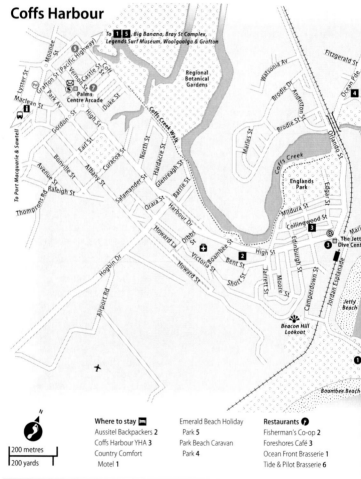

Coffs Harbour

Where to stay 🛏
Aussitel Backpackers **2**
Coffs Harbour YHA **3**
Country Comfort
    Motel **1**

Emerald Beach Holiday
    Park **5**
Park Beach Caravan
    Park **4**

Restaurants 🍴
Fisherman's Co-op **2**
Foreshores Café **3**
Ocean Front Brasserie **1**
Tide & Pilot Brasserie **6**

diving and snorkelling trips to the outlying Solitary Islands. The island group and surrounding coast is gazetted as a marine park and considered to have one of the largest marine biodiversities in NSW.

Other principal attractions include Muttonbird Island, guarding the entrance to the harbour and offering sanctuary to thousands of burrowing seabirds and, in complete contrast, the kitsch Big Banana complex on the northern edge of the town. Often overlooked is the fast developing, but still pleasant, beachside community of Sawtell, which is worth the trip.

South Pacific Ocean

Park Beach

Marina
Booking
Centre

Marina

♦ *Muttonbird Island Nature Reserve*

Bars & clubs 🎵
Ex-serviceman's Club 7
Plantation 5

Arriving in Coffs Harbour
Tourist information VIC ⓘ *corner of Elizabeth St and Maclean St, T6648 4990, www.coffscoast.com.au, 0900-1700.* Ask for the free Coffs Coast visitors' guide.

Places in Coffs Harbour
The rather unsightly and uninspiring main drag, **Grafton Street**, has seen something of an improvement recently, with the creation of the Palms Centre Arcade and redevelopment of the Mall and Park Avenue, which, combined, form the hub of the town centre. From the end of the Mall, **High Street** heads 3 km southeast to the **harbour**, which is hemmed in by the town's three main beaches: **Park Beach**, which straddles Coffs Creek to the north, **Jetty Beach** beside the harbour and **Boambee Beach** to the south. Park Beach is the most popular and is regularly patrolled in summer. Jetty Beach is considered the safest. The view from **Beacon Hill Lookout**, at the end of Camperdown Street, off High Street, offers fine 360-degree views across the harbour, the coast, and the green rolling hills of the Great Dividing Range to the west. There are also numerous other, excellent beaches, stretching 20 km north all the way to Woolgoolga.

Linked to the mainland by the marina's 500-m sea wall is **Muttonbird Island Nature Reserve**, which offers more than just a pleasant walk and some memorable views back towards the town. From October to April Muttonbird Island and others in the Solitary Island group are home to thousands of breeding wedge-tailed shearwaters (muttonbirds) that nest in a warren of burrows across the entire island. The birds are best viewed just after dusk, when they return in number to feed their mates or chicks hiding deep within the burrows. Although the birds were once easily harvested for food, they are now, thankfully, fully protected. For obvious reasons, do not stray from the main pathway. Also keep a lookout for humpback whales which are often spotted just offshore from June to September.

The **Solitary Islands** offer some fine dive sites with such evocative names as Grey Nurse Gutters and Manta Arch, a wealth of marine life (90 species of coral and 280 species of fish) and the densest colonies of anemones and anemone fish (clown fish) in the world. For more details contact the VIC, see above. Coffs Harbour is one of the cheapest places on the NSW coast to get certified for diving. For details of diving and snorkelling trips, see page 136.

It's incredible that by building an oversized banana next to the main highway, you attract people like bees to honey. Coffs' famous icon and monument of marketing genius, the **Big Banana** ⓘ *T6652 4355, www.bigbanana.com, 0900-1600*, located just north of the town on the Pacific Highway, fronts a banana plantation that has 'grown' over the years and now hosts a new 'World of Bananas' attraction. As you can imagine it showcases just about all you need to know about bananas, plus a number of long-established activities, from a lookout (free) to toboggan rides, snow-tubing, ice skating and the obligatory café and shop selling lots of souvenir banana-meets-koala kitsch. It is, however, perhaps entertainment enough to sit in the café and watch people posing for photos in front of the Big Banana. This in itself will without doubt prove the age-old suspicion that human beings are indeed really weird.

Also north of town is the **Legends Surf Museum** ⓘ *T6653 6536, Gauldrons Rd, left off the Pacific Highway, 1000-1600, $8, children $4*, run by enthusiastic and enigmatic Scott Dillon, ex-master of the waves. There are over 120 classic boards on display as well as the odd canoe, photos and other such enlightening memorabilia.

Sawtell, a seaside village 6 km south of Coffs Harbour, is blessed with some fine beaches and a pleasant laid-back atmosphere that has quietly attracted domestic holidaymakers for years. Now the secret is well and truly out; like most of the East Coast's beachside communities the influx of city 'sea changers' may well prove its very demise. Other than the obvious attractions of the beach, the **Cooinda Aboriginal Art Gallery** ⓘ *Shop 1/4, First Av, T6658 7901, www.cooinda-gallery.com.au*, relocated from Coffs Harbour, is well worth a look. It showcases some excellent examples of the unique and spiritually loaded 'dot-style'.

Coffs Harbour to Byron Bay → For listings, see pages 128-140.

The **Clarence Coast Visitor Centre** ⓘ *Ferry Park, just south of the turn-off for Yamba, and 2 km south of Maclean, T6645 4121, www.clarencetourism.com, 0900-1700*, has full accommodation, events and activities listings for the region.

Yamba, Angourie and Yuraygir National Park (North)

The coastal fishing town of **Yamba**, 13 km east of the Pacific Highway (exit just before the Clarence River bridge) and on the southern bank of the Clarence River mouth, is famed for its prawn industry and its fine surf beaches. Serving mainly as a domestic holiday destination, it offers the opportunity to spend two or three days away from the mainstream tourist resorts further north. **Main Beach**, below Flinders Park, is the most popular of Yamba's many golden strands but **Turners Beach**, between the main breakwater and lighthouse, **Covent Beach**, between Lovers Point and Main Beach, and **Pippie Beach**, the most southerly, are all equally good. **Clarence River Delta** and **Lake Wooloweyah**, 4 km south, provide boating, fishing and cruising opportunities. The Yamba-Iluka ferry shuttles back and forth daily, providing access to some sublime beaches and bluffs, a stunning rainforest reserve and the wilderness of Bundjalung National Park.

Iluka and Bundjalung National Park

If you can give yourself at least two to three days to explore the Iluka area, you won't regret it. Other than the superb coastline contained within the southern sector of the Bundjalung National Park and one of the best campsites on the northern NSW coast at **Woody Head**, the big attraction at the sleepy fishing village of **Iluka** is the World Heritage Rainforest Walk through the **Iluka Nature Reserve**. The 136-ha reserve contains the largest remaining stand of littoral rainforest in NSW – a rich forest habitat unique to the coastal environment and supporting a huge number of species such as the charmingly named lily pilly tree and noisy pitta bird. The 2.5-km rainforest walk can be tackled either from the north at the Iluka Bluff Car Park (off the main Iluka Road opposite the golf club) or from the caravan park at western edge of the village (Crown Street).

Iluka Beach is another fine quiet spot reached via Beach Road (head west from the end of Iluka Road). Further north, just beyond Iluka Bluff, **Bluff Beach** and **Frazer's Reef** are popular for swimming and fishing. The Whale Viewing Platform on Beach Road can guarantee panoramic views of the area and the possibility, in season (June to November), of seeing mainly humpback whales migrating up and down the coast.

Two kilometres north of Iluka and Woody Head, the 18,000-ha wilderness of **Bundjalung National Park** with its 38 km of beaches, littoral rainforest, heathlands, unusual rock formations, lagoons, creeks and swamps is an eco-explorer's paradise. Sadly, access from the south is by 4WD only ($16 permit), or on foot. There is better access from the north along the 21-km unsealed road. Go up to Gap Road, off the Pacific Highway, 5 km south of Woodburn, to the Black Rocks campsite. Accommodation and park information, maps and internet are available at the Clarence Coast Visitor Centre (see page 120 for details).

Lennox Head

The small, beachside settlement of Lennox Head is world famous for the long surf breaks that form at the terminus of Seven Mile Beach and Lennox Point. Even without a board, the village offers a quieter, alternative destination in which to spend a relaxing couple of days, away from the clamour of Byron Bay. Just south of the village the eponymous head offers excellent views north to Cape Byron and is considered a prime spot for hang-gliding and dolphin and whale spotting. The **Lennox Reef**, below the head, known as 'The Moat', is also good for snorkelling. At the northern end of the village **Lake Ainsworth** is a fine venue for freshwater swimming, canoeing and windsurfing. **Lennox Head Sailing School**, beside the lake on Pacific Parade, hires water sports equipment and offers lessons. The lake edge also serves as the venue for the coastal markets that are held on the second and fifth Sundays of the month.

Byron Bay → *For listings, see pages 128-140.*

Anything goes in Byron Bay. This town would love to have its own passport control to prevent entry to anyone who is remotely conservative or thinks surfing is something you do in front of a computer. Only three decades ago 'Byron' was little more than a sleepy, attractive coastal enclave. Few strayed off the main highway heading north except a few alternative lifestylers who found it an ideal escape and the land prices wonderfully cheap. But news spread and its popularity exploded. It lacks the glitz of the Gold Coast and the conformity of many other coastal resorts, but there is little doubt it is perilously close to the level of popularity that can turn to a love-it-or-hate-it experience. Despite all this, however, it remains a beautiful place (no high-rise hotels here) and boasts a wonderfully cosmopolitan mix of humanity. Few people leave disappointed.

Arriving in Byron Bay

Getting there The two nearest airports are Coolangatta (north) and Ballina (south) with good daily services and shuttle buses to town. There are plenty of long-distance buses and trains from Sydney, Cairns, Brisbane, etc. Both the train station and bus station are in the centre of town.

Byron Bay

To Julian Rocks
Marine Reserve

Byron Bay

Where to stay
Amigo's Byron Bay
  Guesthouse **1**
Aquarius Backpackers Motel **2**

Arts Factory **3**
Belongil Beachouse **7**
Byron Bayside Motel **9**
Cape Byron Hostel (YHA) **10**

Cape Byron Lodge **5**
Clarke's Beach Caravan Park
First Sun Holiday Park **12**
Holiday Village Backpackers

Getting around You can enjoy all the offerings of Byron Bay on foot, or, to cover more ground, hire a bike. There are local bus services for getting around town and also to sights around Byron Bay such as Ballina and Lennox Head. ➤ *See Transport, page 139.*

Tourist information Byron Bay VIC ① *80 Jonson St, T6680 8558, www.visitbyron bay.com, 0900-1700.* See also page 137, for tour operators.

Places in Byron Bay

The main attractions in Byron, beyond its hugely popular social and creative scene, are of course the surrounding beaches and the stunning Cape Byron Headland Reserve. There are over 37 km of beaches, including seven world-class surf beaches stretching from Belongil Beach in the west to Broken Head in the south. Byron also hosts an extensive array of organized activities to lure you from your beach-based relaxation. Surfing is the most popular pastime. For details, see page 138.

Only metres from the town centre, **Main Beach** is the main focus of activity. It is patrolled and safest for families or surfing beginners. West of Main Beach, **Belongil Beach** stretches about 1 km to the mouth of Belongil Creek. About 500 m beyond that (accessed via Bayshore Drive), there is a designated naturist beach. East of the town centre, Main

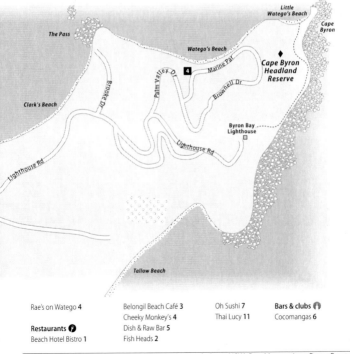

Rae's on Watego **4**	Belongil Beach Café **3**	Oh Sushi **7**	**Bars & clubs** 🎵
	Cheeky Monkey's **4**	Thai Lucy **11**	Cocomangas **6**
Restaurants 🍴	Dish & Raw Bar **5**		
Beach Hotel Bistro **1**	Fish Heads **2**		

Beach merges with **Clark's Beach**, which is no less appealing and generally much quieter. Beyond Clark's Beach and the headland called **The Pass** – a favourite surf spot – **Watego's** and **Little Watego's Beaches** fringe the northern side of Cape Byron, providing more surf breaks and some dramatic coastal scenery. South of Cape Byron, **Tallow Beach** stretches about 9 km to Broken Head and is a great spot to escape the crowds (but note that it is unpatrolled). Several walks also access other more remote headland beaches within the very pretty **Broken Head Nature Reserve**. In the heart of Byron Bay itself, 2.5 km from the shore, is the small and clearly visible rocky outcrop known as **Julian Rocks Marine Reserve**. It is listed as one of Australia's top 10 dive sites, with over 400 species of fish, including sharks and manta ray, and turtles and dolphins often joining the party. If you are not a certified diver, a snorkelling trip to the rocks is recommended.

Crowning the **Cape Byron Headland** is the **Byron Bay Lighthouse** ① *T6685 5955, 0800-1930 (1730 in winter), 30 mins' walk from the town, 40-min tours available*. Built in 1901 it sits only metres away from Australia's easternmost point. As well as the dramatic coastal views east over Byron Bay and south down Tallow Beach to Broken Head, the headland provides some excellent walking opportunities, with the track down from the lighthouse to Little Watego's Beach being the most popular. Humpback whales can often been seen offshore during their annual migrations in midwinter and early summer, while dolphins and the occasional manta ray can be spotted in the clear waters below the cliffs year round.

The town has a number of galleries worth seeing including the **Colin Heaney Glass Blowing Studio** ① *6 Acacia St, www.colinheaney.com,* and the superb works of local photographer John Derrey, at **Byron Images** ① *on the corner of Lawson St and Jonson St, www.johnderrey.com*. The VIC has full gallery listings. Byron also hosts an arts and crafts market on the first Sunday of the month on Butler Street.

Rainbow Region → *For listings, see pages 128-140.*

Inland from Byron Bay lies the so-called Rainbow Region, a collection of bohemian, arty villages famous for their alternative lifestyle. This very pleasant, scenic area, often called the Northern Rivers, stretches from Murwillumbah in the north to Kyogle in the west, Lismore and Ballina in the south and Byron Bay on the coast to the east.

Geologically the region is dominated by the Mount Warning shield volcano and its vast caldera (crater), the largest of its type in the southern hemisphere. The huge volcano, which erupted about 23 million years ago, produced a flat shield-shaped landform with its highest point rising almost twice the height of **Mount Warning** (1157 m), which is all that remains today of the original magma chamber and central vent. If viewed from the air the huge eroded bowl of the caldera can be seen stretching almost 60 km inland from the coast, with the dramatic peak of Mount Warning in its middle. The original lava flows reached as far as Canungra in the north, Kyogle to the west, Lismore and Ballina in the south and almost 100 km out to sea. Today, after millions of years of wind and water erosion, the region is rich in dramatic geological features. Around the rim of the caldera and fringing plateaux lush rainforest-covered landscapes have risen from the ashes, while the floor of the caldera acts as a vast watershed for the Tweed River, which debouches at the border of New South Wales and Queensland. There are no fewer than nine national parks in the area, offering magnificent scenery and walking opportunities.

Visiting the Rainbow Region

Nimbin VIC ① *northern end of Cullen St (71), T6689 1453*, offers transport and accommodation bookings, internet access and maps.

Mullumbimby

Northwest from Byron, the little village of Mullumbimby is about as charming as its name suggests and offers a fine stop or diversion on the way to Nimbin and the Nightcap National Park. There is a scattering of historic buildings along Dalley and Stuart Streets, including the 1908 **Cedar House**, which now serves as an antique gallery, and the old 1907 post office housing a small museum. **Crystal Castle** ① *T6684 3111, www.crystalcastle.com.au, 1000-1700, free*, south of Mullumbimby on Monet Drive, Montecollum, has a fine display of natural crystals, gardens and a café. You could also check out your psychedelic colours as seen through the 'aura camera' or try some crystal healing, tarot card reading or sip a herbal tea in the Lotus Café.

Nimbin

Up until the 1970s, the sleepy dairy village of Nimbin had changed little since its inception by the first European settlers over a century before. Then, in 1973, the Australian Union of Students (AUS) chose the Nimbin Valley as the venue for the 'experimental and alternative' **Aquarius Festival**. The concept was to create 'a total cultural experience, through the lifestyle of participation' for Australian creatives, students and alternative lifestylers. Of course, with many of that generation eager to maintain the ideologies and practices of the sixties, the very concept became like a red rag to the proverbial 'alternative' bull, and when the time arrived it all inevitably went into orbit. In many ways Nimbin never got over the invasion, the excitement or indeed the hangover, and its more enlightened long-term residents have been joined by a veritable army of society's dropouts, man.

In many ways the colourful main street of Nimbin, **Cullen Street**, is the single collective sight in the village and one that speaks very much for itself. Amidst a rash of laid-back cafés, alternative health and arts and craft shops, is **Nimbin Museum** ① *61 Cullen St, T6689 1123, www.nimbinmuseum.com, 0900-1700, $2*. Entirely true to the unconventional and the alternative ideology, it goes deliberately beyond any conventional concepts. It is perhaps simply unique in its creative, historical and often humorous interpretations and expressions of the village, its inhabitants and Australia as a whole.

On the other side of Cullen Street, the loudly advertised **Hemp Embassy** ①, *www.hempembassy.net free*, is also worth a look but, as you can imagine, has little to do with gardening or fashion wear. As well as supporting the multifarious and controversial uses of hemp, the Nimbin Valley is also well known for fruit growing and permaculture. For the visitor the **Djanbung Gardens Permaculture Centre** ① *74 Cecil St, www.permaculture.com.au, T6689 1755, Tue-Fri 1000-1500, Sat-Mon 1000-1200, tours Tue and Thu 1030, Sat 1100*, offers garden tours, herbal crafts, environmental workshops and an organic café.

The most obvious volcanic feature around Nimbin is the **Nimbin Rocks**, which are estimated to be over 20 million years old. There is a lookout on **Lodge Road**, 3 km south of the village. If you fancy a further investigation try a bicycle tour, see page 137 for details.

Nightcap National Park and Whian Whian State Forest

The World Heritage 8145-ha Nightcap National Park is located on the southern rim of the Mount Warning caldera and adjacent is the Whian Whian State Forest Park. Combined, they offer a wealth of volcanic features including massifs, pinnacles and cliffs eroded by spectacular waterfalls and draped in lush rainforest. Some unique wildlife also resides in the park, including the red-legged pademelon (a kind of wallaby), the Fleay's barred frog and the appealingly named wompoo fruit dove.

The main physical features of the park are **Mount Nardi** (800 m), 12 km east of Nimbin; **Terania Creek** and the **Protestors Falls**, 14 km north of the Channon; and **Whian Whian State Forest** and 100-m **Minyon Falls**, 23 km southwest of Mullumbimby. The 30-km Whian Whian Scenic Drive (unsealed), which can be accessed beyond the Minyon Falls, traverses the forest park and takes visitors through varied rainforest vegetation and scenery including the memorable **Peates Mountain Lookout**. Nightcap National Park also holds the rather dubious accolade of receiving the highest mean rainfall in the state.

Popular long walking tracks include the moderate-to-hard 7.5-km **Minyon Loop**, which starts from the Minyon Falls Picnic Area and takes in the base of the falls and the escarpment edge, and the moderate-to-hard 16-km **Historic Nightcap Track**, which follows the former pioneer trails that once connected Lismore and Mullumbimby. Other shorter and easier possibilities are the 3-km **Mount Matheson Loop** and 4-km **Pholis Gap walks**, which both start from Mount Nardi, and the 1.5-km **Big Scrub Loop**, which starts from the Gibbergunyah Range Road in Whian Whian State Forest. It is said to contain some of the best remnant rainforest in the region. Protestors Falls, which were named after a successful six-week protest to prevent logging in the late 1970s, are reached on a 1.5-km return track from the Terania Creek Picnic Area.

The Mount Nardi section of the park is accessed via Newton Drive, which is off Tuntable Falls Road west out of Nimbin. The Terania Creek and Protestors Falls are reached via Terania Creek Road north out of the Channon, and the Minyon Falls and Whian Whian State Forest are reached via Dunoon or Goonengerry southwest of Mullumbimby.

Murwillumbah

The pleasant sugar cane town of Murwillumbah sits on the banks of the Tweed River, at the eastern edge of the Mount Warning caldera, and serves as a major gateway to the Rainbow Region. Most people who visit the town gather what information they need from the World Heritage Rainforest Centre (see below) and then 'head for the hills'; however, if you can spare an hour or so, the small **Tweed Regional Art Gallery** ① *Mistral Rd, T6670 2790, Wed-Sun 1000-1700*, is worth a look. As well as its permanent collection of Australian and international art, it features some fine works by local artists and also hosts the lucrative Doug Moran National Portrait Prize. Murwillumbah VIC shares its office with the NPWS and the **World Heritage Rainforest Centre** ① *corner of Tweed Valley Way and Alma St, T6672 1340, www.tweedtourism.com.au, open till 1600*. Combined they offer insight and information surrounding the region and the parks.

Mount Warning National Park

The 1157-m peak of Mount Warning is all that remains of the magma chamber and vent that formed the vast caldera that shaped much of the Northern Rivers region. Other than its stunning scenery and rich flora and fauna, the great appeal of Mount Warning is the pilgrimage to the summit to see the first rays of sunlight to hit the Australian mainland. The moderate to hard 4.4-km ascent starts from the Breakfast Creek Picnic Area, 17 km southwest of Murwillumbah at the terminus of Mount Warning Road. To ensure you reach the summit for sunrise you are advised to set off about 2½ hours beforehand. Murwillumbah, see above, serves as an overnight stop for those undertaking the dawn ascent. For the less energetic, Lyrebird Track crosses Breakfast Creek before winding 200 m through palm forest to a rainforest platform. Access to Mount Warning is via Mount Warning Road, 11 km south of Murwillumbah on the main Kyogle Road.

Port Macquarie to Byron Bay listings

For hotel and restaurant price codes and other relevant information, see pages 10-14.

● Where to stay

Port Macquarie *p112, map p113*
There are plenty of accommodation options in and around Port Macquarie, from basic NPWS campsites to luxury resorts. During holiday periods and in the high season you are advised to book ahead.

$$$$ HW Boutique Motel, 1 Stewart St, T6583 1200, www.hwmotel.com.au. For a really chic motel in the ideal position, look no further than this. The rooms are well appointed with most offering views across the river mouth and Town Beach.

$$$$ Sundowner Breakwall Tourist Park, beside the river mouth, 1 Munster St, T6583 2755, www.sundowner.net.au. Of the many motor parks in the area this one is hard to beat for position. It has vast and good facilities including a pool and camp kitchen.

$$$ Port Macquarie YHA, 40 Church St, T6583 5512. Closest hostel to the beaches, offering tidy dorms, twins and family rooms, spacious facilities, free bikes, internet, pick-ups from the bus station.

$$ Ozzie Pozzie Backpackers, 36 Waugh St, T6583 8133, www.ozziepozzie.com. More modern, activity-oriented backpackers than **Port Macquarie Backpackers**, well in tune with travellers' needs, good facilities, dorms, doubles/twins, internet, pick-ups, free use of boogie boards, bikes and fishing gear.

$$ Port Macquarie Backpackers, 2 Hastings River Drive, T6583 1791, www.portmacquariebackpackers.com.au. A friendly, family-run historic house with lots of character, dorms, twins and doubles, pool, 24-hr kitchen and TV room, free use of boogie boards, fishing gear, bikes, pool table, internet and pick-ups.

Remote NPWS camping is available at Big Hill and Point Plomer in the Limeburners Creek Nature Reserve, T6586 8300.

South West Rocks and Hat Head *p115*
$$$$ Rockpool Motel, 45 McIntyre St, T6566 7755, www.rockpoolmotorinn.com.au. Modern motel complex 1 km east of the town centre.

$$$$ Smoky Cape Lighthouse B&B, T6566 6301, www.smokycapelighthouse.com. The most unusual accommodation in the area has to be these former keepers' quarters. A totally refurbished interior provides self-contained or B&B options, modern facilities, 4-poster and stunning views south across the national park. 2-night stay minimum. Book well in advance.

$$$ Bay Motel, 1 Livingstone Av, T6566 6909. Another motel only older and cheaper, right on the main shopping street.

$$$ Horseshoe Bay Beach Park, Livingstone St, T6566 6370, www.horseshoebaypark.com.au. Overlooks the river, ocean and the sheltered Horseshoe Bay Beach and is within metres of the town centre. Busy and beautifully placed, this motor park offers cabins, onsite vans and powered sites (some en suite). Hugely popular with locals so book well in advance.

$$ Arakoon State Recreation Area, T6566 6168, Laggers Point, beside the Trial Bay Gaol. Equally fine aesthetics and more seclusion can be secured here. It's a great spot and the best for camping.

$ Hungry Rest Area, south of Hat Head village. Self-registration including day-use fees apply, T6584 2203. Contact for both sites. A good basic NPWS campsite with pit toilets, no water and fires are permitted.

$ Smoky Rest Area, near the lighthouse, see **Hungry Rest Area** for contact details. Excellent for wildlife, a good basic NPWS campsite.

Bellingen *p116*

There are plenty of good B&Bs and self-contained cottages in verdant country settings.

$$$$ Monticello Countryhouse, 11 Sunset Ridge Drive, (2 km), T6655 1559, www.monticello.com.au. Popular B&B, with classy, good value double, twin and singles, within easy reach of the village.

$$$$ Promised Land Cottages, 934 Promised Land Rd, T6655 9578, www.promisedland cottages.com.au. Good value quality self-contained options 15 mins outside of the village. Recommended.

$$$ Bellingen YHA Backpackers, 2 Short St, T6655 1116, www.yha.com.au. Consistently receives rave reviews and deservedly so. Housed in a beautifully maintained 2-storey historic homestead in the heart of the village, with large decks overlooking the river valley, it oozes character and has a great social, laid-back atmosphere. It has a range of dorms, double/twins, family rooms and camping facilities, internet, musical instruments, hammocks and entertaining trips to Dorrigo National Park. Lining the hallways are tasteful photographs of over 200 guests willing to get buck naked in the name of art.

$$$ Fernridge Farm Cottage, 1673 Waterfall Way (4 km west), T6655 2142, www.fernridge.com.au. Peaceful, cosy, self-contained accommodation in a 19th-century 'Queenslander' cottage on a 120-ha alpaca farm.

$$$ Rivendell guesthouse, 12 Hyde St, T6655 0060, www.rivendell guesthouse.com.au. A historic guesthouse with 3 queen rooms situated right in the heart of the village.

Dorrigo National Park

$$$ Fernbrook Lodge, 470 Waterfall Way, 6 km west, T6657 2573, fernbrooklodge@mid coast.com.au. Traditional and homely B&B with great views.

$$$ Historic Dorrigo Hotel, corner of Hickory St and Cudgery St, T6657 2016, www.hotelmoteldorrigo.com.au. Traditional pub rooms at affordable prices in the centre, some with spa bath.

$$ Dorrigo Mountain Resort, on the southern edge of the town, Waterfall Way, T6657 2564, www.dorrigomountain resort.com.au. Standard self-contained cabins, powered and non-powered sites, barbecues, but no camp kitchen.

$$ Gracemere Grange, 325 Dome Rd, 2 km from the Rainforest Centre, T6657 2630, www.gracemeregrange.com.au. Another comfortable B&B option close to the Dorrigo National Park visitor centre.

New England National Park *p117*

$$$ Moffat Falls Cottage, T6775 9219, Point Lookout Rd, www.moffatfalls.com.au. Comfortable, self-contained option in New England National Park with a wood fire and 2 bedrooms. There is also a self-contained room in the lodge and cheaper, value cabins on the property.

Coffs Harbour *p118, map p118*

There is a rash of motels and resorts located along the Pacific Highway on the north and south approaches and along the waterfront on Ocean Pde. There are plenty of motor parks in the area with the best located north or south of the town. The hostels are lively places – very activity- and party-oriented.

$$$$ Friday Creek Retreat, 267 Friday Creek Rd, Upper Orara, 17 km west of town, T6653 8221, www.fridaycreek.com. Sheer luxury, as well as complete peace and quiet in a country setting is offered here. There are 9 superb fully self-contained cottages with spas, open fires, hammocks and great views, free bike hire, complimentary breakfast and dinner by arrangement.

$$$$ Park Beach Caravan Park, Ocean Pde, T6648 4888, www.parkbeach holidaypark.com.au. If you must stay in the town itself this is the beachside motor park with the best facilities.

$$$ Country Comfort Motel,
353 Pacific Highway, T6652 8222, www.countrycomfort.com.au. Next to the Big Banana, this modern, convenient and good value motel is a good choice if you are merely passing through. Pool, sauna and spa.

$$$ Emerald Beach Holiday Park,
Fishermans Drive, Emerald Beach, T6656 1521, www.ebhp.com.au. 18 km north of Coffs, this motor park has luxury villas, standard cabins, onsite vans, powered and shaded non-powered sites in a bush setting with shop, café and pool. The beach is only metres away and is simply superb with headland walks nearby. Recommended.

$$$ Sawtell Beach Caravan Park, 5 Lyons Rd, Sawtell (6 km), T6653 1379, www.sawtell beachcaravanpark.com.au. South of town is this motor park close to the surf beach and local amenities with camp kitchen.

$$ Aussitel Backpackers, T6651 1871, www.aussitel.com. Also near the beach at 312 Harbour Drive, this a social place with emphasis on discounted activities and its own attractive dive packages a speciality. Dorms, twins and doubles, large kitchen, common area, internet, pool, bikes, surf/body boards, wetsuits, etc.

$$ Coffs Harbour YHA, 51 Collingwood St, T6652 6462. Friendly, spotless and well managed. Recently relocated to a spacious modern facility in a suburban setting close to the beach, offering dorms, doubles/twins and family rooms (with en suite), pool, internet, cable TV and free bikes, surf/body boards and pick-ups. Recommended.

Coffs Harbour to Byron Bay *p120*
Most of Yamba's amenities can be found along its main drag, Wooli St, or Yamba St off Wooli St, which terminates at Pippie Beach.

$$$$ Blue Dolphin Holiday Resort,
Yamba Rd, Yamba, T6646 2194, www.bluedolphin.com.au. This 5-star resort offers luxury/standard self-contained cabins, en suite/standard powered and non-powered sites, café, pool and camp kitchen.

$$$$ Surf Motel, 2 Queen St, Yamba, T6646 2200. Modern, well-appointed motel option right next to Main Beach.

$$$ Lake Ainsworth Caravan Park,
Pacific Pde, Lennox Head, T6687 7249, www.lake-ainsworth-holiday-park.nsw.big4.c om.au. For campers and campervans this option is ideally located next to the lake and offers en suite/standard cabins, powered and non-powered sites but no camp kitchen. Activities include windsurfing, sailing and canoeing.

$$ Lennox Head Beach House YHA, 3 Ross St, T6687 7636, www.yha.com.au. Purpose-built hostel with a great laid-back friendly atmosphere, near the beach and Lake Ainsworth. Dorms and small doubles and free use of surf/boogie boards, bikes and fishing gear. Free sailing and windsurfing lessons can also be arranged and there is a natural therapies (massage) clinic onsite, as well as their legendary chocolate cake.

$$ Woody Head Campsite, beside the beach off Iluka Rd, 14 km west of the Pacific Highway, 4 km north of Iluka, T6646 6134, www.nationalparks.nsw.gov.au. This NPSW campsite is simply superb. Non-powered sites, toilets, water, hot showers, boat ramp and fires permitted, plus 3 cabins with cooking facilities. Book well ahead.

Byron Bay *p122, map p122*
There is certainly plenty of choice in Byron, with the emphasis on backpacker hostels and upmarket boutique hotels, B&Bs and guesthouses. There are over a dozen very competitive backpackers in town, all having to maintain good standards. Mostly the choice comes down to availability – book well ahead for all accommodation but particularly the backpackers. If the options below don't suffice, the VIC has an excellent

accommodation booking service. See www.byron-bay.com and www.byronbayaccom.net.

$$$$ Belongil Beachouse, 25 Childe St (Kendal St, off Shirley St), T6685 7868, www.belongilbeachouse.com. East of the town centre, in contrast to the Arts Factory this option offers a wide range of modern, well-appointed options, from dorms and private double/twins with shared facilities, to luxury motel-style rooms with spas, or two-bedroom self-contained cottages. Quiet setting across the road from the beach. Onsite Balinese-style café and float/massage therapy centre. Internet, bike, body/surf board hire and courtesy bus.

$$$$ Broken Head Caravan Park, Beach Rd, Broken Head (8 km), T6685 3245, www.brokenhd.com.au. Further afield and much quieter, the appeal of this motor park is its friendly atmosphere, beachside position and proximity to the Broken Head Nature Reserve. It has cabins, powered and non-powered sites, small shop, barbecue and camp kitchen.

$$$$ Clarke's Beach Caravan Park, off Lighthouse Rd, T6685 6496, www.clarkesbeach.com.au. Further west, with prettier surroundings and right beside Clark's Beach, this motor park offers self-contained and standard cabins, powered and shady non-powered sites, but no camp kitchen, just barbecues.

$$$$ First Sun Holiday Park, Lawson St (200 m east of the Main Beach Car Park), T6685 6544, www.bshp.com.au/first. The most convenient for the town centre and Main Beach, it offers a range of self-contained/standard cabins, powered and non-powered sites, camp kitchen.

$$$$ Rae's on Wategos, overlooking Watego's Beach, T6685 5366, www.raes.com.au. This sits firmly at the top of this price category and is the most luxurious hotel in Byron. It was voted in *Condé Naste Traveller* magazine (and others) as being in the top 50 worldwide. Although location has a lot to do with that accolade, the place itself is superb and cannot be faulted. It has an in-house restaurant that is also excellent and open to non-guests.

$$$ Amigo's Byron Bay Guesthouse, corner of Kingsley St and Tennyson St, T6680 8662, www.amigosbb.com. Doubles (one en suite, one with shared bathroom), bike and body board hire.

$$$ Aquarius Backpackers Motel, 16 Lawson St, T6685 7663, www.byron-bay.com/aquarius. Large and lively complex offering dorms, doubles and spa suites (all en suite, with 'proper beds'), pool, good value licensed café/bistro, internet, free boogie boards, bikes, pool tables and courtesy bus.

$$$ Byron Bayside Motel, 14 Middleton St, T6685 6004, www.byronbayside motel.com.au. This budget 3-star motel is well placed in the heart of town, modern and good value.

The YHA operates 2 hostels in Byron Bay:

$$$ Byron Bay YHA, 7 Carlyle St, T6685 8853, www.yha.com.au. Very similar and just as reliable. **$$$-$ Cape Byron YHA**, corner Byron St and Middleton St, T6685 8788, www.yha.com.au. Offers modern, clean dorms, double and twins (some en suite and a/c) set around a large courtyard with pool. Well managed and friendly. Good kitchen facilities, café, free barbecue nights, large games room, internet and tours desk. Dive shop next door.

$$$ Arts Factory, Skinners Shoot Rd (via Burns St, off Shirley St), T6685 7709, www.artsfactory.com.au. This place takes some beating for the quintessential 'alternative' Byron experience. It offers a wide range of 'funky' accommodation, from the Love Shack and Island Retreats, to the Gypsy Bus, tepees and campsites. Excellent amenities, pool, sauna, internet, café (plus vegetarian restaurant nearby), bike hire, tours desk and unusual arts, relaxation, yoga or music-based activities including didgeridoo making and drumming. It even has its own recording studio should you feel a Susan Boyle coming on. The Byron Lounge Cinema and Buddha Gardens Day Spa are also within the village. It may not be everybody's cup of herbal tea, but for an experience it is recommended.

$$$ Holiday Village Backpackers, 116 Jonson St, south of town centre, T6685 8888, www.byronbaybackpackers.com.au. Offers modern dorms, doubles and motel-style apartments (some en suite with TV), large courtyard with pool, spa, well-equipped kitchen, all-you-can-eat barbecues, internet, free surf/body boards, scuba lessons, bike hire.

$$ Cape Byron Lodge, 78 Bangalow Rd (1 km from the town centre), T6685 6445, www.capebyronlodge.com. Very congenial hostel that more than meets the stiff competition with all the usual facilities and a good atmosphere. Also free shuttle into town and dawn trips to the lighthouse.

Rainbow Region p124

$$$$ Crystal Creek Rainforest Retreat, Brookers Rd, Murwillumbah, T6679 1591, www.crystalcreekrainforestretreat.com.au. This award-winning retreat is located on the edge of the Numinbah Nature Reserve, about 23 km west of Murwillumbah, with modern design, well-appointed self-contained bungalows, spa baths, excellent cuisine, local forest walks and even the odd hammock across the creek. Transfers from Murwillumbah by arrangement.

$$$$ Ecoasis, near the village of Uki, Mt Warning, T6679 5959, www.ecoasis.com.au. These luxury couple-oriented bush chalets are an excellent choice. Indulge yourself.

$$$ Mount Warning Caravan Park, about 3 km up Mt Warning Rd, T6679 5120, www.mtwarningholidaypark.com. Camping is available at this privately run caravan park. It has cabins, onsite vans, powered and non-powered sites (some with fires) and a camp kitchen.

$$$ Midginbil Hill Country Resort, near Murwillumbah, T6679 7033, www.midginbilhill.com.au. Also has a full range of accommodation from B&B to camping with the added attraction of in-house canoe trips and horse riding.

$$ Mount Warning/Murwillumbah YHA, 1 Tumbulgum Rd, Murwillumbah (first right across the bridge, 200 m, across the river from the VIC), T6672 3763, www.yha.com.au. This is the best budget option. Located right next to the river and with a deck overlooking Mt Warning, it is a friendly and homely place, run by a caring and dedicated manager. Dorms and double/twins, free use of canoes and transport to Mt Warning if you stay 2 nights.

$$ Nimbin Caravan and Tourist Park, 29 Sibley St, Nimbin, T6689 1402. Basic facilities, onsite vans, powered and non-powered sites, within easy walking distance of the village.

$$ Nimbin Rox YHA, 74 Thorburn St, Nimbin, T6689 0022, www.yha.com.au. Deservingly popular, this YHA is set in a 10-ha elevated position just west of the village, offering great views across Nimbin Rocks (hence the name). Offers the full range of rooms and modern facilities, including the obligatory tepee for that essential Nimbinesque ambience. Internet, pool and bike hire. Camping sites also available.

$$ Rainbow Retreat Backpackers, 75 Thorburn St, Nimbin, T6689 1262, www.rainbowretreat.net. You are invited to 'Live the Nimbin Dream' at this unusual, good value and suitably laid-back backpackers. Not surprisingly, it provides a wide choice of highly unconventional accommodation options from Malay-style huts to VW Kombis, dorms and secluded campsites, all set in a quiet 7-ha site near the edge of the village. Both the facilities and atmosphere are excellent with regular musical jam sessions, visiting chefs preparing cheap meals, alternative practitioners and performers, not to mention the odd platypus in the creek or harmless python up a tree. Overall, it provides the ideal way to experience the true spirit of Nimbin. Recommended.

Port Macquarie *p112, map p113*
Seafood rules in Port Macquarie, from the full plate of oysters to humble fish and chips. The main outlets can be found at the Wharf end of Clarence St. The vineyards are also worth considering, especially for lunch.

$$$ Fusion 7, 124 Horton St, T6584 1171. Daily for lunch and dinner. Relaxed atmosphere and value, quality Australian cuisine from lauded chef Lindsey Schwab.

$$$ Scampi's, Port Marina, Park St, T6583 7200. Daily from 1800. The best venue for quality à la carte seafood in congenial surroundings.

$$ Beach House, 1 Horton St, T6584 5692. Daily breakfast, lunch and dinner. The most popular venue for locals given the location, with a good atmosphere. Standard pub-style fare with pizza a speciality.

$$ Ca Marche, 764 Fernbank Creek Rd (corner of Pacific Highway), T6582 8320. Daily 1030-1600. Out of town a little but worth the journey is this small, award-winning French/Mediterranean restaurant at the Cassegrain Winery, with a congenial atmosphere and good views across the vines.

$$ Toros Mexican, 22 Murray St, T6583 4340. Long-established and good value venue that does a wicked fajita.

$ Macquarie Seafoods, corner of Clarence St and Short St, T6583 8476. Daily 1100-2100. Great fish and chips.

$ Port Pacific Resort Café, 14 Clarence St, T6583 8099. Breakfast for around $12.

South West Rocks and Hat Head *p115*
$$ Geppy's, corner of Livingstone St and Memorial Av, South West Rocks, T6566 6196. Well known for good seafood, Italian and modern Australian cuisine. Live jazz and blues on Wed.

$$ Pizza on the Rocks, 134 Gregory St, South West Rocks, T6566 6626. Locally recommended.

$$ Trial Bay Kiosk, Arakoon, overlooking the Trial Bay Gaol and beach, T6566 7100. Daily for breakfast and lunch 0800-1600 and Thu, Fri and Sat for dinner. Superb location, alfresco dining and quality, though fairly pricey, fare. Good breakfasts and coffee.

Bellingen *p116*
$$$ No 2 Oak St, T6655 9000. Tue-Sat, from 1800. Recommended for fine dining. Housed in a 1910 heritage cottage it offers an excellent and innovative menu. Book ahead.

$$$ Old Butter Factory Café, 1 Doepel La, T6655 2150. Breakfast and lunch. Good breakfast or light meal venue with indoor or outdoor seating overlooking the golf course. The added attraction is the arts and crafts (see above).

$$ Café Bare Nature & Pizza, 111 Hyde St, T6655 1551. Daily from 1700. For gourmet pizza.

$$ Lodge 241 Gallery Café, Masonic Hall, T6655 2470. Daily 0800-1700. Overlooking the river valley is this café and gallery combined, serving fine local cuisine and good coffee.

Dorrigo and Dorrigo National Park
$$$ Misty's, 33 Hickory St, T6657 2855. Wed-Sat from 1800 and Sun from 0730 for brunch. For fine dining.

$$ Historic Dorrigo Hotel, corner of Hickory St and Cudgery St, T6657 2016. Classic pub grub.

Coffs Harbour *p118, map p118*
$$$ Tide and Pilot Brasserie, Marina Drive, T6651 6888. Daily for breakfast, lunch and dinner from 0700. Quality alfresco dining at this award-winning and friendly restaurant can follow a pre-dinner walk to Muttonbird Island.

$$ Ocean Front Brasserie, Coffs Harbour Deep Sea Fishing Club, Jordan Esplanade,

T6651 2819. Daily 1200-1430 and 1800-2030. Good value and great views across the harbour.

$ Fisherman's Co-op, 69 Marina Drive, T6652 2811. Daily until 1800. *The* place for fish and chips.

$ Foreshores Café, Jetty Strip, 394 High St, T665 23127. Daily. Good breakfast, coffee and lunch. Locals swear by this place.

Coffs Harbour to Byron Bay *p120*
Yamba

$$ Pacific Hotel, 18 Pilot St, T6646 2466. Overlooking the ocean, an old favourite for good value bistro meals daily. Also has budget accommodation.

Iluka
$$ Golf Club, Iluka Rd, T6646 5043. Tue-Sun. The best of a poor selection.

$$ Sedger's Reef Bistro, 5 Queens St, T6646 6119. One of very few open daily.

Lennox Head
$$ Lennox Head Pizza and Pasta, 2/56 Ballina St, T6687 7080. A good option.

Byron Bay *p122, map p122*
Although Jonson St and the various arcades host some good restaurants and cafés, most folk gravitate towards Bay Lane where you will find plenty of atmosphere.

$$ Dish Restaurant, corner of Jonson St and Marvell St, T6685 7320. An award-winning, very chic place with fine innovative international and Australian cuisine. Also runs the **Marvell Bar**.

$$ Beach Hotel Bistro, Bay Lane, T6685 6402. Lunch and dinner 1200-2100. Never fails to attract the crowds and wins hands down for atmosphere. Little wonder it sold for 'Good Lord, how much' in 2007 and will probably do the same in another decade.

$$ Oh Sushi, 90 Jonson St, T6685 7103. Daily 1200-2200. Sushi fans should look no further.

$$ Thai Lucy, Bay Lane, T6680 8083. Daily 1200-1500 and 1730-2200. Offers excellent dishes, good value and lots of atmosphere, but book ahead.

$ Belongil Beach Café, Childe St, T6685 7144. Daily 0800-2200. If a beach stroll is in order you'll find a good coffee and generous breakfasts at this friendly café.

$ Buddha Bar and Restaurant and **Zula** (Arts Factory Village), Skinners Shoot Rd (5 mins west of the town centre), T6680 8038. Daily from 1600. Both good value and always a cosmopolitan crowd. You could combine a visit with a film at the **Lounge Cinema** next door, T5685 5828.

$ Cheeky Monkey's, 115 Jonson St, T6685 5886. Mon-Sat 1900-0300. Backpacker specials are regularly on offer in order to tempt you to stay late at the bar and nightclub.

$ Fish Heads, 7 Jonson St, T6685 7810. Best bet for takeaway fish and chips.

Rainbow Region *p124*
Nimbin
$$-$ Rainbow Café. The oldest of the alternative eateries in Nimbin.

Murwillumbah
$$ Imperial Hotel, 115 Main St, T 6672 1036. Good value pub lunches and dinners. Pub rooms also available.

🎧 Bars and clubs

Port Macquarie *p112, map p113*
For up-to-date listings, pick up the free weekly *Hastings Happenings* at the VIC.

Beach House, on the Green, 1 Horton St, T6584 5692. Nightly, free entry until 2300. Modern popular nightclub with occasional jazz on Sun afternoons.

Finnians Irish Pub, 97 Gordon St. For a quieter night out try this friendly pub which stages live bands at weekends.

Port Macquarie Hotel, corner of Clarence St and Horton St, T6580 7888. Perhaps the most popular pub in town.

Market forces

One of the great tourist attractions in the Rainbow Region is its colourful weekend markets. These operate in a circuit throughout the region, mostly on Sundays. Byron Bay Market is held in the Butler Street Reserve on the first Sunday of the month, while Lismore hosts a regional Organic Produce Market at the Lismore Showgrounds every Tuesday between 0800-1000, as well as the Lismore Showground Markets every second Sunday. The excellent Channon Craft Market, kicks off in Coronation Park on the second Sunday, while the Aquarius Fair Markets in Nimbin are on the third and fifth Sunday and Bangalow holds its market in the local showgrounds on the fourth Sunday.

Coffs Harbour *p118, map p118*
Ex-servicemen's Club, Vernon St, T6652 3888. A popular haunt for cheap food and drinks, especially on Fri night, but ID is needed. **Plantation**, 88 Grafton St. A firm local favourite with regular live entertainment, staying open well into the wee small hours.

Byron Bay *p122, map p122*
Beach Hotel, facing the beach off Bay St, T6685 6402. Huge and the place to see and be seen, popular both day and night, with the lively atmosphere often spilling out onto beer garden. Live bands Thu-Sun.
Cocomangas, 32 Jonson St. 2100-0300, free entry before 2330. Retro 80s on Wed and disco funk and house on Sat.
Buddha Bar and Restaurant, for details see Restaurants, above.

❂ Festivals

Byron Bay *p122, map p122*
Easter Blues and Roots Festival, www.bluesfest.com.au. The most lauded annual festival in Byron is a popular affair attracting its fair share of international stars, wannabes or has-beens.

❍ Shopping

Byron Bay *p122, map p122*
Byron offers a wealth of 'alternative' and arts and crafts shops selling everything from futons to $300 hand-painted toilet seats. With so many image-conscious backpackers around, the town is also becoming saturated with lingerie shops. See also box above.
Byron Bay Camping and Disposals, Plaza, Jonson St, T6685 8085. Camping gear and supplies.
Byron Images, corner Lawson St and Jonson St, T6685 8909, www.johnderrey.com.au. For a lasting image of Byron, see John Derrey's photography work.

⛰ What to do

Port Macquarie *p112, map p113*
Boat trips and cruises
Port Macquarie River Cruise (Port Venture), Clarence St, T6583 3058, www.portventure .com.au. Over 200 passengers can be carried on board the *MV Venture* for a scenic 2-hr river cruise, most days 1000 and 1400, from $25, children $12; 5-hr barbecue cruise at 1000 Wed, from $60, children $20, and a 3½-hr barbecue cruise, from $40, children $20.
Settlement Point Boat Hire 1 Settlement Point Rd (North Shore), T6583 6300. Independent boat hire.

Horse and camel riding
Bellrowan Valley Horse Riding, 35 mins from Port Macquarie, T6587 5227, www.bellrowanvalley.com.au. Professional outfit offering rides of 1 or 2 hrs, $60/85 including refreshments and pick-ups

from Wauchope (transfer from the Port $10). Trek with dinner and overnight accommodation $125.

Port Macquarie Camel Safaris, Lighthouse Beach, T0437 672 080, www.portmacquariecamels.com.au. Daily except Saturday 0930 and 1300, from $30, children $25.

Skydiving and paragliding
Coastal Skydivers, T0428-471227, www.coastalskydivers.com. Offers 10,000-ft tandem skydives for $320.
High Adventure Air Park, Pacific Highway, Johns River, T0429-844961, www.high adventure.com.au. Tandem paragliding (30 mins from $160).

Water sports
Port Macquarie Surf School, T6585 5453, www.portmacquariesurfschool.com.au. Lessons from $40 per hour.
Stoney Park, Telegraph Point, T6585 0080, www.stoneypark.com.au. Specialist water-skiing and wakeboarding complex offering single lessons from $60 or day packages from $199. Recommended. Accommodation also available.

South West Rocks and Hat Head *p115*
This area is renowned for its excellent dive sites including the 120-m Fish Rock Cave. The entrance to the Macleay River offers good snorkelling at peak tide.
South West Rocks Dive Centre, 5/98 Gregory St, T6566 6474, www.southwest rocksdive.com.au. Offers both trips and rooms with dives to see grey nurse sharks and the Fish Rock Cave.

Bellingen *p116*
This is a fine base from which to explore the numerous excellent rainforest walks of the Dorrigo National Park. The river also offers some exciting opportunities either by canoe or on a river cruise.

Bellingen Canoe Adventures, 4 Tyson St, T6655 9955, www.bellingen.com/canoe. Half-day guided trips from $48, full-day trips from $90, 1 hr sunset tour from $25 and independent hire from $15 per hr.
Hinterland Tours, T6655 2957, www.hinterlandtour.com.au. Informative and English/German speaking multi-day eco-walks/tours of the Dorrigo Plateau and national park with accommodation options.

Coffs Harbour *p118, map p118*
The VIC has full activity listings and can offer non-biased advice. **Marina Booking Centre** based at the marina also acts as booking agent for most regional activities and cruises, T6651 4612.

Diving
Jetty Dive Centre, 398 High St, T6651 1611, www.jettydive.com.au. Small group PADI certification from $395, double dives at the Solitary Islands from $115 and snorkelling trips from $65.

Dolphin, whale watching and fishing
Pacific Explorer , T6652 8988, www.pacificexplorer.com.au. Whale and dolphin watching aboard a catamaran, which being quieter often has the advantage of closer viewing, 2½ hrs, from $40.
Various operators and vessels based at the marina offer entertaining fishing trips from around $125 for a half day. Big game fishing is also an option.
Spirit , T6650 0155. Good value whale-watching trips in season (Jun to end of Nov) at 0830 and 1330, from $40.

Horse trekking
Valery Trails, T6653 4301, www.valery trails.com.au. Award-winning outfit suited to advanced and beginners, 13 km south of Coffs. It offers 1-2-hr breakfast; barbecue, moonlight and camp ride-outs from $50.

Skydiving
Coffs City Skydivers, T6651 1167, www.coffsskydivers.com.au. Tandem skydiving, 3000 m, from $325.

Water sports
East Coast Surf School, T6651 5515, www.eastcoastsurfschool.com.au. Lessons at Diggers Beach (near the Big Banana) 1030-1230, private lessons, from $70 per hr, group from $55.
Liquid Assets, T6658 0850, www.surfrafting.com. An exhilarating range of aquatic adventures, including half or full day whitewater rafting on the Goolang River (grade III) and the Nymbodia River (a scenic grade III-V), from $85/$170. Sea kayaking, half day from $50. Surf rafting, half-day from $50 and flat water kayaking in Bongil Bongil National Park, half day from $50. Surfing lessons from $50 and evening trips to observe platypus from $95.

Coffs Harbour to Byron Bay *p120*
Yamba Kayak Tours, Yamba, T6646 1137, www.yambakayak.com.au. 3-hr guided trips exploring the Islands and beaches inside the mouth of the Clarence River, from $70 and half-day or full-day tours on demand.

Byron Bay *p122, map p122*
Diving
Byron Bay Dive Centre, 9 Marvell St, T6685 8333, www.byronbaydive centre.com.au. A range of diving and snorkelling trips from full to half day exploring the wonderful biodiversity of the Cape Byron Marine Park.
Sundive, opposite the Court House, Middleton St, T6685 7755, www.sundive.com.au. Courses, half-day introductory dives from $150 and snorkelling from $50.

Health and spa therapies
There are many alternative and conventional health therapies including the 2 spas below, and the VIC has full listings.

Buddah Gardens Balinese Day Spa, 21 Gordon St, T6680 7844, www.buddhagardensdayspa.com.au.
Byron Bay Yoga, T8007 5128, www.byron bayyoga.com. Yoga classes.
Quintessence, 6 Fletcher St, T6685 5533, www.quintessencebyron.com.au. Spa.

Kiteboarding
Byron Bay Kiteboarding, T0402-008926, www.byronbaykiteboarding.com. Half, 2- or 3-day packages to master the increasingly popular art of kiteboarding, introductory session $49, full day from $250.

Mountain biking
Mountainbike Tours, T0429-122504, www.mountainbiketours.com.au. Great range of informative eco-based biking adventures in the hinterland national parks, full day from $99, coastal half day from $59.

Sea kayaking
Dolphin, T6685 8044, www.dolphinkayaking.com.au. Good trips around the headlands with chance encounters with dolphins, half day departing daily at 0830, from $60.

Skydiving and gliding
Byron Bay Gliding, Tyagarah, T6684 7572, www.byronbaygliding.com. Entertaining trips in a 'motorglider', a sort of glider and microlight cross, of 20 mins to 1½ hrs from $95 to $395.
Byron Bay Skydiving Centre, based near Brunswick Heads, T1800 800840, www.skydivebyronbay.com. Owned by Australian world representative 'skysurfer' Ray Palmer. The team offers a range of professional services including tandems. The views from the jump zone across Byron Bay to the headland and beyond are stunning. Jumps are pretty cheap and range from $239 (2750m) to $324 (4250m).

Surfing

With so many superb surf breaks around Byron there is no shortage of surfing opportunities for pros and grommets alike. Most operators offer surf hire with short boards starting at about $15 per hr, $20 for 4 hrs and around $30 for 24 hrs.

Byron Bay Surf School, T1800 707274, www.byronbaysurfschool.com. 1-, 3- and 5-day packages, from $65 (3-day $165, 5-day $235, private 2-hr lesson from $130).

Style Surfing, T6685 5634, www.stylesurfingbyronbay.com. 3½-hr beginner's package or advanced courses daily at 0900, 1100 and 1300, from $60, or private lessons for 2 hrs, from $180.

Surfaris, T1800 634951, www.surfaris.com.au. This operation is for real enthusiasts or serious learners. Week-long Sydney–Byron trip from $499 or a 4-day/3-night Byron–Noosa– Hervey Bay trip, from $365.

Tour operators

Byron Bay Wildlife Tours, T0429 770 686, www.byronbaywildlifetours.com. Excellent trips to view all the favourite natives, from the ubiquitous koala to flying foxes (bats) and sea eagles. Also offers evening platypus and wildlife photography tours. All tours 5 hrs and great value from $70. Recommended.

Grasshoppers Nimbin Eco-Explorer Tour, The Hub, 9 Marvel St, T0438 269 076. Recommended if you want to see some of the hinterland's best sights, from $45. Transport to the Nimbin backpackers is an additional option.

Jim's Alternative Tours, T6685 7720, www.jimsalternativetours.com. A wide array of entertaining options from simple lighthouse or market trips to dolphin watching and national park ecotours. Day tour departs daily at 1000.

Port Macquarie p112, map p113
Bus

To access the eastern beaches jump on Nos 334, 332 or 324. Long-distance buses stop at the bus terminal on Hayward St. **Busways**, 6 Denham St, T6583 2499, www.busways.com.au, runs both local and regional bus services between **Sydney** and **Yamba**. Greyhound, T1300 473946, www.greyhound.com.au, offers daily state-wide services. **Keans Coaches**, T6543 1322, runs a service from Port Macquarie to **Scone** (via the **Waterfall Way**, **Dorrigo**, **Bellingen**, **Armidale** and **Tamworth**) on Tue, Thu and Sun. **Premier Motor Service** has a booking office at the terminal, T6583 1488, T133410, www.premierms.com.au Mon-Fri 0830-1700, Sat 0830-1200.

Train

The nearest train station is at Wauchope, 19 km west of the city, T132232. The connecting bus to Port Macquarie is included in the fare.

South West Rocks and Hat Head p115
Bus

Busways, T1300 555611, runs **Kempsey** (Belgrave St) to **South West Rocks** (Livingstone St) route 350, Mon-Sat.

Bellingen and Dorrigo National Park p116
Bus

Busways, T1300 555611, runs between **Nambucca Heads**, **Urunga**, **Coffs Harbour** and **Bellingen** several times a day Mon-Fri. See above for **Keans Coaches** service from **Scone** to **Port Macquarie** and **Coffs Harbour**. Long-distance buses do not make the detour to Bellingen. The nearest stop is Nambucca Heads or Urunga.
The nearest train station is in Urunga.

Countrylink, T132232, operates state and interstate services.

From local towns you can catch local services to the national parks.

Coffs Harbour *p118, map p118*

Bus Busways, T1300 555611, www.busways.com.au, is the local suburban bus company with daily half-hourly services from 0715-1730. To get from Park Av in the town centre to the jetty, take 365E. **Ryan**'s Buses, T6652 3201, offers local services Mon-Sat to **Woolgoolga** and **Grafton**. Sawtell Coaches, T6653 3344, offers daily local services to **Sawtell**, No 364. Long-distance buses stop beside the VIC on Elizabeth St. **Greyhound**, T131499 and **Premier**, T133410, offers daily interstate services. See under Port Macquarie for **Keans Coaches** service to **Scone**.

Cycle/scooter Hire from **Bob Wallis Bicycle Centre**, corner of Collingwood and Orlando streets, T6652 5102, from $25 per 24 hrs ($50 deposit).

Train The station is at the end of Angus McLeod St (right off High St and Camperdown St), near the harbour jetty. **Countrylink**, T132232, runs daily services to **Sydney** and **Brisbane**.

Coffs Harbour to Byron Bay *p120*

Bus
Busways, T6645 8941, provides daily services for **Grafton-Yamba-Maclean-Iluka**.

Ferry
The **Iluka-Yamba** ferry, T6646 6163, departs 4 times daily from the River St Wharf, Yamba, from $6.50.

Byron Bay *p122, map p122*

Air
The closest airports to Byron Bay are **Coolangatta** to the north (90 km, Gold Coast) and **Ballina** to the south (31 km). Both are served by **Jetstar**, T131538; **QantasLink**,

T131313; **Regional Express**, T131713, www.rex.com.au; **Tiger Airways**, T03-9335 3033, www.tigerairways.com.au; and **Virgin Blue**, T136789, www.virginblue.com.au. **Airporter Shuttle**, T04-1460 8660, and **Airport Transfers**, T6685 8507, www.airporttransfers byronbay.com, serve Coolangatta and Ballina from about $40 one way.

Bus
Local Blanch's Buses, T6686 2144, www.blanchs.com.au, runs local services within **Byron Bay** (No 637) and also south to **Ballina** via **Lennox Head** (No 640) and north to **Mullumbimby** (No 640).

Long distance The long-distance bus stop is located right in the heart of town on Jonson St. **Greyhound**, T131499, and **Premier Motor Services**, T133410, run daily interstate services north/south.

Northern Rivers Buslines, T6622 1499, run services to **Ballina** and inland to **Lismore** and **Mullumbimby**.

Kirklands, T6622 1499, runs services to **Brisbane**, **Ballina**, **Lismore** and **Coolangatta**. The VIC acts as the local booking agent. Also of note is the **Brisbane Express**, T1800 626222, www.brisbane2byron.com, which operates 2-hr transfers to the city centre for $34 (**Brisbane Airport** $46) and **J and B Byron Bay Express**, T5592 2655, www.byron bay express.com.au, which operates daily services to **Coolangatta** and **Surfers Paradise** from $25 one-way.

Car/motorcycle
Byron Car Hire, corner of Lawson and Butler streets, T6685 6638. **Byron Bus Transit Centre**, T6685 5517, and **Hertz**, 5 Marvell St, T6621 8855. Car servicing at **Bayside Mechanical**, 12 Banksia Drive, T6685 8455

Cycling
Surf and Bike Hire, 1/31 Lawson St, T6680 7066, www.byronbaysurfandbikehire.com.au

and **Byron Bay Bicycles**, T6685 6067. See also Mountain biking, page 137.

Train
The station is located in the heart of town, just off Jonson St. **Countrylink**, T132232, runs daily services south to **Sydney** and beyond, and north (with bus link) with **Queensland Rail**, T132232, to **Brisbane**.

Rainbow Region p124
Bus
Northern Rivers Buslines, T6622 1499, run services to **Lismore** and **Mullumbimby**. For **Brisbane**, Kirklands, T1300 367077, and interstate **Greyhound**, T132030, stop outside **Tweed Valley Travel**, on the corner of Main St and Queen St. Northbound buses and trains both stop in **Murwillumbah**. Nimbin Shuttle Bus, T6680 9189, operates daily, departing from Jonson St, Byron Bay at 1100, returning at 1700, from $40 return.

Train
Murwillumbah station is opposite the VIC and is served by **Countrylink**, T132232.

Port Macquarie *p112, map p113*
Banks All major branches with ATMs can be found along Clarence St and Horton St.
Medical services **Port Macquarie Base Hospital**, Wright Rd, T6581 2000. **Useful numbers** **Police**, 2 Hay St, T6583 0199.

Coffs Harbour *p118, map p118*
Banks Major branches with ATMs are on the Mall or along Grafton St and Park Av. **Medical services** **Hospital**, T6656 7000. **Useful numbers** **Police**, Moonee St, T6652 0299.

Byron Bay *p122, map p122*
Banks Most major branches with ATMs are along Jonson St or Lawsons St. Currency exchange is readily available including **Byron Foreign Exchange**, Shop 4 Central Arcade, T6685 7787. 0900-1800. **Car hire Earth Car Rentals**, Shop 3A, 1 Byron St, T6685 7472, www.eathcar.com.au. The first carbon neutral car hire company in Australia, with a percentage of the fee going to Cool Planet. **Medical services Bay Centre Medical**, 6 Lawson St, T6685 6206, www.byron med.com.au. **Useful numbers Police**, 2 Shirley St.